CREATING THE LAND OF LINCOLN

CREATING THE LAND OF LINCOLN

The History and Constitutions of Illinois, 1778–1870

Frank Cicero Jr.

UNIVERSITY OF
ILLINOIS PRESS
Urbana, Chicago, and Springfield

Cataloging data available from the Library of Congress
ISBN 978-0-252-04167–9 (cloth : alk.)
ISBN 978-0-252-05034–3 (ebook)

For Jan

CONTENTS

ILLUSTRATIONS

Figures

Maps

PREFACE

In 1969, Illinois voters approved a call for Illinois's Sixth Constitutional Convention. I could not resist: I stood for election as a delegate. I had not run for public office before, and I knew much more about the United States Constitution than I did about the Constitution of Illinois. Since high school, however, I had been interested in politics and government. Constitutional law in particular had been a highlight of my studies in those fields in college and graduate schools.

I joined a law firm in 1965 and embarked on what would be a long career in litigation. When the rare opportunity arose in 1969 to participate in rewriting Illinois's constitution, I was eager to join in.

A sense of history was prevalent when 115 other elected delegates and I took our seats on December 8, 1969, for the first session of the convention. We met temporarily in the State House, the present state capitol in Springfield, because renovation of the historic Old State Capitol had not been completed. The awareness of history increased manifold when the convention moved into the Old State Capitol on March 20, 1970. As I climbed the magnificent central staircase and took my seat in the restored House of Representatives chamber on the second floor, feelings of anticipation, excitement, and awe came in a rush.

The building was the Illinois capitol from 1839 until 1876. It was the site of three previous constitutional conventions, in 1847, 1862, and 1869, and numerous other historic events. The House of Representatives chamber in which we met was the site in 1858 of Abraham Lincoln's famous House Divided speech, and where he lay in state in May 1865. The Senate chamber across the hall, and the broad staircase in between where everyone mingled, had seen many of the great men of Illinois history, and some of the great scoundrels. We were walking where they had walked.

The convention was, of course, a worthwhile experience. I made good friends of many delegates, learned much from them, and gained substantial knowledge about the state. We shared the satisfaction at the favorable response of the people of Illinois to the convention's work and their vote ratifying the 1970 Illinois Constitution, which went into effect on July 1, 1971.

I spent little time thinking about state history and constitutions in later years as I pursued an active law practice. That changed a few years ago when I cut back on my legal work to devote time to historical research and writing. Following publication of a book I had written about Chicago immigrant history and my ancestors' experiences as part of it, I was looking for a new project. A friend suggested that I find something of interest to write about Illinois history.

The Illinois and Michigan Canal came to mind immediately. Growing up near the route of the historic hundred-mile-long canal, I knew that extensive water-filled portions of the channel, with its overgrown towpaths, locks, and lock-keepers' houses, still cut through the Illinois landscape. I soon learned, however, that much had been written about the canal, including excellent books published at the time of Congress's 1984 creation of the Illinois & Michigan Canal National Heritage Corridor. There clearly was no need for me to write another.

I was profoundly affected, however, by an almost offhand sentence in Professor James Putnam's landmark work, *The Illinois and Michigan Canal: A Study in Economic History*, published for the Illinois centennial in 1918. Discussing the debates in the 1818 Congress about the law to enable Illinois to write a constitution and become a state, Putnam mentions that "the bill for the admission of Illinois into the Union was so amended as to place the port of Chicago within the boundaries of the State."[1]

I was astounded. I had lived in Illinois my entire life. I never had heard of such an occurrence.

The "what ifs" immediately flooded my mind. If the northern boundary had remained where it was, south of what became Chicago, the city would never have developed as it did. The population growth and economic development of a wide swath of northern Illinois either would not have occurred at all or would not have been within the state's borders. Illinois would have been largely a rural and small-town state, oriented to the South as it was at the time of statehood in 1818. The new Republican Party formed in 1854 would not have rested on the favorable conditions in northern Illinois that enabled it to elect all the state officers in 1856, win all the popularly elected state offices in 1858, and win the popular vote for state offices and the popular vote and Electoral College votes for Abraham Lincoln in 1860.

I soon confirmed in the voting data that my instincts were correct. The votes to give the margins of victory to Illinois Republicans in those three election years and to Abraham Lincoln in 1860 came from the fourteen counties and eighty-five hundred square miles added to Illinois at the time of statehood.

I also learned that the momentous legislative action extending the new state northward was initiated and achieved by one man, Nathaniel Pope. Pope was the nonvoting delegate of the Territory of Illinois in Congress. When the bill to enable Illinois to write a constitution and become a state came before Congress in April 1818, Pope gained the votes for a change in the constitutional specifications of the state's boundaries that moved the northern boundary of Illinois some sixty miles farther north. Pope's avowed purpose was specifically to include within the new state the area of the future city of Chicago and its advantageous site for a canal connection to the Illinois River. The boundary amendment Pope attained was pivotal, but as remarkable were the reasons he argued in support of it, which history proved to be true. His prescience was confirmed by subsequent events.

The state of Illinois that we know now is very different from the state that would have been without the northern territory added by the Pope amendment. Only the first state constitution in 1818 was written in the state that would have been.

Illinois in 1818 was essentially a southern state. It was bordered by slave states to the east, from which came most of the white population, and the slave territory of Missouri, soon to become a state, on the west. Much of the Illinois population was sympathetic to slavery, and many were slave owners. Almost the entire white population of Illinois at the time resided in the south, in a great "Y" along the Ohio and Mississippi Rivers that join and form the state's southern borders, an area that is south of the Mason-Dixon Line. The vast remainder of the state to the north was occupied by Indians and a few French, mixed-race, or other white trappers and traders. The federal government's Fort Dearborn, founded in 1803, annihilated in 1812, and rebuilt in 1816, sat beside the mouth of the Chicago River, but Chicago was not founded until the 1830s and was then a very small village.

By the time of the 1848 Constitution, thirty years later, most of what we know now about Illinois would not have happened at all or would not have been within the boundaries of Illinois: Chicago, with its population of almost thirty thousand; the Illinois and Michigan Canal, opened in 1848; the commerce and development that occurred over the Great Lakes to the east and to the Mississippi in the west—all would not have been in the state and, given the politics over slavery in Congress at the time, might not have occurred at all.

The boundary extension did occur, of course. And the great state we celebrate as the Land of Lincoln was built on it. One man from Illinois accomplished that amendment. No one else in Illinois knew anything about it until days after. Nathaniel Pope is uncelebrated among the founding fathers and state heroes of Illinois. Who he was, what he did, and what his achievement meant to the state were, I thought, worth writing about to a contemporary audience.

In describing the history of the state to 1870, however, why write about constitutions? The simple fact is that constitutional conventions are unique events, different from all other institutions. They exist only one time. They are composed of persons elected from all over the state and are together only for one purpose. They do not stand for reelection as a group. They have lofty goals. Most want to write a document that wins the approval of the voters and makes a better political society. Typically, they are a mix of ages. They may include former holders of public office and judges and, if permitted by the enabling acts, current legislators. Some are trying to redeem lost political careers, and others, especially among the younger delegates, have political ambitions. Many have never held public office.

Important for the study of history, state constitutional conventions reveal and reflect the facts that lead to them. Delegates are free to raise and promote any policy, law, or other issue that they or their constituents want to have raised. They reflect in a singular way the views of the state's people at a particular point in time. The debates of the full conventions often expose in an unrestrained manner the delegates' opinions, sentiments, biases, and prejudices, and those of the people they represent.

State constitutions also may be turning points that move the essentials of state government in a sharply different direction at a specified date. Individual rights may change, such as permitting or forbidding forms of slavery, or allowing voting, not only by white male citizens but also by noncitizens or women or blacks. Structures of government may change, even drastically, as in going from the 1818 to 1848 constitutions in Illinois: the former providing for election of only the governor and lieutenant governor, and a sheriff and coroner in each county, with all other offices and all judgeships appointed by the legislature; the latter providing for popular elections of numerous officers and judges. Powers of government may be expanded or restricted, as in prohibiting whipping as punishment or providing for or disallowing the creation of state banks or the incurring of debt or the granting of privileges such as divorces.

I was fascinated by the little-remembered history of Illinois over two centuries, and the way that history was manifested in the three nineteenth-century constitutions and four conventions. When I related this story to others, uniformly they confirmed how significant but little known to them this history was. As the state approaches its bicentennial, I wanted to share that largely unsung story.

Introduction

When Abraham Lincoln said goodbye to family and friends in Springfield, Illinois, in February 1861 and departed to assume the presidency, he left behind a state that was a microcosm of the United States. Southern Illinois was largely rural, with scattered towns and small cities. Northern Illinois was experiencing rapid economic and population growth, with burgeoning rail routes and a boom in development of counties and cities along the Illinois and Michigan Canal and north to the Wisconsin state line. Chicago in less than thirty years had become the state's dominant urban center and one of the nation's largest cities, blessed by its location at the southwestern shores of Lake Michigan on land that had been engineered to open water routes to the Illinois and Mississippi rivers and rail routes to the West. No other city in America had grown as large as quickly as Chicago.

Illinois had not long been this way. In July 1831, when Lincoln, who described himself later as "a piece of floating driftwood,"[1] returned to settle in New Salem after working on river flatboats, southern Illinois contained almost all the state's non-Indian population. Most of its people came to Illinois from or through the South. They arrived on the Mississippi River from New Orleans or moved across the Ohio River from southern slave states, just as Thomas Lincoln had done, coming from Kentucky through Indiana to Illinois, with young Abe and his family in tow.

Slavery was common in the Illinois country from the earliest days of white settlement by the French in the late seventeenth century. Indian and African American slaves lived in the small farms and homes of trappers and settler families and in sizeable numbers in the founding houses of French priests. For six decades from the 1720s, black slaves were imported openly from New Orleans or, after 1780, brought from other American colonies. From 1787 until 1818, Illinois settlers—first in the Illinois part of the Northwest Territory, later in the Territories of Indiana and Illinois—sought to have slavery legalized. They succeeded by devising euphemistic means of lawfully holding blacks in bondage. The first four governors of the state all were or had been slave owners, as were many holders of public office.

With the first Illinois constitutional convention campaign in 1818, and successive political battles in 1824, in the 1847 constitutional convention, and even into the constitutional conventions of 1862 and 1869, forms of bondage, black codes, and disputes over the presence in the state of free blacks and their civil rights to vote, hold office, or be free of segregation were contested hotly.

The ownership of black slaves and bonded servants existed until the 1850s in the southern half of the state, including, significantly, the capital at Springfield. In Illinois in 1861, as in the nation, there were strong differences of opinion about slavery between the south and north. Sentiment favoring black slavery and slaveholders in neighboring states, and sympathy for recovering runaway slaves, was widespread in the south of the state. Sentiment opposing slavery was widespread in the north, as was advocacy for abolition. In 1861, most white people in the state, even while opposing slavery, did not believe in equality for African Americans. They held views, shared by Lincoln, that blacks were not social and political equals and doubted that blacks might ever be ready to live free in a white society.

Following the Civil War, many continued to harbor antiblack animus. Delegates to the 1869 constitutional convention stridently debated proposals to approve segregation and prohibit black voting. They also created unique provisions for political representation in the 1870 constitution to ameliorate the strongly held differences of political opinion between the southern and northern halves of the state after the Civil War.

The Indian presence, which was pervasive in territorial years and whose members engaged in hostilities against settlers even into statehood, ended little more than a decade later with treaties following the Black Hawk War in 1832, when the last tribe, the Potawatomi, were forced to move west of the Mississippi. The proof of their tragedy and coerced disappearance is the fact that from the mid-1830s the history of Illinois can be written as if Indians never lived there.[2]

Reflecting their times, all four nineteenth-century constitutional conventions were white men's conventions. White males elected the delegates. White males wrote the constitutions. White males voted to ratify or reject them. Women were not mentioned in any of the four. They were excluded by implication from holding office, however, and barred explicitly from voting and from service in the militia, both privileges of white males only.

Blacks, men and women alike, were the subject of severe repressive provisions in the first three constitutions and excluded from service in the militia. Indians were named specifically once in each of the first three constitutions, only to be disqualified from service in the militia.

As with slavery, and often with comparable emotion, political battles in the state culminating in constitutional convention debates and ratification referenda were fought over the forms, structures, and powers of government. Legislative supremacy, executive powers, appointment or election of civil officials and judges, qualifications to vote, public education, taxation, debt financing, regulation of banking, railroads, and warehouses, and the ability of government to incur debt were sharply debated and changed, permitted in one constitution and changed in another.

Internal improvement controversies over roads, bridges, canals, and, especially, railroad charters, excited rivalry among towns and counties. Legislative abuses and extravagances in authorizing improvements in the 1830s led the state to the edge of bankruptcy in the early 1840s. With Illinois on the verge of defaulting on its obligations and becoming a deadbeat state, a strong-willed governor secured adoption in 1844 of legislation to pay off the debt. The legislative plan was reinforced by the 1848 constitution, which severely limited the legislature's power to incur debt and imposed a property tax that enabled final payment of the obligations in 1880.

Illinois, like the Union, became the great state that it is by geographical expansion. The change in the constitutional specifications of the state's boundaries in April 1818 that moved the northern boundary of Illinois some sixty miles farther north added almost 20 percent of the state's area—eighty-five hundred square miles, covering fourteen counties that now include Chicago, Rockford, and other major cities. Building on that base, by 1861 the state had become one of the most populous and economically strong in the nation. The growth and development of the north, fostered by the Illinois and Michigan Canal, the influx of population that included tens of thousands of foreign immigrants, the coming of the railroads, and the boom in agriculture and commerce, were not only remarkable, they changed the course of history.

At statehood in 1818, Illinois barely claimed a population of forty thousand people. In just forty-two years, in 1860, led by the growth in the north, Illinois ranked fourth in the Union in population and wealth. Flourishing even more during the Civil War, and tripling in size in a decade, by the time of the postwar constitution in 1870, Chicago, which did not exist before 1831, was the fifth-largest city in the nation, with just under three hundred thousand people.

The growth in population and prosperity of the land area added to the state in the 1818 constitution changed state politics in the 1850s and fostered events that were of historic national significance through the 1860s and thereafter. Beginning immediately with his assassination, Abraham Lincoln has attained an immortality that generally places him in modern rankings as the greatest of American presidents. It is easily assumed that he was the preeminent leader in his home state before rising to the presidency. That, of course, is not the fact. Stephen Douglas was the foremost Illinois politician on both the state and national stage for more than two decades, until 1860.

Within a decade after arriving in Illinois in 1833, intelligent and exceptionally ambitious Douglas rose rapidly through several state offices, a presidential appointment in Illinois, and appointment to the supreme court before he was elected to Congress in 1843 at age thirty. In an expansionist nation, Douglas attained a preeminent position and national fame from the time of his arrival in Washington.

Abraham Lincoln in the same period was one among many whose political attainment was far less than Douglas's. Before 1860, Lincoln held two elective offices, serving in the state legislature for four two-year terms, retiring to private life in 1841, then serving one term in Congress. After election to Congress in August 1846, Lincoln took his seat in the House of Representatives in 1847 on the same day Douglas moved to the Senate. In contrast to Douglas, Lincoln became unpopular in his home state and known in the nation because of his denunciation of President Polk for leading the United States into the expansionist Mexican War. In 1848, he declined to seek reelection and returned to private life in Springfield.

Douglas's key role in events that changed the nation and state began in 1850, when he laboriously garnered the votes for the compromise that opened the possibility of slavery's expansion into southwestern territories acquired in the Mexican War. After quelling heated opposition to that proposal, Douglas then heightened the controversy in 1854 when he promoted a bill to repeal the Missouri Compromise of 1820 and organize the vast Kansas and Nebraska territories with popular sovereignty to decide whether they would be slave or free. The bill opened the possibility that slavery would expand into areas from which it previously had been banned.

Douglas succeeded in gaining passage of the Kansas/Nebraska legislation. As he ironically had predicted, however, a "fire-storm" erupted in Illinois and other northern states. Political alignments in Illinois changed quickly. Support for Douglas's position came primarily from Democrats in the south of the state. Longtime Democratic voters in the north, including large ethnic immigrant groups, opposed the legislation, as did prominent Democrat officeholders.

The focus of political effort in Illinois became the November 1854 elections of representatives in Congress and the elections for the state legislature that would choose the U.S. senator to fill the seat held by Douglas ally James Shields. In the November elections, anti-Nebraska candidates won five of Illinois's nine House of Representative districts. Among the victors was Illinois Supreme Court justice Lyman Trumbull, who resigned his secure position on the court to win election as an anti-Nebraska Democrat.

Abraham Lincoln, also, was "aroused . . . as he had never been before"[3] by the Kansas-Nebraska Act. He quit retirement to seek election to the Senate as a Whig when the new general assembly would vote in February 1855. Trumbull, who had taken his seat in the House of Representatives, also entered the Senate contest, as did others. Lincoln would have known that his quest was unprecedented. Since the 1820s, when political parties emerged in Illinois and Elias Kent Kane was elected as a Jacksonian Democrat, all eight men elected senators by the legislature in ten elections were Democrats.[4]

Lincoln led the initial general assembly vote for the Senate in February, falling five votes short of the necessary majority, with Shields a close second and Trumbull a distant third. When Lincoln could not gain the needed votes, he urged his supporters to vote for Trumbull, whom he knew well and liked, and who he believed would be a capable foe to Douglas in the Senate. Trumbull was elected on the tenth ballot. He became a staunch Republican in the Senate, campaigned for Lincoln in the 1858 and 1860 elections, supported him through the Civil War, played a key role in the passage of the Thirteenth Amendment outlawing slavery, and ultimately became the first Illinois senator to serve three full terms.

During the 1854 turmoil, a collection of antislavery groups in Michigan and Wisconsin had combined to form the emerging Republican Party. Lincoln declined to join that effort, believing that they were too abolitionist and radical, and choosing to remain a Whig as he sought election to the Senate. In 1856, however, Lincoln assumed a leadership role in organizing the Illinois Republican Party at its state convention. Believing that only a former Democrat could win the governor's office as a Republican, he assembled the necessary support for Mexican War hero and former congressman William Bissell to lead a slate of candidates for election in the fall, all with little involvement from residents in southern Illinois.

Democrat James Buchanan narrowly won the state's votes for president in 1856. Bissell was elected governor, beginning a thirty-six-year string of Republican governors. The other Republican candidates swept all the statewide offices for the first time. Republicans carried the counties stretching across the north of the state in the area added by the 1818 enabling act by almost twenty-four thousand votes, overcoming the Democratic lead in the rest of the state.[5]

In 1858, Lincoln opposed Douglas's effort to win a third term in the Senate. Launching his campaign at the Republican convention with his famous House Divided speech, Lincoln ran on his differences with Douglas over slavery. The seven Lincoln-Douglas debates during that campaign gained international attention and earned for Lincoln recognition as a worthy opponent for the famed "Little Giant." In the general election in November, Republicans won the state's popular vote, again with the votes assuring victory coming from the northern counties added to the state by the constitutional boundary amendment in 1818. The members of the gerrymandered general assembly elected Douglas by a 54 to 46 vote, however, returning him to the Senate.[6]

Lincoln, of course, was successful in 1860 when he defeated Douglas in the four-way presidential race, receiving a narrow 50.7 percent majority of Illinois's popular vote. He won that election and Illinois's electoral votes with the votes of the counties added to the state by Nathaniel Pope's 1818 boundary extension.

That boundary change, written into the constitution of 1818 and perpetuated in the Illinois constitution of 1848 and later constitutions, enabled Lincoln's success in 1860 and set the stage for the preservation of the Union.[7]

Illinois voters in the November 1860 general election also elected the Republican ticket of candidates for state office, headed by Richard Yates as governor, and a Republican-dominated general assembly. In January 1861, the new legislature elected Lyman Trumbull to a second term in the U.S. Senate.[8]

In the November 1860 election, Illinois voters approved, by a greater than 2 1 vote, the call for Illinois to hold its fourth constitutional convention. The convention would not occur, however, until January 7, 1862, more than a year later, with delegates to be chosen from each of the state's seventy-five legislative districts on November 5, 1861. In the year before the election of delegates, the start of the Civil War changed the political climate. Half as many voters as in the 1860 general election produced a sharp reversal for the Republican Party, with twice as many Democrats as Republicans chosen to be delegates.

The convention moved in sharply partisan and controversial directions. In the end, opposition to the proposed constitution was overwhelming. Only forty-six of the seventy-five delegates were present for the final vote in March 1862; only four of them were Republicans, who all voted against the document. The voters rejected the proposed constitution in June, 53 percent to 47 percent.

In November 1864, as the Civil War moved toward its conclusion, Abraham Lincoln carried the presidential vote in all but three of the twenty-five states that voted. The Republican Union ticket won the Illinois state elections with large margins and won eleven of the fourteen congressional races. Events of the next five years changed forever the state of the law in Illinois and the United States. The adoption of the Thirteenth Amendment ending slavery, which Illinois was the first state to ratify, the conclusion of the war, Lincoln's murder, and the adoption of the Fourteenth and Fifteenth Amendments that can fairly be called a Lincoln Legacy set the stage for the Fourth Illinois Constitutional Convention that began in December 1869.

The delegates who drafted the 1870 constitution were elected in a state that was sharply divided politically between north and south in the aftermath of the Civil War. Many in the state retained southern attitudes toward African Americans. Convention battles sought to limit the effect of the Civil War amendments and deny to blacks full civil rights. The convention, however, bridged those divisions and adopted progressive and even unique provisions on many subjects that gained overwhelming favor in the ratification votes in 1870 and remained in effect for a century.

Illinois's three eighteenth-century constitutions were adopted in a span of only fifty-three years. They reflected the momentous changes during that period that made Illinois one of the most populous, economically strong, and socially and politically progressive states in the nation, the state that in the twentieth century came to be known as the Land of Lincoln.

CHAPTER 1

Illinois before Statehood

Slave Country of the Northwest Territory

On July 4, 1778, the second anniversary of the Declaration of Independence, George Rogers Clark, in a surprise nighttime attack, secured the first American rule over the land that would become the State of Illinois. Not yet twenty-six years old at the time, Clark was a patrician Virginian and a neighbor and friend of Thomas Jefferson and other Virginia leaders. He was also an experienced frontiersman and wily pioneer.[1]

In 1776 Clark had led a company of settlers into Virginia's far western Kentucky territory. Charged with protecting the new settlements against increasing Indian attacks stimulated by the British, he returned to Williamsburg in December 1777 to meet with Virginia officials. He secured the long-sought recognition of Kentucky as a county of Virginia and received authorization and money from Virginia governor Patrick Henry to take the offensive and stop the Indian raids by capturing the British headquarters at Detroit and clearing the British from the Old Northwest. Secretly, Governor Henry also authorized Clark to seek control first of Kaskaskia and the other old French-settled villages in the Illinois country along the east side of the Mississippi River, the western boundary of the British territory. Clark had received information from frontier friends that the villages were defenseless and that the French settlers would welcome the Americans.[2]

The villages along the Mississippi River that came to be called the American
Bottom were the first white settlements in the Illinois country. In March 1699
priests of the Seminary of Foreign Missions established a settlement east of the
Mississippi River, some eight miles south of the present site of St. Louis, in an
area populated primarily by Cahokia Indians. Traders soon gathered nearby. The
mission, which they named Cahokia, survives today as the oldest continuously
occupied community in the American interior.[3]

In 1703 the Jesuits followed, establishing a settlement some sixty miles south
of Cahokia. They named it Kaskaskia for the Indians who lived in nearby villages. Other settlements were established between the first two, as was Fort de
Chartres, the seat of civil and military power, built in 1720 fifteen miles upstream
from Kaskaskia. Kaskaskia flourished. It became the center of French colonial
life in the Illinois country and for more than one hundred years remained the
commercial, cultural, and governmental center of Illinois.[4]

These few settlements were the only population centers in Illinois. Most remained important in the Territory and State of Illinois well into the nineteenth
century, long after French sovereignty ended.

Although Clark was authorized to raise a force of three hundred men, he was
able to recruit little more than half that number by May 1778. After training on
Corn Island at the Falls of the Ohio, now Louisville, his force set forth in late
June 1778, during an eclipse of the sun, rowing in keelboats down the Ohio River
to Fort Massac, which was east across lower Illinois from Kaskaskia. Disembark-
ing there, they marched 120 miles in six days over previously uncrossed Illinois
wilderness and quickly captured Kaskaskia the evening of July 4 without firing a
shot. Clark promptly sent a small body of his forces north along the Mississippi,
accompanied by friendly Frenchmen, to occupy the other villages, which also
surrendered without opposition.[5]

Clark spent several months organizing his control over the old French villages
and calming the alarmed inhabitants. Representing Virginians who believed in
local self-government and who despised autocratic rule, Clark devised a form
of government in which the people would participate. He distributed commissions to the necessary militia officers. He served as the first American judge in
the region and inaugurated a system of courts to which the people would elect
the judges.[6]

Clark then turned his attention east across Illinois to Vincennes, on the Wabash River. The notorious British governor Henry Hamilton had fortified the

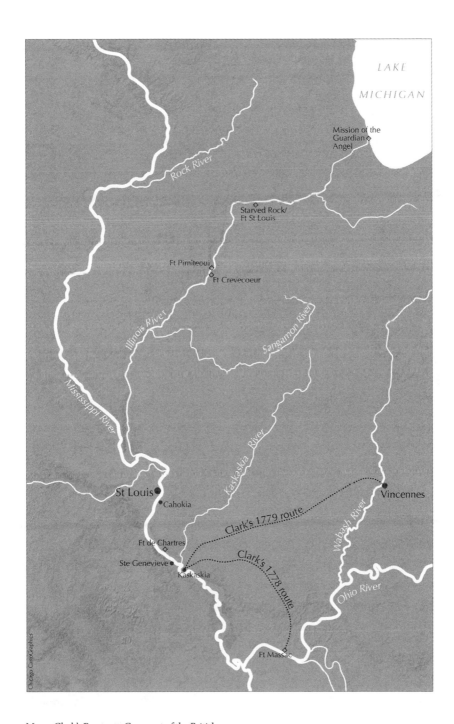

Map 1. Clark's Routes to Conquest of the British

sleepy town. Receiving word from informants that French settlers in Vincennes also would welcome the Americans, Clark did the unexpected in presumably impossible February conditions. With fewer than 170 men, he marched the 140 miles from Kaskaskia to Vincennes through swamps and flooded rivers. Aided by friendly settlers, Clark overwhelmed Hamilton and the British garrison in a surprise attack on February 25, 1779. Hamilton was sent to the Virginia capital at Williamsburg as a prisoner and remained in a dungeon there until March 1781.[7]

Clark had a clear and immediate opportunity to accomplish his original goal by capturing Detroit. His force dissipated, however, as Kentuckians departed to attempt an attack elsewhere and others were impatient to return to their homes. Clark and his remaining forces spent the rest of the war on the defensive, keeping possession of the former French villages, preventing Indian raids where they could, and blocking the British from establishing a new base south of Detroit.[8]

A County of Virginia

As soon as word of Clark's victory at Kaskaskia reached Williamsburg, Virginia took steps to secure its claim and create a government for the huge northwestern territory. On December 9, 1778, invoking entitlement from ancient charters, the House of Burgesses created the Virginia County of Illinois, a vast area of indefinite boundaries that encompassed all British territory west to the Mississippi and north to Canada. Governor Henry appointed the county lieutenant, the chief executive officer, and the militia commandant. Local residents were authorized to choose civil officers and judges of the courts. These officials were to administer the law already in force in the area, the *coutume de Paris*, modified in some ways by the law of Virginia. French residents were given assurance that they could freely exercise their religion.[9]

The area was almost entirely in the undisputed possession of Indians. For all practical purposes, the government was concerned only with the old French Mississippi River villages and a few other outposts as far away as Peoria and Vincennes. The entire population of these locales totaled fewer than two thousand white persons and their one thousand slaves.[10]

By the summer of 1779, the harmony and good will that had met the new governors was fading. Antagonisms grew between the longtime French inhabitants and the American frontiersmen increasingly arriving in the country. Their cultures and attitudes differed in almost every respect. The French were Catholics;

the newcomers mostly Protestants. The French lived on good terms with the Indians; the pioneers believed the only good Indian was a dead one. The French had been educated to respect law and government imposed by authorities; the frontiersmen wanted to live free of the law and solve disputes on their own. Their opposing attitudes foreshadowed a fundamental difference between those who favored orderly authoritarian rule and those who desired populist democratic government—a difference that would mark Illinois for decades.[11]

The Virginia County of Illinois lasted three years. Unrest against the military governors, confiscation of property to support the soldiers, and ineffective courts and other officials were widespread. A steady stream of emigration by the French to the Spanish side of the Mississippi depleted village populations. Unable to support effective government in the huge territory, Virginia allowed the law creating the Illinois County to lapse on January 5, 1782.[12]

Britain Cedes the Northwest Territory

British sovereignty over the northwest territory had endured barely twenty years. Great Britain had obtained dominion over the area in 1763 as a result of the Treaty of Paris, which ended the Seven Years' War between France and Great Britain (the American French and Indian War). France ceded to Great Britain all French possessions on the North American continent east of the Mississippi, encompassing the present states of Illinois, Indiana, Michigan, Ohio, Wisconsin, and an eastern portion of Minnesota that includes St. Paul and Duluth. In a separate treaty the same year, France ceded to Spain its Louisiana Territory west across the Mississippi River from the Illinois country.

The destiny of Britain's northwest country was in play in Paris again in 1783 at the negotiations that ended the Revolutionary War. The bargaining proceeded along unexpected lines. Factions in London and in Spain were pressing to have Britain retain dominion over the region. However, Lord Shelburne, the British minister in charge of the negotiations, did not make a strong effort to do so.[13]

Shelburne was a friend and admirer of Benjamin Franklin, the American commissioner in Paris. He was impressed by Franklin's arguments that generosity in giving up the region could lead to centuries of Anglo-Saxon friendship. He also believed that if Great Britain retained the territory, the inevitable thrust of the American population westward would always be a source of friction, and there might well be conflict also with the Spanish west of the Mississippi. As a result, the Treaty of Paris of 1783 fixed the international border with Britain along the Mississippi River and the upper Great Lakes.[14]

The success of the American diplomats in the treaty negotiations can be attributed in large measure to the idealism of the British minister. Lord Shelburne felt justifiable pride in this act. In 1797 he wrote to an American friend, "I cannot express to you the satisfaction I have felt in seeing the forts [of the Northwest] given up. . . . The deed is done, and a strong foundation laid for eternal amity between England and America." That amity, of course, was interrupted fifteen years later by the War of 1812.[15]

Eight Years of Unrest and Anarchy

Clark's ouster of the British and the failure of Virginia to institute effective administration left the Illinois villages in a period after 1782 that has been described as anarchy and chaos. Each village was left to its own resources. The French, with their imbued tradition of authoritarian rule, had no talent for self-government. Courts fell into disuse. Debts could not be enforced. Although Virginia had prohibited settlement, English-speaking settlers pushed in, attracted by the stories that Clark's soldiers and others told of abundant fertile land, opportunity, and independence. Among them were the elder Shadrach Bond, who served in Clark's force, and his nephew and namesake who became a prominent political leader in the Indiana and Illinois territories and the first elected governor of the new state of Illinois. Many of the new settlers became squatters, developing and cultivating the free land and eventually creating legal controversy.[16]

The Spanish government west of the Mississippi abetted the disintegration, luring Illinois settlers across the river with land grants and other inducements. Prominent priests and lay leaders as well as prosperous landowners were persuaded to make the river crossing. After 1787 the clause of the new Northwest Ordinance prohibiting slavery caused the French residents anxiety, which the Spanish exploited with warnings that they would lose their slave property if they stayed in Illinois.[17]

The Articles of Confederation

The task of governing the vast land area that the United States had obtained from the British ran into conflicting claims by several of the original states. The largest was Virginia's. Connecticut also declared that its colonial charter gave it rights to a strip extending into northern Illinois. New York, Pennsylvania, and Massachusetts claimed areas that were smaller and closer to the Appalachians.[18]

The Second Continental Congress drafted the Articles of Confederation to be the governing document or constitution of the original thirteen states. They were completed and sent to the states for ratification in 1777, with the stipulation that they would not become effective until all thirteen states approved them. Virginia was the first state to ratify on December 16, 1777. Eleven others followed by February 1779. Maryland, however, refused to ratify unless Virginia and the four other states gave up their western claims.[19]

Virginia led the way in solving the problem by agreeing in 1781 that it would keep title to Kentucky and relinquish all claims north of the Ohio River if others did the same. The others agreed. The articles went into effect with Maryland's ratification on February 2, 1781.[20]

Thomas Jefferson and three other Virginia delegates signed a deed on March 1, 1784, ceding the area to the United States while keeping title to Kentucky. The other states followed Virginia's lead. Virginia's deed of cession to the United States included a significant condition: that settlers in the ceded territory "shall have their possessions and titles confirmed to them and be protected in the enjoyment of their rights and liberties." This was understood to mean that settlers in the conceded territory could continue to own slaves, as French settlers in Illinois had for eighty-five years. The condition would perpetuate forms of slavery in Illinois for another sixty years.[21]

African American Slavery: Pervasive and Persistent

Slaveholding in the French villages, both of Indians and later of African Americans, existed from the first days of white presence. Louis Jolliet and Father Jacques Marquette had brought Indian slave boys with them in their epic 1673 exploration when they crossed the future state of Illinois on the Illinois and Des Plaines Rivers to Lake Michigan. By the 1720s, households in the villages of the American Bottom included families with their children and also their slaves. All lived in close quarters, worked together, and worshipped together. Priests were a constant presence, as were Indians resident in nearby villages.[22]

Beginning in 1719, the first black African slaves were brought in numbers to the Illinois country, transported up the Mississippi from lower Louisiana. By the early 1720s, black slaves were brought to work in commercial mining ventures in the lead mines and salines west of the Mississippi, across from Kaskaskia. Many lived among the other residents in the villages east of the river, crossing to the west to work.[23]

In the late 1740s, Ste. Genevieve, the first permanent European settlement west of the Mississippi River other than New Orleans, was established across from Kaskaskia. Initially, Ste. Genevieve existed largely as an agricultural annex of Kaskaskia, formed by French and Creoles who moved across the river from the American Bottom. By the end of the French and Indian War in 1763, it was a firmly rooted, independent civic and sacramental parish. It became substantially larger than any of the towns east of the Mississippi by the end of the century.[24]

Censuses by French authorities of the communities in the American Bottom register the growth in population and also the relatively high percentages that slaves comprised, percentages that equaled or exceeded the proportions of slave ownership in the American South on the eve of the Civil War. Between 1726 and 1752, the total resident population increased from 512 to 1,380 persons. Of those, black slaves' numbers increased from 129 to 446 and Indian slaves from 68 to 149. The percentage of slaves to the entire population thus approximated 40 percent at each census, culminating in 43 percent in 1752. That year, sixty-nine of the 167 white heads of household owned one or more black slaves.[25]

Slaves represented a huge portion of the society and were a significant component of the Illinois country's economy in the eighteenth century. Their labor was important to productivity. Their value was a substantial capital asset. The institution of slavery was firmly established.[26]

Most significant, the slavery of the French colonies later was legitimized by Illinois's constitutions, which perpetuated bonded servitude in Illinois until the eve of the Civil War. Illinois is not thought of today as having been a slave state, but slavery was an important part of its origins and history.

The Northwest Ordinance

On March 1, 1784, the same day as the Virginia deed of cession, the Congress appointed a committee, with Thomas Jefferson as chairman, to plan for government of the huge new territory. Jefferson submitted a report proposing to organize the area into seven rectangular states with fancy names, supposedly of Greek and

Indian origin. Notably, Jefferson's report also proposed that after 1800, "there shall be neither slavery nor involuntary servitude in any of the said states otherwise than in punishment of crime whereof the party shall have been duly convicted."[27]

No official action to govern the northwestern territory was taken for three years. While the Congress could not agree on any plan to organize its new land riches, large numbers of squatters illegally settled along the Ohio River and its major tributaries. Increasingly, as federal military action could not manage the influx, settlers rejected any notion that Congress should control their communities. The Congress, and particularly Federalist leaders, feared discord and possible fragmentation of the vast and rich western lands. Supporters of the newly drafted Constitution of 1787, which was at the time being circulated among the states for ratification, shared a belief that a strong federal or national government was necessary to preserve the Union.[28]

Early in July 1787 representatives of a prominent group of Federalist Revolutionary War veterans, motivated by their political beliefs as well as their interest in speculation in valuable public lands, presented to the Congress a plan to purchase five million acres of land in the territory. Congress acted promptly. On July 9 a committee of the Congress met at the capital in New York to finish a proposal even while the constitutional convention was meeting in Philadelphia revising the Articles of Confederation. Several men were members of both bodies. At the last moment, committee chairman Nathan Dane added Article VI, which provided, "There shall be neither slavery nor involuntary servitude in the said territory," wording that proved acceptable to the slave states as long as it applied to the territory northwest of the Ohio River. To make the plan even more tolerable to slave owners, Dane added a fugitive slave clause.[29]

The ordinance was reported to Congress on July 11. The next day it was read a second time. The Northwest Ordinance was adopted on July 13, 1787, receiving the unanimous vote of all eight states present: Virginia, Massachusetts, Delaware, New York, New Jersey, North Carolina, South Carolina, and Georgia. At the time, slaves were held in all the states except Massachusetts. When the government under the new constitution was inaugurated in 1789, Congress affirmed the territorial law.[30]

One of the final actions of the Continental Congress, the Northwest Ordinance is considered by many to be second in importance only to the Constitution of 1787 as a foundation document of the United States and achievement of the

Confederacy. It provided a system of government for the territory, with power concentrated in the hands of nationally appointed officials, that proved to be a catalyst of discontent and a motivating force in the drive for Illinois statehood and the weak executive of Illinois's first constitution. Officers, all to be nominated by the president and appointed by Congress, were a governor, a secretary, and a court of three judges. The governor, acting with at least two judges, had legislative functions; together they could adopt civil and criminal laws from among those of the existing states. The governor also was commander in chief of the militia, with power to commission and appoint all officers below generals, who

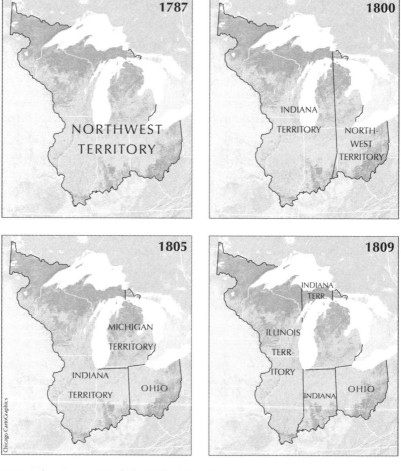

Map 2. Northwest Territory Evolution to Illinois Territory

were named by Congress. He had the power to appoint magistrates and other civil officers in each county or township "as he shall find necessary for the peace and good order."[31]

The governor could invoke a second grade of government when the territory's population reached "five thousand free male inhabitants of full age." The second grade introduced an element of democracy by providing for "a general assembly, or legislature," that consisted of the governor and a house of representatives elected by male voters. A legislative council, or upper house, of five members was to be appointed by Congress. Bills needed to be approved by majority votes of both the council and the house of representatives but would become laws only with the governor's assent, giving him an absolute power of veto. The governor also had the power to establish counties and appoint their officials.[32]

An important provision was that the council and legislature acting as one body could elect a delegate to Congress who would have the right to debate but not vote. In fact, as was demonstrated in 1818 when the Illinois statehood bill came to Congress, the delegate could be very influential, working in committees, writing legislation, lobbying members of the House and Senate, and participating in debates.[33]

Significantly, the phrase "free male inhabitants" in section 9 of the ordinance was understood to include free blacks. In the Ohio area of the territory and under the 1802 Ohio state constitution, free blacks were allowed to vote.[34]

The ordinance provided for the establishment in the Northwest Territory of "not less than three, nor more than five states." It set forth boundary and population conditions and also specified that new states would be "on equal footing with the original states, in all respects whatever."[35]

The final section comprises six articles that declare certain fundamental rights. Article VI was a categorical declaration outlawing slavery. Echoing Jefferson's earlier report, it stated, "There shall be neither slavery nor involuntary servitude in the territory, otherwise than in the punishment of crime, whereof the party shall have been duly convicted." Despite the absolute nature of this prohibition, creative provisions in constitutions and laws perpetuated slavery in the form of indentured servitude in Illinois until the 1850s.[36]

The first governor appointed by the Continental Congress, former revolutionary general Arthur St. Clair, was serving at the time as its president. As news of Article VI circulated in the territory, residents interpreted it as an abolition law. A group of slave-owning residents, including some French settlers, organized to negotiate with the Congress to rescind or modify the clause. St. Clair was not impartial on the subject. While resident in western Pennsylvania, he had purchased two slaves whom he brought to the territory and held in bondage in violation of Article VI. St. Clair endorsed the theory that to apply the provision to slaves in the territory would make it a retrospective law and issued an edict declaring the article enforceable against slaveholding immigrants only. When St. Clair informed President Washington of his decision, Washington offered no objection. The clause was interpreted thereafter as a ban on importing slaves into the territory.[37]

Government under the Northwest Ordinance was slow to materialize, especially for the Illinois country. St. Clair did not travel to the new territorial capital at Marietta for more than a year. Almost two years passed after he first arrived in Marietta before he finally visited the Illinois country, and even then only after prodding by Congress and President George Washington.[38]

Although slow to bring his office to Illinois, after finally arriving in March 1790, St. Clair was prompt in creating a county and naming it after himself. St. Clair County covered almost a third of the present state. He appointed his nephew, William St. Clair, clerk and recorder of deeds of the new county.[39]

Governor St. Clair remained in Illinois some three months, visiting the old settlements at Kaskaskia and Cahokia. He assessed Illinois as being in deplorable condition. He found it difficult to establish civil government, he said, because "not a fiftieth man could read or write" and the entire area "afforded barely a sufficient number of persons . . . qualified to fill offices."[40]

Departing on June 11, 1790, St. Clair did not return to Illinois for five years. In that time, the U.S. government, like Virginia before it, did little to administer the country. William St. Clair, after three years, reported that court sessions were sporadic and organized government almost nonexistent. Indian raids, thefts, shortages of food and salt, plague, and crop failures all caused hardship. Numbers of the French crossed the river to Spanish territory.[41]

Boding well for the future, however, the same decade also saw the arrival of men with money and business acumen. Some crossed the Ohio River from Kentucky. Others were French Canadians who would play major roles in the region's development. Principal among the latter was Pierre Menard, who opened a store in Kaskaskia in 1791 and in subsequent decades became a leading merchant in the American Bottom and in Ste. Genevieve and St. Louis. Menard served in the

Indiana and Illinois territorial legislatures as a three-year resident, although not a citizen. Later, in the 1818 Illinois constitutional convention he was the subject of a special schedule provision to allow him to serve in office as lieutenant governor although a citizen for only two years.[42]

The persistent threat from Indians presented a major problem for the territorial government. Indians were stimulated to hostility in part by the continued presence of British forts in the northwest despite the cession of the region in the Treaty of Paris in 1783. Major Indian attacks occurred in present-day northern Indiana and northwest Ohio. In 1790, General Josiah Harmar lost a battle against Indian tribes in which 180 U.S. soldiers died. The following year St. Clair himself suffered a humiliating defeat while leading an army against Miami Indians near Fort Wayne. American casualties included 630 dead and 285 wounded. Three years later, on August 20, 1794, as the confident Indians demanded peace negotiations and evacuation by whites from the Northwest Territory, General "Mad Anthony" Wayne routed the Indians in the Battle of Fallen Timbers, fought in the forest wreckage of an Ohio tornado. Following his victory, in 1795 Wayne bullied the Indians into signing the Treaty of Greenville, which gave the Americans undisputed control of much of the northwest territory. The Jay Treaty, negotiated in London in 1794 by Supreme Court chief justice John Jay, who was sent by President Washington, finally required that the British forts be relinquished, effective in 1796.[43]

Discontent in the Territory

By 1800, after more than a decade of territorial government based in Ohio under Governor St. Clair, residents in Illinois and Indiana were expressing their discontent. Settlers in the western part of the huge territory complained that the seat of government at Marietta, some five hundred miles east of Kaskaskia and three hundred miles east of Vincennes, was too distant, that judges rarely visited their villages, that territorial government was too expensive and afforded them no benefits, and that the government headed by the stiff-necked Federalist Arthur St. Clair was unconcerned with the western reaches. The complaints and petitions of the westerners meshed nicely with the ambitions of William Henry Harrison.[44]

Harrison was long known for being the oldest person elected to the office of president of the United States—until Ronald Reagan in 1981—and for serving the shortest time in office. Sixty-eight years old when he was elected as the ninth president, he died only thirty-one days after giving an inauguration address of more than two hours outdoors, wearing neither coat nor hat, on a cold, rainy March 4, 1841. He was the last president born as a British subject before the Declaration of Independence, which his father signed as a delegate from Virginia. Left impoverished at age eighteen when his father died, he joined the army in 1791. When General Wayne took command of the western army in 1792 from Arthur St. Clair, Harrison was soon promoted, first to the rank of lieutenant and, shortly thereafter, to serve as an aide-de-camp to Wayne. Harrison, at age twenty-one, served in that position with General Wayne at the Battle of Fallen Timbers.[45]

Harrison had a long career in military service and in political office. After holding territorial offices, he served Ohio as a U.S. congressman and senator. He was an unsuccessful candidate for president in 1836, losing to Martin Van Buren, but he won election over Van Buren in 1840.

The Territory of Indiana

Astute and ambitious politically, William Henry Harrison resigned from the army in 1797. The next year he gained congressional appointment to serve under Governor St. Clair as the secretary of the Northwest Territory. From that position, he won election the following year to be the first delegate to Congress of the newly second-grade territory. Harrison won the position by one vote over Arthur St. Clair Jr., who was serving as attorney general of the territory after appointment by his father in 1796.[46]

Although Harrison did not have a vote in Congress, he secured the key position as chairman of the House Committee on Public Lands. From that post, he maneuvered passage of a law, effective July 4, 1800, creating a new Territory of Indiana. The territory was large: with its capital at Vincennes, the Indiana Territory covered the present states of Illinois, Indiana, Wisconsin, most of Michigan, and part of Minnesota, yet its population was less than six thousand. The smaller territory remaining to the east retained the name, the Northwest Territory.[47]

Not surprisingly, President John Adams nominated Harrison, and Congress confirmed him the next day to be the first governor of the new Indiana Territory. Also no surprise: the residents of Illinois soon made it clear that they were not satisfied to be part of this new territory either. As with Ohio, the Mississippi villages lamented that the seat of government, the legislature, and the courts at Vincennes were too far away. They complained bitterly about Harrison's use of his appointment power, charging with justification that he chose the great majority of his officials from Knox County, which covered Indiana, to the detriment of St. Clair and Randolph Counties in Illinois. In addition to local favoritism, they also complained that he used his patronage power to cultivate factions loyal to him.[48]

As early as July 1788, settlers in what became the Illinois Territory conveyed threats to future governor St. Clair that if slavery were prohibited in the territory, they would move west of the Mississippi to Spanish country, where slavery was legal. After formation of the new national government in 1789, St. Clair's interpretation of Article VI—that it did not apply to existing slavery—did not satisfy new settlers in Illinois. They agitated for the repeal or suspension of the slavery prohibition. Thus, in 1796, four leading men of St. Clair and Randolph Counties in Illinois sent a petition to Congress asking for repeal of the article. After 1800, when the Territory of Indiana was split off from Ohio, Illinois settlers requesting repeal or a ten-year suspension of Article VI filed numerous petitions with Congress. In 1802, and again in 1805, 1806, and 1807, petitions were filed with Congress asking for repeal or modification of Article VI of the ordinance. Antislavery interests in Congress blocked all these efforts.[49]

Indiana Permits Slavery by Indenture

Unable to persuade Congress to permit slavery, officials in the Indiana Territory adopted the artifice of voluntary indentured servitude to accomplish continued ownership of blacks and their labor. Such an indentured servitude provision had been included in the Ohio statehood constitution of 1802.[50]

In 1803 Governor Harrison, a slave owner himself and sympathetic to the slavery cause, with the support of two of the appointed judges, promulgated the first of a series of laws that permitted bondage and involuntary servitude under allegedly voluntary contracts. The 1803 Indiana Territory "Law Concerning Servants," derived from the slave codes of Virginia and Kentucky, stated that all persons brought into the territory "under contract to serve another"—the persons to whom the law was applied were always slaves in their former location—were required to serve the full terms of their contracts. Such contracts often obligated service of fifty or more years, including many for ninety-nine years. Sales from one master to another were permitted. The law also specified rules of conduct, providing for punishments, including whipping, for servants who would not perform their duties. As with slaves, the contract for the indentured black could be sold or assigned to a new master and bequeathed to the master's heirs. Third parties were prohibited from doing business with bound servants or entertaining or harboring them. The 1803 law, along with similar laws in 1805 and 1807, became the basis of involuntary servitude in the Indiana Territory until 1809 and in Illinois until decades after statehood.[51]

In 1804 Indiana became a territory of the second grade. The next year the newly elected legislature—five of its seven members were settlers from the slave states of Maryland and Virginia, and a sixth a slaveholder from Illinois country—adopted another law that provided that a person older than age fifteen who was a slave in another state could be brought into the territory and within thirty days sign a contract to serve as an indentured servant for a specified number of years. If the slave refused to sign within thirty days, the master was required to deport him or her from the territory within the next thirty days. Thus, a slave who did not "consent" to the "voluntary" contract was exiled into chattel slavery elsewhere.[52]

The 1805 law also included two provisions binding children and young people. If an owner brought a black or mulatto younger than age fifteen into the territory, the young slave could be held to service until age thirty-five if male and age thirty-two if female. The owner had the obligation to register such young slaves with the county clerk. Significantly, the 1805 law also stated that children born to an indentured woman during her service became servants of the owner, thus making the bondage hereditary without consent from the children. Male children could be held to service until age thirty and females until age twenty-eight without indenture contracts.[53]

In 1807 Indiana moved beyond questions of defining bondage to issues of the treatment of blacks. A new statute, titled "An Act Concerning Slaves and Servants," was adopted. This law was a "Slave Code" or "Black Code," as severe as any in the southern states, regulating the conduct of servants and slaves. It provided penalties for slaves, including whipping for being more than ten miles away from their usual residence or their master's home without a pass or letter of permission, for engaging in trespass, riot, or unlawful assembly, or for giving "seditious speeches." Persons harboring slaves or aiding runaways also could be punished.[54]

Chattel Slavery in the Salines

Outright and explicit chattel slavery, with no pretense of voluntariness, was utilized for years to labor in the salt wells in Gallatin County, southwest of Shawneetown, Illinois. Traditions long held that the saline flats and streams southwest of Shawneetown were a major source of salt for native peoples. In 1778 government geographer Thomas Hutchins said of that region, "The Northwest abounds with salt springs and any quantity of salt may be made from them in a manner now done in the Illinois country."[55]

Congress in 1796 directed U.S. surveyors working in the territory northwest of the Ohio River "to observe closely" for salt mines, springs, and wells. Two potent springs were identified and a ten-by-thirteen-mile reservation created for salt mining. Congress withheld the area from public land sales and in March 1803 authorized the secretary of the treasury to lease the springs. In June, Governor Harrison, who was also named superintendent of the saline, negotiated a treaty with five Indian tribes that ceded to the United States two million acres of lands that included the salines. The same summer, he leased the Saline River springs to a private operator.[56]

From the outset, salt mines and processing facilities used slave labor. Some historians estimate that from one thousand to two thousand blacks worked in the salt wells, although that number is disputed. Most workers were slaves leased from owners in Kentucky and Tennessee. They cut trees, split and hauled wood used to boil the hundred-gallon cast-iron kettles of saltwater as they moved along a row firing twenty to thirty kettles. At the end of the line, they scooped the salt into barrels made at the scene and hauled the fifty-pound containers by oxcart to Shawneetown, where they loaded them into keelboats for transport to market.[57]

When the Territory of Illinois was separated out of Indiana in 1809, Governor Edwards assumed the duties of saline superintendent. In 1814 a territorial law made the leasing of slaves legal for up to one year at a time for any type of labor. The law was a clear contradiction of the Northwest Ordinance. The rationale was that the scarcity of white labor hindered the erection of facilities for salt production, but the law did not prevent leasing anywhere in the territory for any type of labor. Leased slaves were used in other labor than salt production. The salines became the property of the state of Illinois in 1818. The reservations were sold in stages between 1829 and 1847. The salines near Shawneetown finally closed in 1873.[58]

The Territory of Illinois

By 1808, the views of Indiana residents toward slavery were changing rapidly. Many northern migrants with strong antislavery sentiments had settled in the Indiana part of the territory. They were opposed to Governor Harrison because of his proslavery proclivities. They had no objection, however, to uniting with Illinoisans seeking to separate from Indiana as long as their proslavery attitudes would be confined to Illinois. In 1806 a House of Representatives committee had deemed as "inexpedient" a petition from Illinois to Congress asking for separation from Indiana. In 1808, however, after an election had changed the composition of the Indiana territorial legislature by electing representatives from Illinois who favored separation, a deal was made with Jesse B. Thomas, speaker of the Indiana Territory house of representatives, who lived in eastern Indiana.[59]

Thomas was a slaveholder. As speaker in Indiana, he signed both the 1805 and 1807 slave laws. He won election as the Indiana Territory delegate to Congress with the support of anti-Harrison, proslavery Illinois residents to whom he had pledged to achieve separation. Once in the U.S. House of Representatives, in just four months he achieved enactment of the law, on February 3, 1809, establishing the new Territory of Illinois.[60]

It did not concern Thomas that he was hanged in effigy and vilified in Indiana. As soon as the Illinois Territory was formed, Thomas moved there and secured appointment as one of the first territorial judges. He held that position until 1818, when he was elected a delegate and then president of the Illinois constitutional convention. After statehood later in the year, the new Illinois General Assembly elected him to the U.S. Senate, where he served Illinois, with one reelection, until 1829. A bitter rival of President Andrew Jackson, he did not run for reelection that year and moved his home to Ohio.[61]

The new Illinois Territory was large. It covered an area two and one-half times that of the present state, extending on the south from the Mississippi and Ohio rivers—as does the present state—on the east from the Wabash River and Vincennes north all the way to Canada, and on the west along the Mississippi River north to Lake of the Woods on the Canadian border. It also was sparsely populated, with white residents estimated at some nine thousand and Indians an estimated eighteen thousand occupying the larger portion.[62]

Along with Thomas, the two Kentucky senators, Henry Clay and John Pope, played key roles in achieving the vote in Congress for the creation of the Illinois

Territory and the organization of the territorial government. On March 7, 1809, President James Madison, newly in office, selected John Boyle, a stranger to Illinois who was sponsored by Senators Clay and Pope, to preside over the new territory as governor. Boyle was an associate justice of the Kentucky Court of Appeals. The same day, the president appointed Nathaniel Pope, the senator's young brother, to the important position of secretary of the territory. Boyle declined the appointment, preferring to remain on the Kentucky court. With that, twenty-five-year-old Nathaniel Pope became the first holder of an executive office in the Illinois Territory. Pope would serve Illinois with great distinction for four decades, first as territorial secretary for eight years and, for a key period from 1817 to 1818, as the territory's elected delegate to Congress. Later, after statehood, he would serve as Illinois's only federal judge for more than thirty years.[63]

Nathaniel Pope personified the frontier spirit of untold numbers of settlers in new territories. Pope was born in 1784 in the Falls of the Ohio. He was the sixth generation in America of a family that had emigrated from England and distinguished itself in Maryland and Virginia. Nathaniel's father, William, who served as a militia captain in the revolutionary army, was one of thousands of residents of Virginia and elsewhere in the East who, in middle age, headed for the lands beyond the Alleghenies after George Rogers Clark's capture of Kaskaskia in July 1778 and Vincennes in February 1779. Successfully established among the three hundred residents of Falls of the Ohio, he sent for his wife and three children. Among them was John, born in 1770, who later became a prominent lawyer and U.S. senator from Kentucky. During the first few years, the Pope family, like others, lived in a small log cabin with unglazed windows, wore rude clothing, cultivated crops with neighbors in a small clearing adjacent to the stockade, and maintained a wary watch for Indians.[64]

Despite the rough surroundings, Nathaniel was raised in a family culture of education and civic leadership. He attended private schools in Louisville and went on to college at Transylvania University in Lexington, which numbered among its population prominent political and civic leaders, including Henry Clay, John Breckinridge, U.S. senator and attorney general under Jefferson, Joseph H. Daviess, the first western lawyer to appear before the U.S. Supreme Court, and John Pope. After older brother John established his law practice in November 1803, Nathaniel worked there and studied law while he remained in Lexington.[65]

In 1803 the exciting news reached Lexington that the United States had purchased the vast territory of Louisiana from France. For nineteen-year-old lawyer

Nathaniel Pope, fluent in French, the new upper Louisiana Territory offered opportunity. Leaving his family connections behind, Pope promptly moved to Ste.
Genevieve, Louisiana. There he practiced law for five years, attaining a position
of leadership among the small bar.[66]

Although Ste. Genevieve at the time had only twenty-five to thirty American
residents among a population of some one thousand French, and although relations between people of the two heritages were not always cordial, Pope apparently enjoyed the community's respect. He was elected to positions of trust in
the higher education academy and the town.[67]

Slavery was widespread among the French settlers in the Louisiana Territory.
One of the first tasks falling to town secretary Pope was to transcribe the recently
adopted code governing slave behavior. It was severe, regulating conduct, adopting curfews, and imposing other restrictions, with penalties up to twenty-five
lashes for some violations. Pope himself was a slaveholder, owning three slaves
in Missouri whom he brought with him when he moved his residence across the
river to Kaskaskia at the end of 1808.[68]

Within a few months after Pope's move to Kaskaskia, President Madison appointed him secretary of the new Illinois Territory. Although the president made
the appointments to the offices of governor and secretary of the Illinois Territory
on March 7, 1809, Pope did not take the oath of office until April 25, apparently
after he learned of Justice Boyle's decision to decline the appointment as governor. Not knowing when a governor would be appointed, Pope believed it was his
duty under the law to organize the new territorial government. By proclamation
as acting governor on April 28 he established two Illinois counties, St. Clair and
Randolph, with boundaries the same as under the Indiana territorial government.
He also acted promptly to make appointments, issuing commissions to a sheriff,
several justices of the peace, and a number of militia officers.[69]

On April 24 President Madison, again because of the sponsorship of Henry
Clay, John Pope, and others, appointed Ninian Edwards, chief judge of the same
Kentucky Court of Appeals, to become governor of the Illinois Territory. Edwards
was an aristocrat and prominent lawyer who achieved great success financially
and politically in Kentucky and, later, in Illinois. A cousin of the Pope brothers
and son of a Maryland congressman from a prominent family, he was born in
Maryland in March 1775. He completed courses at Dickinson College in Pennsylvania. At age nineteen, bankrolled by his father, he moved to Kentucky to buy

lands for the family and was successful in laying out farms, building tanneries and distilleries, and erecting houses. He also apparently sowed his wild oats. In the words of an adulatory biography by his son, he is said to have "entered without restraint into all the excesses of society . . . and became dissipated."[70] The details are never given, but the period is recited as a morality tale of overcoming excess and reforming to lead a distinguished and exemplary life.

Despite these claimed derelictions, during the same period young Edwards twice won election to the Kentucky legislature, the second time almost unanimously. He also continued his legal studies. Licensed to practice law in Kentucky in 1798 and Tennessee the next year, he soon became a leading lawyer in the two states, amassed a large fortune in business and land speculation in a few years, and became a justice of Kentucky's highest court and chief justice of the state in 1808.[71]

Thirty-three years old when he was appointed territorial governor, Edwards abandoned the practice of law after moving to the Territory of Illinois. He was elected as one of Illinois's first two senators after statehood and later served as the state's third governor. He became the foremost merchant of his day, garnering riches in land speculations and commercial pursuits on an extensive scale in Illinois cities from Kaskaskia to Springfield and in several cities in Missouri. During his lifetime, he owned, bought, and sold many slaves and bonded servants in Illinois and Missouri. An aristocrat in bearing and dress, he traveled, even in campaigning for governor, in an elegant open carriage with a black slave as his driver.[72]

Following his appointment as governor, Edwards required time to transport his household, slaves, and livestock from Kentucky to Kaskaskia. In the interim, Nathaniel Pope continued to act as governor of the Illinois Territory for six weeks, until Edwards took the oath of office on June 11, 1809. On June 16 Governor Edwards and the three appointed judges, among them Jesse Thomas, acting as the legislative body, met to complete the organization of the territorial government.[73]

Edwards was an able and intelligent territorial governor. An aristocrat in background, he was democratic in practice for his time. Although he made full use of his power to appoint, from the outset in 1809 he allowed the men of each county to select their own civil and military officers.[74]

Early in 1812 Edwards took another step toward more democratic civil government at all levels. The Northwest Ordinance provided that only landowners could vote in elections, a requirement that created unrest in the Illinois Territory, where few could demonstrate land ownership, and numerous unresolved land claims left their settlers without title. In response to public agitation, in 1812 a referendum called by Edwards demonstrated an overwhelming majority in favor of enlarging the franchise. In response, Edwards successfully petitioned Congress for a law granting Illinois second-grade territorial government and giving the right to vote to all free white males who had lived in the territory one year and paid any tax, no matter how small. At Illinois's first general election, in October 1812, squatters and landowners voted, electing Shadrach Bond, nephew of one of the first English-speaking arrivals, as representative to Congress, as well as the territory's first legislature.[75]

During much of 1812 and into 1813, Edwards was required to devote attention to Indian hostilities that had intensified in 1811 and after the beginning of the War of 1812. Indian discontent was inspired by British agitation and by unhappiness among many tribes over the huge cessions of land in Illinois and much of Wisconsin that Governor Harrison obtained in six treaties between 1803 and 1809. By the end of 1811, Indian attacks on settlements in Illinois became more frequent.[76]

Edwards, who also was commissioned as superintendent of Indian affairs, hastened to make preparations for defense of the territory. He summoned the militia, raised several companies of mounted volunteers, and provided large sums of money himself to purchase arms, build a line of forts from the Mississippi River across the territory to Indiana, and prepare other defensive works. In 1812, with companies of mounted federal rangers authorized by Congress also present in Illinois and war declared on Great Britain in June, defensive efforts intensified. The annihilation of Fort Dearborn at Chicago on August 15 increased the clamor for war against the Indians.[77]

Ambitious for a military career, Edwards determined to take action against the nearest concentration of Indian villages, at Peoria. He organized a mounted army of four hundred men at Fort Russell, which he had built in 1811 just north of Edwardsville. In the last two weeks of October 1812, the Illinois troops launched attacks against several Indian villages near Peoria. A portion of Edwards's men turned into a mob, killing fleeing Indians as well as some inhabitants. The force burned Indian towns and returned to Fort Russell, concluding the expedition thirteen days after it started.[78]

In the spring of 1813 the national government formed a military district to manage operations in the territories of Illinois, Indiana, Missouri, and Michigan. Indiana governor Harrison was given overall command. Missouri governor Benjamin Howard resigned that position to accept appointment as a general commanding a subdistrict of Illinois and Missouri. Edwards's military authority was superseded. Chagrined at the slight, Edwards turned over government of the territory to Nathaniel Pope, returned to Kentucky, and seriously considered resigning his office. For six months, from late June until early December 1813, Pope as acting governor was again in charge of the territorial government.[79]

In a coda demonstrating the frontier's hatred of the Indian, on Christmas Eve 1814, ten days after the War of 1812 ended officially, the Illinois legislature enacted a law "to promote retaliation upon hostile Indians." The territory promised to pay a fifty-dollar bounty for killing an Indian who shall "commit any murder or depredation" in any settlement. Bounties of fifty dollars were offered for each Indian woman or child taken prisoner, and one hundred dollars for citizens or rangers who had official permission for an expedition and killed any Indian warrior or captured any woman or child. There apparently is no record of anyone ever collecting.[80]

In 1815, as Nathaniel Pope's term as secretary of the territory was ending, the general assembly asked him to carry out an important undertaking. The laws of the territory had been adopted from those of several other states as well as enacted by the Illinois General Assembly after 1812. No authoritative compilation of the laws had ever been made, a fact that caused much confusion and uncertainty. The legislature contracted with Pope to take on the task. The reference work, which became familiarly known as *Pope's Digest*, was published in Kaskaskia by the press of Matthew Duncan on June 2, 1815. The widely used work was the first comprehensive collection of Illinois laws and the first book printed in the state.[81]

Following almost a year in private life after writing *Pope's Digest*, in May 1816 Pope announced that he would seek election as the Illinois Territory delegate to Congress. After winning election in early September, Pope embarked on the thirty-five-day trip on horseback and by stagecoach to Washington. Seated in the House of Representatives on December 2, 1816, for the second session of the fourteenth Congress, Pope joined distinguished colleagues, including Henry Clay, back in the House as speaker, Daniel Webster, John C. Calhoun, and future president John Tyler. When the session finished, he returned home to Kaskaskia for the summer recess in 1817.[82]

The Push for Statehood Begins

Tentative movements for admission to statehood began during Illinois's first decade as a territory. They were motivated primarily by the desire for self-government because of dissatisfaction with undemocratic territorial government. In 1808, while still part of the Indiana Territory, in 1814, and in early 1816, elected Illinois members of the territorial legislature sent to Congress resolutions requesting repeal of the power given to the territorial governor to veto legislative acts and to prorogue and dissolve the general assembly. They argued that the veto was a form of despotism that frustrated the expensive and diligent efforts of electing representatives and having them convene to consult for the public good. Congress denied all the requests.[83]

In late 1817 a precocious Kentucky native, Daniel Pope Cook, began an aggressive effort to attain statehood for Illinois. Cook had lived in Illinois for barely two years. In that time, he had benefited from the friendship and patronage of Governor Edwards, who had appointed Cook at age twenty to be the first statewide auditor of public accounts. Cook's advocacy for statehood, however, was directed in strong and even vituperate terms against the autocratic powers of the governor.[84]

Daniel Pope Cook was born in Kentucky in 1794. He spent his childhood there. Physically he was frail and delicate. In later life, he was often ill. With poor parents, he had little formal education. As a youth, he was sent to the thriving town of Ste. Genevieve, Missouri, where, after a short time working in a shop, he studied law under the tutelage of his uncle, Nathaniel Pope. In 1815, he was admitted to the bar in Kaskaskia, where Pope had become territorial secretary and Edwards, who was to become Cook's father-in-law, was territorial governor.[85]

Cook soon established a good law practice. He also gained appointment to an important position in the territorial government. In January 1816 Governor Edwards appointed him to the new position of auditor of public accounts, in which he served only a few months. The same year, he purchased an interest in the territory's only newspaper, the *Illinois Herald*, which changed its name first to the *Western Intelligencer* and later to the *Illinois Intelligencer*.[86]

In February 1817 Cook departed Kaskaskia for Washington to seek a position as a federal official. President Madison declined to appoint him to succeed Nathaniel Pope as Illinois territorial secretary. Shortly, however, he was sent on a mission from newly inaugurated President James Monroe as a bearer of dispatches to John Quincy Adams, then in London as minister to the Court of St. James. The principal message was a summons back to Washington to become secretary of state in the new Monroe administration. The mission served Cook well, providing not only an opportunity to travel and to see London but also the beginning of a close political and personal friendship with Adams.[87]

After their return to Washington, Cook obtained Adams's assistance in an effort to gain appointment by President Monroe as secretary of the Alabama Territory. Awaiting that assignment, he refused a clerkship in the State Department at a good salary. On September 25, 1817, Cook wrote to Governor Edwards evaluating likely job possibilities and concluding that it was not worthwhile for him to stay in Washington. "I shall know in a few days whether I go as Secretary of Alabama Territory or not," he wrote. "The President, it is feared, has made up his mind; if so, I shall fail; there is no situation vacant at present for me but that." In a postscript, Cook added, "I am not yet well. May it not be better for me to return to Kaskaskia and wait for prospects in that country if I don't go to Alabama." A week later, on October 2, Cook wrote to the governor again, confirming that he had decided "to return to the West, and remain there until an opportunity presents itself for my advancement."[88]

Cook traveled back to Illinois from Washington in the fall of 1817. At the same time, Nathaniel Pope was heading in the opposite direction. Traveling with his family to Louisville, where he left them before continuing on, and delayed further by bad weather and bad roads, Pope did not arrive in Washington until the first week of December 1817. While Pope was out of communication for three months, events were occurring back in Kaskaskia that would place Pope at the center of Illinois history.[89]

Cook Incites Action for Statehood

Daniel Pope Cook arrived in Kaskaskia in mid-November and immediately initiated a campaign for Illinois statehood that not only succeeded but also made him a leading political figure in the new state. On November 20, 1817, two days after arriving back in Kaskaskia, Cook published in the *Western Intelligencer* the first of two articles arguing the case for statehood. The second, lengthier piece was published a week later, on November 27.[90]

Cook based his case almost entirely on what he described as the unrepresentative, autocratic, and even despotic nature of the territorial government—which, of course, was headed by his patron, Governor Edwards. In the first article, Cook framed the issue he later would argue at length: "While we are laboring under so many of the grievances of a territorial, or semi-monarchical government, might not our claims to a state government be justly urged?" The territory, he stated, would be willing to take on the burdens of statehood "rather than submit any longer to those degradations which they have so long been compelled to put up with."[91]

Cook published again on November 27, signing as "A Republican." He asserted that the territory's population, which he estimated, quite generously, at forty thousand to forty-five thousand, had "increased to a sufficient number to enable us to take into our own hands the reins of self-government." He contended that the autocratic territorial political structure placed "shackles" on the people's legislative functions. Cook took particular issue with the governor's veto power. The territorial legislature, he wrote, was subject to the arbitrary actions of a governor who, "owing no responsibility to the people has the power of closing their deliberations at pleasure." The governor's veto impaired good government because "men of lofty feelings and useful intelligence reject, what would be under other circumstances, an elevated situation," and consequently legislation was left to inferior individuals.[92]

The legislature assembled in Kaskaskia on December 1, four days after the second *Intelligencer* editorial. The next day, Governor Edwards delivered a message concerning statehood to the two houses of the legislature. He congratulated the members and the "citizens at large" because the "astonishingly rapid increase of population" meant that "our present temporary governments must soon give place to one more congenial to the principles of natural liberty." He called for the legislature to facilitate and prepare for "this desirable event" by providing for a census with the results reported back to the legislature at its next session. This would have been the normal procedure, but it would have postponed action seeking statehood until the next year. Not only was that timeline much too leisurely for Cook's personal campaign, it also did not satisfy the sense of urgency others felt because agitation had begun in Missouri to seek statehood. Many believed it important that Illinois be first for its honor but also understood that, because Missouri likely would be a slave state, the existence of slavery there would be the strongest argument for allowing it in Illinois also.[93]

Cook had secured a position as a clerk in the territorial house of representatives, enhancing his ability to influence members. The same day the governor's message was delivered, the house appointed a committee to move forward by drafting a memorial to Congress asking that the territory be admitted into the Union. Four days later, on December 6, the house unanimously adopted the memorial. On December 10 the council approved it and sent it to the governor for his concurrence. Putting its gloss on the prompt action, the *Intelligencer* asserted that "the rapidity of its passage was possible only because of the lack of opposition, it being the 'unanimous voice of our representatives from every part of the territory, that are desirous to enter into a state government.'"[94]

The memorial, comprising two long paragraphs, shows Cook's hand in its writing. Much of the first paragraph tracks his article in the November 27 *Intelligencer* about the oppressive nature of territorial government, which is characterized as "'a species of despotism' in direct hostility with the principles of a republican government, which ought to exist no longer than *absolute necessity* may require it." He emphasized the fitness for self-government of the population of the territory, estimated at "not less than forty thousand souls."[95]

Fig. 1. Architects of Statehood: Nathaniel Pope, Daniel Pope Cook. Courtesy of the Abraham Lincoln Presidential Library and Museum.

The memorial dealt with a number of practical concerns as well. It requested that Congress grant to the state the lead mines and salt springs and their adjoining lands, that it reserve section sixteen of every township for school use, that it designate part of the proceeds from the sales of public land for roads, and that Congress grant the same gifts and privileges that had been given to Ohio, Indiana, and Mississippi.[96]

Pope Pushes Promptly for Action by Congress

Nathaniel Pope, unaware of the drive for immediate statehood being pressed by Cook, received the Illinois memorial in Washington in mid-January 1818. He was not expecting it. When he had departed Kaskaskia in October, public attitudes did not favor putting forth the matter of statehood at that time. Pope feared that such an effort was premature and might fail because of an inability to demonstrate by census a sufficient population. Nevertheless, having received the legislature's petition, he determined to move forward "with that candour and good faith becoming my station."[97]

Pope presented the Illinois memorial to the House of Representatives on January 16, 1818. The house established a five-person select committee, with Pope as chairman, to consider the petition and draft appropriate legislation. The committee endorsed the idea of Illinois's admission.[98]

Pope moved quickly. Six days later, he presented the committee with a draft of "A Bill to enable the people of the Illinois Territory to form a constitution and State Government," modeled primarily on the 1816 act for Indiana's admission and that of Mississippi in 1817. The bill first requested authorization for the territory's inhabitants to draft a constitution and form a state government. It next asked that the boundaries be fixed as at present with the exception that the northern boundary was to be "an east and west line drawn through a point ten miles north of the southern extreme of Lake Michigan." This was farther north than the line prescribed by the Northwest Ordinance. Article V had directed that "not less than three nor more than five States" should be formed out of the Northwest Territory. If Congress determined to create five states, two should be northern ones "in that part of said territory which lies north of an east and west line drawn through the southerly bend or extreme of Lake Michigan."[99]

The provision for such a line touching only the most southerly point of the lake, if applied to determine the northern boundary of Illinois, would leave the new state with no shoreline or direct access to Lake Michigan. To avoid this impractical result and give the state an outlet to the lake, Indiana's northern boundary had been fixed ten miles north of the "southern extreme" of the lake. Pope's draft requested the same for Illinois.[100]

The committee approved the draft bill on January 22. The next day Pope reported the bill to the House, where it was read twice and scheduled to be taken up the following Monday, January 26.[101]

Although communications with Illinois were very slow, Pope sought to keep his constituents informed. The day before the select committee approved his draft, on January 21, Pope wrote to the *Western Intelligencer* describing the status of the matter, expressing his optimism about passage, and explaining that he proposed to deal with doubts concerning whether Illinois in fact had the population it claimed by providing that a census should be taken before the constitutional convention met.[102]

The next week, Pope wrote again. Although he had sought in the petition to avoid controversy by asking no more than was granted to Indiana, he told his Illinois constituents that he intended to obtain more. As soon as the bill was printed, Pope sent a copy to the *Intelligencer.* "You will remark," he wrote to the editors, "that the northern line is ten miles north of the southerly extremity of Lake Michigan—Indiana goes as far north. When the bill is taken up, I will endeavor to procure twenty or thirty miles further north."[103]

Adding territory thirty miles or more northward was necessary, as Pope knew, to include the mouth of the Chicago River in the new state and accomplish an important and long-discussed strategic and economic objective. For almost 150 years, dating back to the Jolliet and Marquette expedition in 1673, men dreamed of cutting a canal across the short portage that native peoples had used from time immemorial to travel between the south branch of the Chicago River, which opened into Lake Michigan, and the Des Plaines River, which flowed into the Illinois River watercourse that emptied into the Mississippi and south to the Gulf of Mexico.[104]

The great economic benefits of such an undertaking began to be discussed in the late 1700s. The 1795 Treaty of Greenville had obtained three tracts of land that were of importance to an Illinois canal: a six-mile square at the mouth of the Chicago River where Fort Dearborn would be built to dominate the portage, a six-mile square at Peoria, and a twelve-mile square at the mouth of the Illinois River on the Mississippi.[105]

Stimulated in part by the planned Erie Canal, in 1810 Congressman Peter B. Porter of New York urged the federal government's aid for a system of waterways extending from the St. Lawrence and Hudson Rivers to the Gulf of Mexico. He referred specifically to the ease with which a canal could be constructed to connect Lake Michigan with the Illinois River. Others also promoted the idea. In 1814 *Niles' Weekly Register*, a prominent journal of opinion in Baltimore, proclaimed, "Buffalo in New York may be united with New Orleans by inland navigation. . . . What a route! How stupendous the idea." It predicted that such a canal at Chicago would make Illinois "the seat of an immense commerce and a market for the commodities of all regions."[106]

Years before the statehood petition, Edwards, Pope, and other political leaders in Illinois as well as Governor William Clark and others in Missouri were already working to achieve the envisioned inland navigation and resulting commerce. In August 1816 Edwards traveled to St. Louis to join Clark and Auguste Chouteau, prominent trader and a founder of St. Louis, in negotiating a treaty with the Potawatomi, Ojibwa, and Ottawa tribes. The treaty ceded a tract of land required for the Illinois and Michigan Canal. Twenty miles wide and one hundred miles long, it extended from the mouth of the Chicago River at Lake Michigan southwest along the proposed route of the canal to the Illinois River. Edwards reported to the Illinois legislature that the Indians "ceded the land for a trifle" because they "were induced to believe that the opening of the canal would be very advantageous to them."[107]

In the same treaty, the U.S. negotiators retroceded to the Indians all the territory of Illinois north of a line through the most southern point of Lake Michigan. The Illinois lands were not thought to be of immediate use for settlement. Two years later Nathaniel Pope, with a different vision, added a sizeable portion of this land to the state of Illinois through the northern boundary amendment he negotiated in Congress.[108]

In March 1817 army engineers sent their report in response to a request from Congress to evaluate "the practicability of uniting, by a canal, the waters of the Illinois and those of Lake Michigan." The report described such a waterway as "the first in importance of any in this quarter of the country, and, at the same time, the construction of it would be attended with very little expense compared with the magnitude of the object."[109] By January 1818 Pope and members of the select committee likely would have known of the report. And Pope, for his part, intended to assure that this stupendous project would be entirely within Illinois.

Although the House had scheduled the Illinois bill to be taken up on January 26, other congressional business intervened. Pope waited impatiently but hopefully. On February 21 he wrote to the *Intelligencer* that the bill "will be taken up in all probability early next month." He added that he was "not without sanguine expectation of its success."[110] Congress instead became engaged in a lengthy debate on internal improvements in other western areas—specifically, roads and canals—with the result that the matter of Illinois admission was not considered until April 4.

Pope Achieves Most Favorable Terms

On April 4, when the House finally considered the Illinois bill, it became apparent immediately that Pope harbored ambitions for the new state that were greater than he had revealed to anyone. As soon as the debate began in the House, Pope moved to amend the future state's northern boundary by moving it to latitude 42°30' north, a line some sixty miles north of the southernmost point of Lake Michigan. Pope nowhere stated why he chose to move the line more than the thirty miles he referred to earlier and why he specified that precise latitude for the northern boundary. In the two months that passed, he may have learned that thirty miles north, about which he had written in February, would have set the boundary at or barely north of the Chicago River, and not as far north as the lakefront point established by the twenty-mile width of the 1816 treaty tract. Such a line would have left no room for growth of a city and area surrounding the harbor.[111]

It is clear also, in the far northwest of the added area, that Pope wanted the lead deposits around the future city of Galena to be within the state. The financial terms of the proposed enabling act already asked that Illinois be granted all lead mines and salt springs in the state. These resources were expected to be "immensely valuable" in paying expenses of the new state government as well as providing lucrative patronage opportunities by leasing them to entrepreneurs.[112]

In addition to the financial benefits to be expected from the canal, Pope also had in mind long-range political objectives. The *Annals of Congress*, an abridgement published in 1854 of the proceedings in the House on April 4, 1818, summarized the argument Pope made in support of the amendment:

The object of this amendment, Mr. P. said, was to gain, for the proposed State, a coast on Lake Michigan. This would afford additional security to the

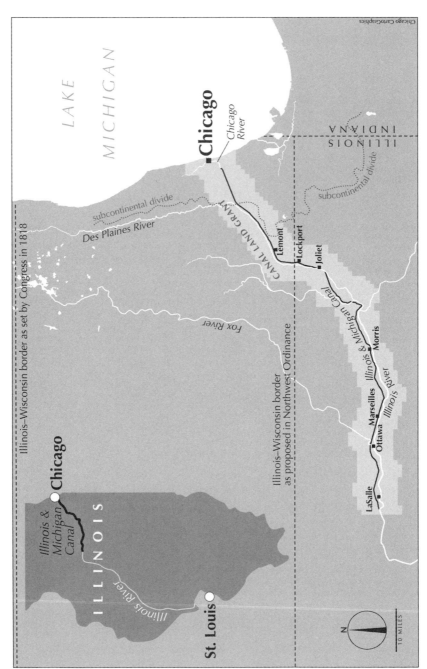

Map 3. Northern Boundary Extension/Illinois & Michigan Canal

perpetuity of the Union, inasmuch as the State would thereby be connected with the States of Indiana, Ohio, Pennsylvania, and New York, through the Lakes.[113]

The state's eighth governor, Thomas Ford, who knew Pope well, attested years later that Pope warned, "In all confederated republics there was danger of dissolution." Pope was concerned, Ford wrote, that if Illinois were restricted to water access solely by way of the Mississippi and Ohio Rivers, its economic interests might compel it to join a southern and western confederacy:

> If left entirely upon the waters of these great [south-flowing] rivers, it was plain that, in case of threatened disruption, the interest of the new state would be to join a southern and western confederacy.[114]

On the other hand, Ford wrote,

> if a large portion of it could be made dependent upon the commerce and navigation of the great northern lakes, connected as they are with the eastern states, a rival interest would be created, to check the wish for a western and southern confederacy.[115]

Thus, Governor Ford said, Pope saw the importance of giving to Illinois control of the projected route for an Illinois and Michigan canal, including a port at Chicago and "a considerable coast on Lake Michigan, with country back of it sufficiently extensive to contain a population capable of exercising a decided influence upon the councils of the state."[116]

Subsequent events confirmed Pope's prescience. Had the site of the future Chicago not been included in Illinois by his maneuvers in 1818, Chicago probably would not have grown into the great metropolis that it did. The growth in commerce and communication to the west might well not have occurred until the expansion of railroads in the 1850s or later. By that time, there would have been little reason for railroad terminals and facilities connecting the East and the West to pass as far north as Chicago instead of the northern Indiana area where Gary and other cities were built later.[117]

Pope's proposed amendment to move the boundary north passed the House without a division. There was at the time, of course, virtually no white population either in the area being added to Illinois or in the future Wisconsin to the north.[118]

Pope next dealt with Section 6 of the draft bill that related to the financing of internal improvements. This section, like the previous one concerning boundaries, showed Pope's objective to achieve statehood on the most advantageous terms possible. Pope proposed no changes to three provisions of the section; those remained as he drafted them in committee. The first granted to the state section sixteen in every township, or equivalent lands, to be used for schools. The second provision gave to the state all salt springs and lead mines in the state. The fourth provision stated that the president would designate thirty-six sections, or one township, for a "seminary of learning."[119]

Pope did, however, offer and obtain passage of a significant amendment to the third directive of section 6, which specified that 3 percent of the proceeds of federal land sales in Illinois should be used for the development of roads and canals. Pope proposed that, instead of roads and canals, the state's monies would "be appropriated, by the legislature of the State, for the encouragement of learning, of which one-sixth part shall be bestowed exclusively on a college or university."[120]

In support, Pope observed that in other states the federal proceeds set aside for the development of roads instead had been distributed to local governments and misused or dissipated. He argued that the "importance of education in a Republic . . . was universally acknowledged" and that education badly needed improvement in Illinois. This amendment also passed the House without a division.[121]

Pope was disappointed, however, in his hope that Congress would omit a population requirement. Instead, the House required a census showing that the state population exceeded forty thousand inhabitants. Pope did succeed in striking a provision that a federal marshal conduct the census; an honest census by a disinterested official would have been fatal. Other minor amendments were adopted. Thereafter, the bill passed the House unanimously on April 4, 1818.[122]

The House bill was reported to the Senate on April 7. On April 14 the Senate passed the bill by a large majority after some unimportant amendments in which the House promptly concurred the next day. Pope reported his success to his Illinois constituents in an enthusiastic—and prophetic—letter:

> Some jealousy was felt against our gaining so much territory north, say sixty miles, but the bill passed. We may say with truth, that we will enter upon a state government with better prospects than any state ever did.—The best soil

in the world, a mild climate, a large state, with the most ample funds to educate every child in the state; *however poor, a man may well hope to see his child
rise to the head of this mighty nation, if he have talents and virtue.* Our avenues
for navigation are towards the east and the west, the north and the south.[123]

President Monroe signed the bill into law on April 18, 1818. The process Daniel
Pope Cook had initiated the previous November was complete. Ahead was the
task of organizing and taking a census and writing a new state constitution.[124]

The shrewd political maneuvering of Nathaniel Pope, although he was caught
off guard by the territorial legislature's petition, had succeeded in his single-
minded objective of achieving statehood for Illinois on the best possible terms.
The financial terms provided much-needed funds for education and exempted
from taxes large areas of public land. The boundary change, adding eighty-five
hundred square miles and fourteen counties in the north of the state, provided
the land area that enabled Illinois in a few decades to become one of the largest
and most powerful states in the union. One of the smallest states in population
ever admitted, Illinois by 1860 was the fourth most populous state. A distant
isolated wilderness region in 1818 saw huge growth in commerce, agriculture,
and industry as well as population.

Settlement of the added fourteen counties also changed the course of history.
Without that area, Illinois likely would have been a Democratic state in 1860.
The northern counties were filled largely by immigrants—from New England,
elsewhere in the Northeast, and foreign countries—who held antislavery views.
Their votes sustained the new Republican Party organized in 1854, elected a Re-
publican governor and the rest of the state ticket for the first time in 1856, and
in 1860 culminated in the Republican convention in Chicago that nominated
Abraham Lincoln and the general election that gave him the state's electoral votes.

Nathaniel Pope singlehandedly achieved history-making terms for Illinois's
entry into the Union. Prominent historian John Moses wrote in 1918, in the first
volume of the Illinois Centennial Commission History, "No man ever rendered
the State a more important service in congress than did Nathaniel Pope, to whom
the people of Illinois are indebted for securing the passage of this enabling law."[125]
A century later, at this writing on the eve of the bicentennial, that assessment is
still true.

CHAPTER 2

The Constitution of 1818

Slavery, a Bogus Census, Feeble Executive Power

The first Monday in August 1818, twenty-nine delegates pushed their way through the gathered spectators into Bennett's tavern in Kaskaskia for the beginning of Illinois's first constitutional convention. Four delegates elected from the nearby counties of Washington and Jackson inexplicably did not appear until the second day. There is no record that any woman was present. Nor is there any mention of black presence, although there certainly would have been slaves and perhaps other servants in attendance.[1]

Delegate elections July 6, 7, and 8, in each of Illinois's fifteen counties, were the culmination of seven months of political activity in Illinois and Washington—activity remarkable in its urgency in a time of poor communications and difficult travel. At each county seat, votes were cast for delegates by voice vote, *viva voce*, declared to each county sheriff, who proclaimed the vote aloud and provided a tally.

The enabling act specified that two delegates would be elected from each of twelve counties, with three to be elected from each of the three largest. No delegate came from north of the far south ends of today's Madison, Bond, and Crawford Counties; thus all the delegates resided in the most populous southern one-third of the state.[2]

Seven months earlier, in December 1817, the first formal steps toward statehood began. On December 1, four days after the second of Daniel Pope Cook's

Intelligencer editorials arguing the case for statehood, the territorial legislature assembled in Kaskaskia for its regular session. The next day, Governor Edwards delivered his message concerning statehood in which he congratulated the state's citizens for the "astonishingly rapid increase of population" and called for a census. Four days later, on December 6, the house of representatives adopted the memorial to Congress asking that the territory be admitted into the Union. On December 10, the council approved it. With the governor's concurrence, the document was sent to Nathaniel Pope in Washington.[3]

While Nathaniel Pope waited in Washington from January until April 1818 for the Illinois statehood bill to be taken up in the Congress, preparations in Illinois for the census moved slowly. Governor Edwards had appointed census commissioners in all but two counties by mid-January, but final appointments were not completed until June, after it was known in Illinois that, contrary to Pope's hopes, the Congress required a census showing that the state population exceed forty thousand inhabitants.

The Territorial Census of 1818

When census returns were reported in June 1818, they showed a population of 34,610, far short of the requirement. Forewarned that the process was failing to reach the required number, the legislature provided for a supplementary census to continue counting until December 1, on the premise that a large increase in population would occur later in the year.[4]

The prediction of an increase in population was made true, at least in the census commissioners' reports. As the count continued, there were reports of census takers who were not doing their jobs, failing to record citizens of their counties. There also were many indications of overzealous counting by census takers that amounted to padding the numbers, if not fraud. Families were recorded at more than one place as they transited through Illinois on their way to settle in Missouri. Some were listed two and three times as they crossed one county and met different census takers. Without an actual count, "good faith" estimates were made of persons in distant forts, including Fort Crawford at the junction of the Wisconsin River with the Mississippi, well north of Illinois's boundaries. Eventually the count was reported at 40,258, which was taken at face value and reported to Congress.[5]

The 1820 federal census bears out the charge of padding. The population of several counties was less than the number reported in the 1818 Illinois census, even though it was clear that the permanent population had increased in the intervening two years. Illinois's boosters, in their zealous desire to become a state, simply cooked the books.

The Delegate Campaigns

Little information exists describing electioneering or issues that may have been disputed in particular delegate election contests. It is clear, however, that two overriding concerns dominated the public's thinking about the new constitution. The first, on which there was widespread agreement and little dispute or discussion, was to have relief from the autocratic governor-dominated system of government that existed in the territory. The second was the issue of slavery. These two matters had coalesced in the December 1817 session of the territorial legislature.[6]

On December 10, 1817, the same day the council approved the memorial to Congress asking for statehood, opponents of slavery in the legislature made a preemptive strike against the indentured slavery system by introducing a bill to repeal the state's indenture laws. The intention apparently was to establish a precedent, before a statehood constitutional convention, for a slavery prohibition and a free-state constitution. Earlier in 1817, petitions asking for admission to the union began to be circulated in Missouri. The common belief was that Missouri would be admitted as a slave state and, if that occurred before Illinois statehood, the existence of slavery in Missouri would be the strongest argument for allowing it also in Illinois.[7]

The indenture repeal passed the legislature and was sent to the council on December 13. After being twice debated there, it passed without amendment by a 3–2 vote on December 17.[8]

Governor Edwards vetoed the bill on January 1, 1818, returning it to the house of representatives with a lengthy statement, described as "a message of masterful double-talk," stating his objections.[9] Focusing on the preamble's declarations, Edwards observed that the indenture laws of the Indiana Territory had been reenacted unanimously by the general assembly in Illinois and acquiesced in by subsequent legislative sessions. He argued at length that the indenture laws were not a violation of the Ordinance of 1787 because of the Virginia deed of cession. He concluded with the bold declaration that he was "no advocate for slavery, and if it depended on my vote alone, it should never be admitted in any state or Territory, not already cursed with so great an evil. I have no objection to the repeal which I suppose was intended."[10] (Four years later, during his service as one of Illinois's first two U.S. senators, Edwards voted to admit Missouri to the Union as a slave state.)

Edwards prorogued the legislature two weeks after his veto, explaining that he believed terminating the legislative session was necessary to prevent "misapprehension" by further discussion of the subject. He claimed that it had not been his desire "to defeat the measure that was intended" and attempted to justify his good faith by asserting that a better bill could have been offered after his veto and the objective could have been achieved "by limiting the period of service to one year only." He also asserted that indenture contracts were "reasonable in themselves, beneficial as to the slaves, and not repugnant to the public interest."[11]

The repeal of the state's indenture laws followed by Governor Edwards's veto furnished a dual argument for those who opposed slavery and those who had long complained about the governor's autocratic power and absolute veto. The result of this antislavery effort, and its failure by veto, was to make those two issues dominant in the 1818 delegate election campaigns and in the convention.

Slavery

Slavery was an institution firmly rooted in the Illinois Territory. The territorial census in 1818 recorded more than a thousand slaves owned by territorial residents. The political leaders of the territory, and of the state after admission in 1818, were largely slave owners. Included in this number were Governor Edwards and Secretary Pope, as well as the territorial delegates to Congress, Shadrach Bond and Benjamin Stephenson, who preceded Pope. Two of the five members of the territorial legislative council, Pierre Menard and Thomas Browne, were slave owners. Both voted against the abolition of the indentured slavery system in December 1817. The first state governor, Shadrach Bond, elected in September 1818, owned more than a dozen slaves, as did Pierre Menard, the first elected lieutenant governor. Elias Kent Kane, prominent leader in the constitutional convention, elected secretary of state by the legislature in 1818, was a slave owner, as, of course, were the state's first two U.S. senators, Ninian Edwards and Jesse Thomas, who also was president of the constitutional convention.

Daniel Pope Cook was a notable exception to the panoply of influential slave-owning political leaders. In the spring of 1818 Cook turned his advocacy efforts from the subject of the governor's autocracy to the subject of slavery. Following optimistic reports about the prospect of statehood from Nathaniel Pope in Washington, Cook, on February 4 and April 1, published two articles in the *Western Intelligencer*. Signing as "A republican," he presented arguments against slavery as an institution.

Slavery became the subject of more intense discussion after the *Western Intelligencer*, on April 29, informed its readers that the enabling act had passed Congress and been signed into law. Adding to the interest, the paper on April 29 also informed readers that the elections for delegates to a constitutional convention were scheduled for the first Monday in July and the two following days, and the convention itself was to meet the first Monday in August.

The most cogent of the writings in the *Intelligencer* were signed by "Agis." Agis was in fact future governor Edward Coles, a newly arrived Virginia aristocrat and ardent opponent of slavery who wrote eloquently against slavery and also about the injustice of the veto. "It must be a subject of regret to every lover of liberty," he wrote, "that although our last legislature passed an act to repeal the odious [slavery] law . . . the repealing act has been defeated by the *veto* of his excellency, the governor. Let us hail the approach of that period," he continued, "when it shall not be in the power of an individual, in whose appointment we have no voice, to set aside the will of the people, as expressed by their representatives."[12]

The Convention Delegates Act Quickly

The thirty-three men who were elected to serve as delegates were all white citizens who resided in the county from which they were chosen. As has been usual in state constitutional conventions, which are one-off events of limited duration, the delegates included a few holders of public offices and several former office-holders. There were young ambitious lawyers hoping to establish reputations and older established citizens well known to their local electorates. Five of the fifteen men who had been census takers that summer, and thus in personal contact with many residents of the counties, were elected. Only two delegates appear to have been born in Illinois, while more than a dozen had lived less than ten years in the area that became the state. Many listed farming as their occupation. Five had legal training, including three who had served as judges. Three were physicians, two sheriffs, one a minister, one a storekeeper, another a land-office official. Four were connected with the salt industry, which was worked almost entirely by slave labor. Ten of the thirty-three delegates (30 percent) were owners of slaves, a disproportionately high percentage compared to the general population.[13]

Facts concerning the convention proceedings are, unfortunately, only partially known. No transcript or record is known to exist, other than one copy of the convention's journal that was discovered later. It was presented to the state in 1905 by a nephew of Joseph Kitchell, a member of the convention from Crawford County. Published verbatim in the 1913 *Journal of the Illinois State Historical Society*, it is a brief document that summarizes the actions, textual proposals and revisions, and numerical votes at the convention, but not verbatim remarks or the names of delegates voting yea and nay.[14]

The delegates who gathered in Kaskaskia on August 3 proceeded with dispatch to complete the convention's work in a session that lasted only until August 26. Of the twenty-five session days, however, excluding two Sundays, only nine were spent on substantive discussion of constitutional issues. The first ten days, until a draft of the constitution was taken up on August 12, were devoted to preliminary matters, including election of officers, rules, and naming and meetings of committees. Unexpectedly, the subject of moving the state capital from Kaskaskia to a new site was broached for the first time on August 18. Three groups of speculators sought to have their lands named in the constitution as the new capital site. More time was consumed in discussion of that matter in the remaining days than any other subject except slavery.

As soon as the delegates were seated on August 3 and the roll called, they elected officers. Jesse Thomas of St. Clair County was named president by the first ballot. Thomas was the most prominent man elected to the convention. Speaker of the Indiana territorial legislature from 1805, elected the Indiana territory delegate to Congress in 1809, he was a leader in separating a new Territory of Illinois from Indiana. When the new territory was formed, he moved to Illinois and secured appointment as one of the first territorial judges and thereby as a member of the legislative council. He served in that position in 1818 while a delegate to the constitutional convention. Thomas was known as a strong advocate of slavery. He is recorded as owning five slaves at the time of the convention.

With Thomas as president, Elias Kent Kane, a young delegate from Randolph County, dominated the proceedings. Twenty-four years old, son of a prominent New York family, he had graduated from Yale in 1812, read law in

New York, immigrated to Tennessee in 1814, and later that year moved to Kas-kaskia, where he established a successful law practice. Apparently the youngest delegate, he was also the most outwardly ambitious. The May 6 issue of the *Intelligencer* that announced the Senate's passage of the enabling act also carried Kane's announcement that he would be a candidate "for the Convention from the county of Randolph." He was the first to announce.[15]

Kane took the initiative from the first day of the convention. He served on important committees, researched precedents, and was largely responsible for drafting the constitution in his law office. As soon as Thomas was elected president, Kane moved the creation of a three-man committee, including himself, to propose rules and examine the credentials of the delegates. With that approval, after disposing of other routine organizational matters, the convention adjourned to the next morning.

The second day of the convention, August 4, the four missing delegates from Jackson and Washington Counties were seated. On Kane's motion, a committee was appointed to examine the returns of the special census and "to receive and report such other evidence of the actual population of the territory" in order to establish that the convention was authorized to proceed, as specified in the enabling act. Kane and two others were appointed to that committee, with Kane as chairman, after which the convention adjourned.[16]

The next morning, Kane reported that the committee had examined the census returns and, despite many discrepancies, affirmed that the territory population was 40,258. No question was raised to the accuracy of the census; the convention "read, considered, and concurred in" the report. The delegates next adopted a resolution declaring, "there are upwards of 40,000 inhabitants in the territory," therefore "it is expedient to form a constitution and a state government."[17]

The convention next created a committee composed of one delegate from each of the fifteen counties "to frame and report to this convention a constitution for the people of the territory of Illinois." Although the committee's chairman was a delegate from Gallatin County, Kane was the principal draftsman and directing spirit. The committee prepared its draft in a week. On Wednesday, August 12, the draft was reported to the convention. In the meantime, the convention met two days to adopt an elaborate set of rules of procedure, provide for printing of the journal, and deal with other routine matters. The rest of the week it convened daily and promptly adjourned.[18]

The draft constitution was read and debated three times over the next two weeks. The delegates proceeded through the draft in the order of its provisions, with no more than two votes on most issues. As finally approved on August 24, the concise document comprised eight articles. It provided a basic framework for state government. Occasionally rudimentary in form, it reflected the sentiments of a majority of settlers in a frontier state. It also included provisions that were tailored for immediate needs and for specific persons and thereby would pose significant problems for the future.

The preamble recited the intention to form a free and independent state named Illinois, on an equal footing with the original states, consistent with the U.S. Constitution, the Northwest Ordinance of 1787, and the Enabling Act of Congress. It also ratified the enlarged boundaries of the new state as set out by Congress in the enabling act.

Article I provided for the separation of the powers of government into three departments.

Article II established a bicameral general assembly composed of a senate and a house of representatives, to be elected biennially. Representatives, elected for two-year terms, were required to be citizens, to be at least twenty-one years old, to be resident in their districts for twelve months preceding election, and to have paid a state or county tax. The qualifications for senators were the same, except that the minimum age was twenty-five and they were elected for four-year terms. The legislature was to establish legislative districts that would be apportioned according to the number of white inhabitants and would provide for twenty-seven to thirty-six house districts and one-third to one-half as many senate districts. To aid in reapportionment, the legislature was to provide for a census "of all white inhabitants of the state" to be conducted every five years beginning in 1820.[19]

The debates over two sections of Article II dealing with "ministers of the gospel" are notable. In the later territorial period and during the campaigns for election of delegates there had been extensive discussion in the *Western Intelligencer* about political activities of clergymen. Several ministers had preached that only "professors of religion" should be elected to office, a position denounced as "religious tyranny" by writers to the newspaper. The draft of Article II disqualified ministers from serving in the legislature: "Whereas the ministers of the gospel are by their professions, dedicated to God and the care of souls, and ought not to be diverted from the great duties of their functions: Therefore, no minister of the gospel or priest of any denomination whatever, shall be eligible to a seat in either house of the legislature." A later section was a corollary to this directive, stating, "No minister of the gospel or priest of any denomination whatever, shall be compelled to do militia duty, work on roads or serve on juries."[20]

Motions to strike these provisions were voted down on second reading. On reconsideration later, both sections were dropped from the constitution.[21]

The question whether citizenship should be required for voting was a recurrent issue in every Illinois constitutional convention. The 1818 convention approved the committee draft that gave the right to vote to all white male inhabitants, citizens or not, above age twenty-one who had resided in the state six months before the election. Noncitizens had been allowed to vote in the Territory of Illinois and also under the Ohio constitution of 1802. However, Indiana, in its 1816 constitution, limited the franchise to citizens. The tension between the desires of the frontier to encourage settlement by being liberal in allowing elective participation and the hostility of those who opposed giving the vote to aliens, whom they derided as "subjects of foreign powers" who had never complied with naturalization laws, provoked continued controversy.[22]

The constitution also specified that the manner of voting would be *viva voce*, unless later changed to ballot by the legislature. This issue was decided in the opposite way in the Indiana constitution of 1816, which specified ballot voting unless later changed by the legislature. The 1802 Ohio constitution required that all elections would be by ballot.

The Illinois draft provisions setting forth the structure and powers of branches of government were copied largely from the Ohio constitution of 1802. Jeffersonian Republicans overwhelmingly dominated the Ohio constitutional convention, which met in Chillicothe in November 1802. The constitution they drafted was a radical departure from the Ordinance of 1787. It entrusted power in the state almost entirely to the legislature, rejecting the undemocratic territorial system in which a governor, himself an appointed official, had broad powers of appointment of other officers and wielded an absolute veto over actions of an elected legislature.[23]

The Illinois draft provided for the governor to be elected by the voters but left blank the length and number of terms he could serve as well as a required age and how long he must have been a citizen and resident of the state. The blanks were filled in on first reading to specify that he should hold office for four years but be ineligible for "more than four years in any eight years," be at least thirty years old, a citizen of the United States for ten years, and an inhabitant of the state for two years. On second reading the requirement of citizenship was changed from ten to thirty years, an exceptionally long time. The 1802 Ohio constitution set two-year terms for the governor and a required residence in the state of twelve years. The Indiana constitution of 1816 set three-year terms and required ten years of residence in the state. No explanation is found in the journal or elsewhere for Illinois's change to a thirty-year citizenship requirement.[24]

The governor was given the power to fill by appointment only the office of secretary of state, with the advice and consent of the senate. He could fill other offices only if later so provided by the legislature (Article III, Sections 20, 21).

In the last days of the convention, on third reading, four other constitutional offices were created in the executive branch. On August 20, Kane proposed, and the convention accepted, adding the offices of state treasurer and public printer. Both were to be elected biennially by the legislature in joint vote of the two houses of the general assembly (Article III, Section 22). The next day, the convention in the schedule provided for two additional constitutional officers, an attorney general and an auditor of public accounts. Both, along with "such other officers of the state as may be necessary," were also to be appointed by the general assembly, which would specify their duties (Schedule, Section 10).[25]

Thus, the legislature, although in session only a few months in alternate winters, had the power to elect the two U.S. senators, the four justices of the supreme court, lower court judges, the auditor of public accounts, the attorney general, the state treasurer, the public printer, other secondary state officials, and the occupants of any other offices of the state it chose to create, as well as most local officers. The people could elect statewide only the governor and lieutenant governor and, locally, sheriffs, coroners, county commissioners, and, from their apportioned districts, state senators, state representatives, and U.S. congressmen. These limits on the governor's appointive power gave the legislature a firm grip on patronage and provided great opportunity for future mischief.

The governor's power also was limited significantly by withholding from him any veto power over acts of the legislature. Instead, a council of revision made up of the four justices of the supreme court, who were to be appointed by the legislature, or "a major part of them," together with the governor, could "revise all bills about to be passed into law" and return them with stated objections to the legislature. The council's revisions could be overridden by a simple majority of the two houses of the legislature. This provision was copied almost verbatim from the New York constitution of 1777 but departed in important ways from its requirement of a two-thirds vote to override the council's objections.[26]

The Illinois version of the council of revision system thus allowed a simple legislative majority to impose its will without a serious check. The system also had implications for the separation of powers by requiring supreme court justices to become directly involved in the legislation-writing process. It had consequences for the judiciary when legal questions about laws, which had to have been approved by the council, were raised on appeal. At minimum, judges may have found themselves embarrassed to consider issues of law that they had previously approved; under present-day ethical rules of judicial conduct they would be obligated to withdraw from consideration of such appeals.

Two provisions of the executive article were written to achieve statewide office for specific persons. The clause in the schedule that allowed the legislature to appoint "such other officers of the state as may be necessary" was inserted because the delegates wanted Elijah C. Berry, the territorial auditor, to continue in the job but feared that Shadrach Bond, whose election as governor was assured, would not appoint him.[27]

The second provision anointing a specific person for office also was achieved through the schedule, which nullified the requirement in the body of the constitution that the governor and lieutenant governor be U.S. citizens and residents in the state for thirty years. Pierre Menard was the popular choice to be lieutenant governor. Menard, a French Canadian, had come to Kaskaskia in 1791. He had prospered in business, first as a storekeeper in Kaskaskia and later as an import-export trader based in Ste. Genevieve. He had served in the territorial legislatures of Indiana and Illinois; in the latter, he was president of the five-man council advising Governor Edwards after the Illinois Territory achieved the second grade. He also had served as an Indian subagent under Edwards. Menard was never a citizen, however, until he was naturalized "a year or so" before the convention. To accommodate him, the schedule changed the residency requirement for lieutenant governor to two years before election and required citizenship only upon assuming office.[28]

The judicial article was dealt with expeditiously. Article IV established a supreme court, comprising initially a chief justice and three associate justices, and such inferior courts as the legislature might establish. All judges were to hold office during good behavior. The number of supreme court justices could be increased by the general assembly after 1824. That did not occur until 1840, when the Democrat-dominated legislature increased by five the number of justices and appointed five Democrats to fill the new seats, initiating a partisan controversy that helped promulgate the calling of the 1847 constitutional convention. The supreme court was authorized to have appellate jurisdiction only, except in certain specified cases.[29]

Further confirming legislative power, the Illinois constitution followed the precedent of Ohio, giving the general assembly sitting in joint session the power to elect all justices and judges. In contrast, under the 1816 Indiana constitution, the governor appointed supreme court judges, with the advice and consent of the senate. The legislature in a joint ballot elected the presidents of county courts. The electorate chose the associate justices of the county courts.[30]

In yet another augmentation of legislative power at the expense of the governor, the final version of the constitution gave the legislature the right to determine how justices of the peace in each county would be chosen and what their terms of service, duties, and powers would be. The committee draft had stated that the governor would have the power to "nominate, and by and with the consent of the senate, appoint a competent number of justices of the peace in each county." On third reading, a substitute was adopted providing for the election by the voters of justices of the peace. Delegates reconsidered that action in the last days of the convention, with the legislature given the power to determine justices of the peace in each county.

Slavery Contested and Continued

The most bitterly contested issue in the convention was the subject of slavery. The individual delegates' positions on the issue in the convention are difficult to determine from available sources. All recognized, however, the need to have the new constitution approved by Congress yet feared that the northern majority there would reject a constitution containing an explicit provision admitting slavery. They also knew that after the constitution had been approved and statehood achieved, another constitutional convention could allow the introduction of slavery.[31]

The delegates had before them the slavery provisions of two constitutions of states that had been under the same obligation to harmonize them with the

Ordinance of 1787 and satisfy Congress. Section 2 of the bill of rights of the Ohio constitution of 1802 illustrated in one long paragraph the delicate position that had evolved to deal with the slavery issue. The first clause stated succinctly the slavery prohibition of the Northwest Ordinance: "There shall be neither slavery nor involuntary servitude in this state, otherwise than for the punishment of crimes, whereof the party shall have been duly convicted." Read with the St. Clair gloss, that provision was understood to protect the right of slave ownership of the "French slaves." It did nothing to protect slave ownership by others.[32]

The Indiana constitution of 1816 included a categorical prohibition on slavery. That provision was the culmination of a remarkable eight years of legislative activity. In 1803, 1805, and 1807 the Indiana Territory adopted stringent laws governing the behavior of black slaves and servants. By 1809, when the Illinois Territory was separated out from Indiana, opposition to slavery had become increasingly strong in Indiana as more settlers from the Northeast moved in. In 1810 the legislature of the newly constituted Indiana Territory repealed all indenture laws and prohibited the introduction of any new slaves or indentured servants. Indiana governor William Henry Harrison signed the law repealing all the indentured servitude laws that he had instituted and signed from seven to two years earlier.

The 1816 constitution followed, stating: "There shall be neither slavery nor involuntary servitude in this state, otherwise than for the punishment of crimes, whereof the party shall have been duly convicted. Nor shall any indenture of any negro or mulatto hereafter made, and executed out of the bounds of this state be of any validity within the state."[33]

In the Illinois convention, the first draft of Article VI copied the Ohio clause exactly. On Monday, August 17, during second reading, this forthright clause was amended to state, "Neither slavery nor involuntary servitude *shall hereafter be introduced* into this state otherwise than for the punishment of crimes whereof the party shall have been duly convicted" (emphasis added).[34] This change constituted implicit approval of continued slavery for more than one thousand persons openly considered slaves.

The second clause of section 2 of the Ohio constitution was intended to secure what the first clause prohibited, that is the legally bound service under the guise of voluntary indenture contracts of the type of persons referred to as slaves in the first clause. Ohio residents were using indentured servitude as a way to continue to exact labor from their former chattel slaves.[35]

The Illinois clause concerning indentures was copied exactly from the Ohio constitution, with the addition on August 17 of the first "hereafter" and other minor language changes to read:

> nor shall any male person arrived at the age of twenty-one years, nor female person arrived at the age of eighteen years be held to serve any person as a servant under any indenture *hereafter* made, unless such person enter into such indenture while in a state of perfect freedom, and on condition of a bona fide consideration received or to be received for such service. Nor shall any indenture for any negro or mulatto hereafter made and executed out of this state, or if made in this state, where the term of service exceeds one year, be of the least validity except those given in cases of apprenticeship. (Emphasis added.)[36]

The purpose of this provision was, again, not to interfere with the bondage of indentured servants who had been introduced during the territorial period and to provide such a system for the future. The provision that such contracts be entered while "in a state of perfect freedom" implicated the same issues of voluntariness relating to all indentures; they were described as freely entered into by slaves who in fact had little freedom of choice. Second, it did not free minors who by birth were indentured until ages twenty-one and eighteen. At that age, they would be "in a state of perfect freedom" and could themselves be contracted for the future. Third, the provision regarding "bona fide consideration," which simply means that real value must be exchanged, was given no special meaning in the clause and does not suggest anything new in the treatment of indentured servants. Typical indenture contracts stated that service was obligated "in consideration of," that is, in exchange for, room, board, lodging, clothing, and maintenance during the servant's natural life. Some more "generous" contracts also provided for one or two changes of clothing and perhaps a blanket at the end of the service term.[37]

The potentially most significant provision allowing black persons to be bound to service for more than a year was the blanket exception for "cases of apprenticeship." Indentures called "apprenticeships" were relatively common both before and for decades following the 1818 constitution. In the obligations of both servants and masters, there were no material differences from other service of slaves.[38]

The vote approving the proposed amendments to the first section was perhaps the most important on the slavery issues in the Illinois convention. The yeas carried it by 17 to 14.[39]

On second reading, on August 20, a new Section 2 was added to Article VI to permit bringing in slaves from other states to work in the salt mines near Shawneetown in Gallatin County for periods of one year at a time until 1825. Although slaves were to be hired only for salt making at the salines, they easily could be assigned other work. Later, a motion on third reading to strike this special section for salines was defeated by a vote of 10 yeas to 21 nays.[40]

Not satisfied with the approval of existing indentured service in Section 1, General Leonard White, a proslavery delegate from Gallatin County, offered an additional section specifically to approve continuation of the supply of bound labor in Illinois. The section stated that persons who were bound to service by a contract or indenture under the Illinois Territory laws would be held to specific performance of their contracts or indentures and "such negroes or mulattoes who have been registered in conformity with [those] laws, shall serve out the time appointed by said laws." Thus, slaves over age fifteen brought in from another state could be bound to long contracts. Enslaved youths imported under age fifteen could be bound to serve until age thirty-five, if male, or thirty-two, if female. Children of slaves and indentured servants "hereafter born" in the state were bound to serve the mother's owner until adulthood; that hereditary service would last until age twenty-five, if male, or twenty-eight, if female. Addition of this section was approved by a 17–14 vote, mirroring the vote on the first section. The alignment was different, however, with four delegates switching sides. On third reading, by approval without a division, the required age for such hereditary service was changed to age twenty-one for males and eighteen for females.[41]

These sections taken together thus approved continuing bondage under indentures made during the territorial period, even for contracts for the expected lifetime of the servants. Moreover, it also assured that the children of such servants could be held in bondage until adulthood because of birth to an indentured mother, without a contract. There were no protections, as in emancipation provisions in other northern states, to assure that such children eventually would gain their freedom. Nor were there penalties for masters who might remove children from the state before the end of their terms and take or sell them elsewhere into lifetime slavery.

The Illinois constitution omitted a provision that was in the Ohio and Indiana constitutions expressly prohibiting future changes in the constitution to allow the introduction of slavery. Some writers have treated that omission as significant. While this fine point may have been considered significant to antislavery advocates looking to prevent slavery, in fact such a prohibition would not likely have been binding to prevent future constitutional conventions from enacting a provision allowing slavery, particularly since the 1818 Illinois constitution was not submitted to the voters for ratification.

Antislavery advocates could take little comfort from the terms of Article VI Proslavery forces may well have been encouraged by their success in adopting artifices that permitted continuation of bound labor for decades. Their hopes or expectations may have stimulated the campaign that occurred six years later to call a proslavery constitutional convention in Illinois.

The constitution included other articles. Article V established a state militia composed of "all free male able bodied persons"; it expressly excluded negroes, mulattos, and Indians. Article VII provided, as was the custom at the time, that the constitution could only be amended by a two-thirds vote of the general assembly setting a date for the voters to approve calling a convention. The Indiana constitution of 1816 provided that every twelve years at the election for governor the question whether to call a convention to revise the constitution should be placed before the voters. If a majority voted for a convention, the legislature was obligated to set dates for election of delegates and the holding of a convention.[42]

The final article, Article VIII, was a twenty-three-section bill of rights, mostly adopted from the Ohio constitution with little discussion, with some sections taken from the constitutions of Kentucky, Tennessee, and Indiana. The first right, the usual statement that "all men are born equally free" with the right "of enjoying . . . liberty," was adopted with no thought, of course, of how it might relate to the slavery provisions of Article VI.[43]

Section 20 states, "The mode of levying a tax shall be by valuation, so that every person shall pay a tax in proportion to the value of the property he or she has in his or her possession." This section appears to be original, perhaps inserted in response to complaints about the "oppressive system of taxation" in the territories. Section 21 deals with the subject of banking, a matter of great interest in Illinois and elsewhere in the West. A number of banks had been chartered during the territorial period, and one had been established. The new section stated that there shall be no other banks except a state bank and its branches. This provision caused much mischief in later years. Sections 22 and 23, added at third reading, provided for freedom of the press and of "thoughts and opinions" and for the right to offer the truth in evidence "in prosecutions for the publication of papers investigating the official conduct of officers, or of men acting in a public capacity, or where the matter published is proper for public information."[44]

A portion of section 8 of the bill of rights dealt with real property law peculiar to the old French communities of the American Bottom. Lands granted and held in common to the inhabitants of these towns were guaranteed "forever [to] remain common to the inhabitants" and never to "be leased, sold, or divided under any pretense whatever."[45]

Future Site of the Capital

Departing from the substantive questions of governmental structure and powers, the convention devoted substantial time in its final days to a bitter debate over the future location of the state capital. Three groups of speculators, two of which comprised prominent men allied with convention delegates, vied to have their properties specified as the future site. In the end, none could garner sufficient votes for any of the proposed sites. Instead, the convention adopted a provision designed to take the question away from private speculation. Section 13 of the schedule specifies that Kaskaskia would remain the capital until changed by the legislature. It also directs the legislature to petition Congress for a grant of public land to be the new seat of government for twenty years. Vandalia eventually became that site. The capital was moved there from Kaskaskia in 1819.[46]

The convention completed its work on August 26, 1818, after being in session twenty-one days. The residents of Kaskaskia celebrated their approval of the convention's work. The governor, delegates, and other officials gathered in front of the capitol, along with many residents and the company of militia with officers in uniform. With flags flying, there were speeches and a twenty-round salute by field cannon, with an extra round for the new State of Illinois. The *Intelligencer* proclaimed,

> This was a proud day for the citizens of Illinois—a day on which hung the prosperity and hopes of thousands yet to follow—a day which will long be remembered & spoken of with enthusiastic pride. . . . The united exer-

tions of our representatives have furnished us with a wise and republican constitution—distributing to all classes their just rights. It now behoves [*sic*] us as faithful citizens to protect it from encroachment.[47]

Approval by Congress and the President

The first election of state officials was held in September while the new constitution was being printed and forwarded to Washington. Shadrach Bond was elected governor. Bond had lived in Illinois for twenty-four years. A gregarious farmer, he was little educated—some sources say he was illiterate—but had been popular with the frontier voters for many years. He had served in the Indiana legislature as long as Illinois was part of that territory. At the first elections held in Illinois Territory, he had been voted into the highest elective office, that of delegate to Congress.[48]

Pierre Menard, the French leader, was elected lieutenant governor, as was anticipated in the special citizenship provision created for him by the constitutional convention. In a surprise, the other major elective office, to be the state's first congressman, was won by John McLean of Shawneetown, another young and brilliant southerner. By fourteen votes, McLean defeated Daniel Pope Cook, the man most responsible for the successful drive for statehood.[49]

On October 5, the First General Assembly of the state—thirteen senators and twenty-seven representatives—convened in Kaskaskia. New men held most of the seats. Only two members of the general assembly had served in the Illinois territorial legislature. Twelve members of the constitutional convention were elected: five to the senate and seven to the house.[50]

Following the installation ceremony, Governor Bond nominated Elias Kane to serve as secretary of state; the senate confirmed Kane the same day. Kane had many talents useful to a secretary of state, but he was of particular value to Bond. Bond's state papers and addresses as governor were attributed in large part to Kane, and it is generally agreed that Kane dominated the administration and was the most influential person in the first years of the state's history.[51]

The third day of the joint legislative session was devoted to the election of two U.S. senators. Ninian Edwards was elected on the first ballot with the vote of thirty-two of the forty members. Three more ballots were required before Jesse Thomas was elected to the second senate seat with a bare majority of twenty-one votes. The next day, the legislature in joint session elected the four justices of the supreme court.[52]

Congress Approves the New Constitution

Senators Edwards and Thomas and Congressman McLean were all in attendance
in Washington when Congress took up the question of Illinois's admission on
November 16. Speaker Henry Clay placed the Illinois constitution before the
House, where it was tabled for later consideration. On November 20, the select
committee reported a resolution to admit Illinois "on an equal footing with the
original states." The discussion that day related principally to the question of
population. Several members expressed doubts that sufficient population had
been demonstrated. Verbal assurances were given in reply.[53]

The principal debate, which began on November 23, related almost entirely
to the question of slavery. Many considered the deliberations over Illinois to be
a prelude to a later fight over admission of Missouri as a slave state.[54]

Representative James Tallmadge of New York, who was to lead the fight later
against Missouri's admission, opposed acceptance of the Illinois constitution
because "the principle of slavery, if not adopted in the constitution, was not sufficiently prohibited." Each section of the sixth article of the new constitution,
he asserted, "contravened" the prohibition against slavery of the Ordinance of
1787, "either in the letter or the spirit." Each of those sections, he concluded,
"embraced a complete recognition of existing slavery" and a tolerance for its
future introduction, particularly in the passage "wherein they permit the hiring
of slaves, the property of non-residents, for any number of years consecutively."
Referring to the "excellent" provisions of the prohibition against slavery in the
Indiana constitution, he declared, "no involuntary service" should be permitted
"in the constitution of any state to be formed out of that territory."[55]

In response, George Poindexter of Mississippi, one of the members of the
select committee, first expressed, rather disingenuously, his concurrence in the
"solicitude to expel from our country, whenever practicable, anything like slavery."
He argued that the indenture registration provisions made sense, but also that it
did not matter that the constitution be as strict as Indiana's, because a state once
admitted could call a convention and "shape its constitution as it thought proper.
The whole power would be with the people," he said, and "no provision" like that
of Indiana's "can control." Richard Anderson of Kentucky, also a member of the
select committee, agreed with Poindexter but maintained further that there was
nothing binding about the Ordinance of 1787, since "the people of the Northwestern Territory" were not "represented at all, nor consulted on the occasion."[56]

William Henry Harrison, now a representative from Ohio, spoke for admission in response to Tallmadge. Harrison said that the people of his state would never seek to alter their constitution to permit slavery, which was the object, he said, of his abhorrence, as it was Tallmadge's. He sincerely wished, he said, "that Illinois had either emancipated its slaves, or followed the example of Indiana" and "left the question . . . for decision of courts," but no compact from 1787 bound Illinois or had shorn its people of their sovereignty.[57]

The resolution for admission carried in the House by a vote of 117 to 34, with all thirty-four opposing votes, except Reed of Maryland, coming from the New England states, New York, New Jersey, and Pennsylvania. The statehood bill passed the Senate without a division on December 1. With President Monroe's signature on December 3, Illinois became the twenty-first state in the Union. The following day, Ninian Edwards and Jesse Thomas took their seats in the Senate and John McLean was seated in the House.[58]

As the year 1818 drew to a close, Illinois was a new state on the edge of the frontier. Its people had their ardently sought opportunity to govern themselves. Its location and resources offered the prospect that the state would serve as a fulcrum in the prosperity and the politics of the Union.

The Failed Fight for a Slavery State

The issue of slavery bubbled up anew almost immediately after Congress's approval of the new constitution. In February 1819, Congress debated the question of Missouri's admission as a slave state for the first time. Illinois residents had a keen interest in the matter. Although many opposed admission of another slave state bordering Illinois, the state's two senators, Jesse Thomas and Ninian Edwards, and representative John McLean voted to permit slavery in Missouri Territory. Six months later, in August 1819, Daniel Pope Cook won election to Congress over McLean, to whom he had narrowly lost the prior year, largely because of McLean's vote and Cook's outspoken opposition to slavery.[59]

The antislavery attitudes of many in Illinois, their efforts against Missouri's admission as a slave state, and Cook's fiery antislavery speeches in the U.S. House of Representatives during the winter of 1819 to 1820 stimulated animosity on the part of Missouri slaveholders, who determined to retaliate by provoking a contest in Illinois over slavery. They found ready allies among Illinois owners of indentured blacks who were anxious to introduce in their state an unrestricted

Fig. 2. First Three Governors of Illinois: Shadrach Bond, Edward Coles, Ninian Edwards. Courtesy of the Abraham Lincoln Presidential Library and Museum.

indenture system or outright slavery. A scheme was soon agreed to call for a convention to revise the 1818 constitution.[60]

Proslavery sentiment became more vocal after the 1820 financial crisis from those who contended that out and open slavery would help the state's economy by attracting prosperous planters. Following admission of Missouri as a slave state in 1821, they argued that their case had been justified by Missouri's attraction of wealthy slaveholding settlers.[61]

The slavery question became the determining issue in the 1822 election of state officers. Edward Coles was elected as the state's second governor, as advocates of slavery split their votes among three other candidates. Proslavery men won the lieutenant governorship and control of the legislature. Coles was an improbable abolitionist. An aristocrat from a prominent Virginia family, he moved in the circles of the leading Virginia statesmen. Thomas Jefferson, Patrick Henry, and James Monroe were frequent overnight visitors at the Coles family plantation. After graduating from the College of William and Mary, Coles spent six years in the White House as private secretary to President Madison. Curious about the old Northwest, Coles made a trip to Shawneetown and Kaskaskia but shortly was called back by Madison for a diplomatic mission to Russia. He later returned to Kaskaskia, where he attended the 1818 constitutional convention.[62]

Coles had inherited a plantation and its slaves at age twenty-three. Slave ownership had long troubled his conscience, however. He returned to Virginia, sold his plantation, and started westward with his slaves. In April 1819, on an Ohio River flatboat on his way to Illinois, he told his slaves that they were free men and women. They could remain with him if they wished; if so, he would pay them wages to work for him and arrange for each family to be settled on a 160-acre farm. They were also free to go their own way if they chose.[63]

Before Coles left Virginia to settle in Illinois, President Monroe appointed him to the post of register of the Edwardsville land office. From that base, Coles soon became well known in the state. Three years after returning to Illinois he won a four-way contest for governor as the choice of most slavery opponents.[64]

The blunt-speaking Coles stirred up the slavery issue in his inaugural address in December 1822. In addition to taking an unpopular stand on a banking issue, he also called for abolition of the slavery that was permitted by the constitution, for repeal of all black codes, and for laws against the kidnapping of free blacks. Legislators retaliated with a drive to legalize explicit slavery by amending the state constitution.[65]

Amendment required calling a convention by a two-thirds majority vote in each house of the legislature, followed by a favorable vote for a convention by those casting ballots at the next general election. The proslavery forces achieved their needed legislative action to put the issue before the electorate, but only after a melodrama that outshone even the narrow gubernatorial election.

The senate acted first, approving the call for a convention by an exact two-thirds vote of 12 to 6. Proslavery men were sanguine about their prospects in the house of representatives, but they found themselves temporarily thwarted when Nicholas Hansen of Pike County, who had been counted as a supporter, voted against the convention call, causing it to fail by one vote.[66]

Hansen's election to the house, however, had been contested by one John Shaw. The committee on elections had seated Hansen after a unanimous recommendation in his favor. Advocates of the convention, furious at Hansen's betrayal, moved to reconsider the vote by which he had been seated. After various procedural maneuvers, the vote on the election contest was reconsidered and Shaw was elected in place of Hansen, with eleven members changing sides on the question of seating him. A messenger was dispatched to Pike County—a distance of more than one hundred miles—to inform Shaw of the unexpected honor conferred on him. Shaw proceeded promptly to the capital. After further maneuvering over rules, he was seated and duly provided the requisite twenty-fourth vote to call a constitutional convention. The process consumed nine weeks from the time the earlier vote regarding the convention call had failed in the house.[67]

Pro-convention men lauded this triumph of democracy in a raucous noctur-
nal celebration in the streets of Vandalia. Two supreme court justices, a future
governor of Missouri, a future lieutenant governor of Illinois, and most of the
proslavery legislators blew on horns and beat drums and tin pans as they marched
to the residence of Governor Coles and the boardinghouses of convention opponents.[68]

This taunting demonstration was the beginning of a heated eighteen-month
campaign leading to the vote by the electorate on the call for a convention. Governor Coles led the opposition and promptly organized an antislavery society.
Similar societies were formed in other counties. Coles worked tirelessly writing
pamphlets on his own behalf and anonymously for others. He campaigned in
every county and enlisted antislavery businessmen from other states, including
Nicholas Biddle, president of the Bank of the United States, to support the cause.
He also contributed the salary of his four-year term to the campaign as well as
spending heavily from his own funds.[69]

Three of the state's five newspapers supported the side of slavery. The two
opposed included the *Illinois Intelligencer*, which had switched its position on
the convention issue after a group headed by Coles bought it.[70]

The ablest public man speaking against the convention was Congressman Daniel Pope Cook, who returned from Washington in 1824 and devoted himself to
that cause and to his own reelection campaign against former governor Shadrach
Bond. Cook had been an ardent antislavery advocate in Congress after his election in December 1819. As Illinois's only congressman, he had voted against the
admission of slave state Missouri in 1821, while his father-in-law, Senator Ninian Edwards, and the other Illinois senator, Jesse Thomas, voted for it. Ninian
Edwards, who was claimed by both sides in the convention controversy, never
took a discernible position on the issue. Prominent slavery advocates included
six present or future U.S. senators, former governor Shadrach Bond, a future
governor, the chief justice of the Illinois Supreme Court, and a large number of
other officials.[71]

Out-of-state advocates joined the fight as well. Slavery proponents, including
many Missourians, used the settlement of Missouri by wealthy immigrants from
the south as an argument for the economic benefits that would accrue to Illinois.
Antislavery advocates argued as vigorously against slavery on moral grounds and
because of the national turmoil that would follow the incursion of slavery north
of the Ohio River.[72]

The "long, excited, angry, bitter, and indignant contest" over calling a convention ended with the general election on August 2, 1824. The result was decisive. The anti-convention cause triumphed by a vote of 6,640 to 4,972. The vote followed sectional lines, with southern counties supporting the convention and more northerly counties opposing it, several by majorities of better than 80 percent.[73]

Governor Coles delivered his valedictory message on December 6, 1826. As in his inaugural address four years earlier, he expressed his views on the slavery question. A new criminal code and digest of laws were to be adopted during the next legislative session. Coles urged that the laws referring to blacks be revised and made less oppressive. If the general assembly would not abolish slavery immediately, he urged adoption of measures that ultimately would end it. He pressed specifically for abolishing the constitutional provision compelling children brought into the state before age fifteen or born of indentured slaves to remain in bondage until they reached adult ages. He also urged more protections for free blacks.[74]

Coles's idealism was not soon realized. To the contrary, during the term of Governor Ninian Edwards over the next four years and until the 1840s, legislation was increasingly burdensome on free blacks and black servants and slaves and increasingly solicitous to slaveholders.

The successful fight on the constitutional convention referendum was Coles's last political victory. He made a poor showing in a later race for Congress. Similarly, few of his antislavery colleagues were successful in running for political office. In contrast, the proslavery campaigners secured victories in a number of elections for higher positions. Among them were John McLean, who later served as a U.S. senator, secretary of state and future senator Elias Kent Kane, and Chief Justice Joseph Phillips.[75]

Daniel Pope Cook was reelected to Congress in 1820, 1822, and 1824. Cook played a significant role in the presidential election of 1824. None of the four candidates received a majority of electoral votes, thus throwing the election into the House of Representatives. Cook, who was the only representative of Illinois at the time, cast the state's decisive vote in favor of his friend and patron John Quincy Adams, who was elected over Andrew Jackson. The Illinois electorate was ardently Jacksonian, however. In 1826 Cook lost his bid for reelection to Congress in a surprise upset to little-known Joseph Duncan. Cook's health, which had always been poor, had deteriorated, hindering his ability to campaign. During the last weeks of the congressional session of 1826–27, he was confined to his home in Washington.[76]

In the spring of 1827 President Adams sent Cook on a secret mission to Cuba. He returned in June, very ill, to his home in Edwardsville. Frail and failing, he traveled back to his family home in Kentucky in the fall to spend his last days there. He died at age thirty-three on October 16, 1827. In January 1831, the Illinois legislature named Cook County in his honor.[77]

Edward Coles retired to a bachelor's life on his Edwardsville farm when his term as governor ended. He was successful as an investor in St. Louis real estate and traveled widely. In 1832, after living in Illinois only thirteen years, he left the state for the life of a wealthy aristocrat in Philadelphia. No other governor lived in Illinois so short a time, and few did as much to influence life in the state.[78]

CHAPTER 3

Black Codes and Bondage, Settling the North, Legislative Follies

The First General Assembly of the State of Illinois met in Kaskaskia on January 4, 1819, one month after admission to statehood. The legislature faced many challenges. Composed of novices to the legislative process, it had to grapple with issues of civil and criminal law, in a state that had no penitentiary and few county jails, and revenue and finance, in a state where land ownership was overwhelmingly either in the federal government or nonresident speculators. Treatment of blacks in bondage and, later, of free blacks, created conflict and stirred emotions greatly out of proportion to their small and diminishing proportion of the population. No state north of the Ohio River had so many slaves or came closer to providing constitutional protection for slavery.[1]

A New Capital on the Frontier

In the first months of 1819, the constitutional mandate to establish a new capital was going forward. Senators Thomas and Edwards persuaded their congressional colleagues that a grant of land for a new capital would increase the value of unsurveyed public lands. Just before the close of the session, a bill granting to the state four sections of public land passed both houses of Congress and was signed by President Monroe on March 3, 1819.[2]

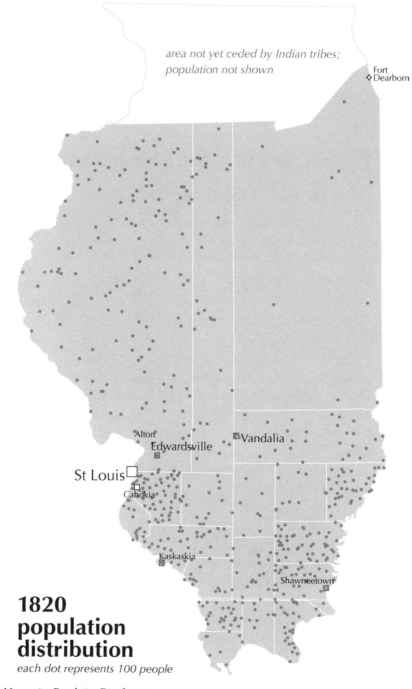

area not yet ceded by Indian tribes;
population not shown

◇ Fort
Dearborn

Alton
Edwardsville
St Louis
Cahokia
Vandalia
Kaskaskia
Shawneetown

**1820
population
distribution**
each dot represents 100 people

Map 4. 1820 Population Distribution

In June, four legislators appointed as commissioners rode eighty-two miles northeast from the capital along the Kaskaskia River to a point where a local settler helped them select a beautiful site on high ground in the virgin forest a few hundred feet west of the river.[3]

The commissioners acted promptly to establish the capital. A survey platted a spacious town, reserving a large square in the center for public use. After 150 lots were sold at inflated prices to officials and other speculators, a simple two-story frame statehouse was constructed in the spring and early summer of 1820. Forty by thirty feet at the foundation, with a thirty-foot-square house of representatives chamber on the first floor and a smaller senate chamber on the second, it was nondescript among its neighboring frame and wood-planked structures.[4]

The state moved what there was of its government to Vandalia in the summer of 1820, in time for the Second General Assembly to convene there in the fall. On December 4, 1820, the town was overcrowded with legislators, clerks, other state employees, spectators, lobbyists, and office seekers. The governor and others moved in with relatives or to private homes. Some clerks slept in the statehouse. Governor Bond devoted much of his opening address to the idealistic promise of Vandalia as a place of culture and learning, a modern center of good public buildings, home to college professors teaching in seminaries and institutions of higher learning.

Vandalia never attained that promise. Legislatures were unwilling to invest state funds in a temporary capital. The first statehouse was home to the Second and Third General Assemblies. Predictably a fire hazard, it burned down in December 1823 due to a wayward stove. The town promptly constructed a ramshackle two-story brick structure—partly a reconstruction of a fire-gutted bank—to serve as a new capitol. This building also failed to provide adequate space and became legendary for its sagging floors and bulging and cracking walls.

Legislators worked in this structure for twelve years, through six general assemblies. It was abandoned in 1836—after warnings about its safety. The building was significant historically, however, having housed important legislative sessions and because Stephen Douglas, Abraham Lincoln, Lyman Trumbull, and many other illustrious Illinois officeholders began their political careers there. A new statehouse was constructed in 1836. Vandalia remained the seat of government until 1839.[5]

New Codes, Old Laws

The First General Assembly adopted a code of statute law compiled by secretary of state Elias Kane, for the most part copied from the statutes of Virginia and Kentucky. The revenue laws placed the burden of raising money for state purposes on nonresident landowners, contrary to the provisions of the enabling act. County revenue was derived from taxation of residents' personal property and, at lesser burdens, real estate.[6]

Criminal codes were constrained by the impossibility of providing for punishment by imprisonment. The state had no penitentiary, and counties were reluctant to undertake the expense of providing jails. Fines were the prescribed remedy in numerous cases. Whipping was prescribed when fines could not be collected and as punishment for more serious offenses. The 1819 code provided for as many as five hundred lashes for some offenses. Punishment of death by hanging was prescribed for four offenses: rape, arson, horse stealing, and murder.[7]

The most comprehensive set of laws was the 1819 Black Code, which was more stringent in regulating the conduct of blacks than the codes in many southern states. The act of March 30, 1819, "respecting free Negroes, Mulattoes, and Slaves," was largely a re-adoption and codification of civil and criminal codes that previously had been enacted by the territorial legislature. The code was important, however, not only as the first for the state but also as the forerunner of many enactments to follow.[8]

The 1819 Black Code dealt in large part with matters related to the presence of free blacks in the state. The perceived threat from free blacks would be a hotly contested issue for fifty years in public debates, in the legislature, and in constitutional conventions in 1847 and 1862. The 1819 law required a black or mulatto to produce a court-issued certificate of freedom before settling in Illinois. That document was to be registered in the county where he wished to live, along with names, dates, and descriptions of himself and family.

Section 3 of the act made it unlawful for anyone to bring a slave into the state for the purpose of freeing him. The hostility felt toward those who sought to shelter a slave from the law or interfere with the property rights of slave owners was manifested in Section 6, which stated that anyone knowingly harboring a slave or preventing the recapture of an escaped slave was guilty of a felony to be punished according to the laws concerning the receipt of stolen goods.

The requirements of registration and restrictions on movement were a burden. The greatest danger, however, was the active commerce in kidnapping free blacks and selling them into slavery in the South. The 1819 code prohibited kidnapping. It provided that anyone forcibly taking a free black or indentured servant out of the state—excepting masters removing their own runaway slaves—was to pay a fine of $1,000 to the injured party.

The act's final provisions dealt with the behavior of the servant or slave and the duties of servants to master. The master was to provide "wholesome and sufficient food, clothing, and lodging" and, at the end of the term of service, "a coat, waistcoat, a pair of breeches and shoes, two pair of stockings, two shirts, a hat, and a blanket." There were no penalties on the master, however, for failure to fulfill his obligations.

On order from a justice of the county, disobedient, lazy, or disorderly servants could be punished by whipping. Blacks who refused to work or attempted to run away were obligated to spend extra time in service and work off any expenses of recapture. Blacks were forbidden to own a servant not of their own color; there were to be no white slaves to blacks. Commercial dealings were prohibited, travel was severely restricted, and a slave visiting dwellings other than his own was punishable by severe whipping. Any person permitting dancing or reveling by slaves on his premises was subject to a twenty-dollar fine.

Like the territorial codes that were the pattern for the Black Code of 1819, certain provisions on paper were not followed in practice. Punishments by whipping often were meted out by masters but seldom after the required official process. The act stated that the servant could sue the master in circuit court for injurious demeanor; undeserved correction; insufficient food, raiment, or lodging; or other grievances. In practice, servants whom the law said could seek redress in the circuit courts in the event of mistreatment had no such recourse.

Any theoretical right of servants to seek redress in court was effectively nullified by an act of February 2, 1827, which stated, "A negro, mulatto, or Indian shall not be a witness in any court, or in any case, against a white person." The act specified that "a person having one fourth part negro blood shall be adjudged a mulatto."[9]

More repressive provisions were added two years later when the legislature in January 1829 enacted a major revision of the 1819 Black Code. The new act comprised four significant sections. The first dealt with the same subject of free blacks entering the state, as did Section 3 of the 1819 act. However, instead of placing any burden on the owner to provide a bond and register, the new law placed the onus on the servant. A black seeking to reside as a free man in Illinois was required to produce a certificate of freedom and also give a bond in the amount of $1,000—a huge amount—conditioned on not becoming a charge "as a poor person." The section also imposed a $500 fine on any person hiring, harboring, or giving any sustenance to a black who was not in compliance. The sizeable bond requirement and its conditions of compliance made it virtually impossible for a free black to gain lawful residence. The 1829 amendments also added a new provision barring marriage between a white person and a black or mulatto. Such marriages were not only declared null and void; offenders were subject to a fine, whipping up to thirty-nine lashes, and imprisonment for at least a year.[10]

Bondage by Contract Servitude Flourishes

Under the 1818 constitution, hundreds of "French slaves" and black servants bound by contracts during the territorial years remained in bondage in Illinois through the 1820s and 1830s, and into the 1840s and 1850s. Many were required to serve out lengthy terms that could last the rest of their lives.

In 1810, after he moved to Illinois to become governor, Ninian Edwards registered in Randolph County (Kaskaskia) five servants brought from Kentucky: in April, Anthony, a mulatto, age twenty-one, for a term of thirty-five years; in June, Strass, a black male, age forty, for fifteen years, Rose, a mulatto, age twenty-three, for thirty-five years, and Joseph, a black, age one, for thirty-four years; in July, Maria, a mulatto, age fifteen, for forty-five years. In June 1811 Edwards registered Charles, a mulatto, age twenty-two, for thirty-six years, and Jesse, a black male, age twenty-five, for thirty-five years. In December 1814 he registered Charlotte, a mulatto, age twenty-seven, for a term of thirty-six years, and in 1815, William, a black, age thirty-six, for twenty years, Milley, a black, age thirty-nine, for twenty years, and Gracey, a black, age five, for twenty-five years. All were brought to Illinois from Kentucky.[11]

Nathaniel Pope registered three indentured servants in Randolph County in June 1810: Patience, a black, age twenty-three, with seventeen years left on her term; Isaac, a black, age eleven, with a term of twenty-four years; and Frederick, a mulatto, age seventeen, with a term of twenty-three years remaining. All were his slaves in Louisiana. Ten years later, the 1820 census recorded seven "people of color" as part of Pope's household, not specifying whether they were free blacks, servants, or slaves. Pope's indentured slave Frederick was punished in a public whipping in 1814, receiving twenty-five lashes and a fine of fifty-four dollars after conviction by a jury of larceny at the home of another settler in December 1813.[12]

Elias Kent Kane registered Rebecca, whom he brought from Kentucky, in Randolph County on December 6, 1816, at age sixteen. She was required to serve a forty-year term that would end in 1856 when she would be fifty-six years old. Shadrach Bond registered more than a dozen indentured servants. Benjamin Stephenson was reported in the 1810 census as owning five and in the 1818 and 1820 censuses as owning eight.

These are some of the more modest indentures. Many contracts obligated service for terms of ninety-nine years. It is difficult to fathom the motivation for such unrealistic provisions other than the desire to make a point about ownership and bound labor in defiance of the avowed "free" and "voluntary" purpose of the indenture device. These "Negroes" and "Mulacttoes," held as "servants," tilled the soil on plantations, as farms in southern Illinois were then called, but also labored in all kinds of household work and as waiters in taverns, as dairymen, as shoemakers, and as cooks, in the salt mines, and in other hard labor.[13]

Slaves and indentured servants were a property right. They and their service could be conveyed as other property. Advertisements offering slaves and servants for sale or rent were common in Kaskaskia newspapers. Frequently, they warned that if the servants were not rented in Illinois they would be sold in Missouri.[14] In 1810 Ninian Edwards, who owned slaves in Illinois and Missouri, advertised to sell almost two dozen slaves, including children, and, notably, to sell this human property alongside animals:

> Notice: I have for sale twenty-two slaves, among them are several of both sexes between the years of ten and seventeen; if not shortly sold I shall seek to hire them in Missouri territory. I have also for sale a full blooded horse, a very large English bull and several young ones.[15]

Edwards's will gave his wife, Elvira, full discretion to deal with his property interests as she thought proper. He expressed his desire that she "procure a farm for her wherever she may choose one," of not more than four hundred acres and with improvements that were not "unreasonably costly or extravagant." He added that she should obtain a sufficient number of servants for housework and for cultivation of the farm. For that purpose, he said, she should "keep any or

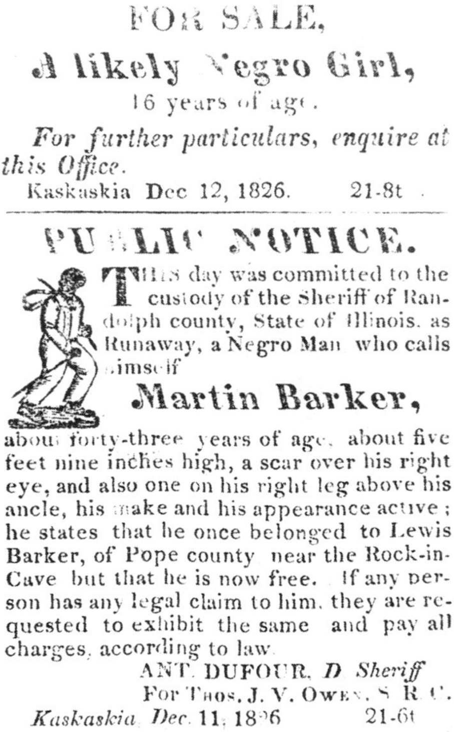

FOR SALE,
A likely Negro Girl,
16 years of age.

For further particulars, enquire at this Office.

Kaskaskia Dec 12, 1826.   21-8t

PUBLIC NOTICE.

This day was committed to the custody of the Sheriff of Randolph county, State of Illinois. as Runaway, a Negro Man who calls himself

Martin Barker,

about forty-three years of age, about five feet nine inches high, a scar over his right eye, and also one on his right leg above his ancle, his make and his appearance active ; he states that he once belonged to Lewis Barker, of Pope county near the Rock-in-Cave but that he is now free. If any person has any legal claim to him, they are requested to exhibit the same and pay all charges, according to law.

ANT. DUFOUR, *D Sheriff*
For Thos. J. V. Owen, S R C.

Kaskaskia Dec. 11, 1826   21-6t

Fig. 3. Kaskaskia Newspaper Notice: Slave Girl for Sale; Captured Runaway Being Held. Courtesy of the Abraham Lincoln Presidential Library and Museum.

all of my servants, or sell them to purchase others." The extensive probate file of the will, opened on August 7, 1833, after Edwards's death in July, does not list an inventory of servants. It does, however, list the proceeds of a private sale in September, which included "Richard," sold for $375, "Runaway negro," for $500, and "Catherine," for $400. The record of a distribution to Elvira in September 1834 listed various monies and other assets, including "Negroes" valued at $1,300.[16]

Shadrach Bond owned many slaves and indentured servants over the years, including fourteen in 1820 while he was governor. Like many others, he desired to keep them in the family beyond his lifetime. Thus, he provided in his will, "I give to my loving wife, Achsah Bond, all of my personal property . . . [and] my negro Frank Thomas. . . . I give to my daughter Julia Rachel five hundred dollars and my negro girl Eliza. And to my daughter Achsah Mary five hundred dollars and my negro girl Harriet and to my wife Achsah I give all the rest of my negroes to be disposed of as she thinks best having entire confidence that she will make proper use of it."[17]

In the 1820s and into the 1840s there are records of many other transfers of indentured servants from one master in Illinois to another, sometimes of one servant many times over. Such transfers were common and legal. They illustrate the routine treatment of people as property.

The indenture system and the condition of indentured blacks were of little concern to the public as a whole in the 1820s and early 1830s. Few disputes were brought to court, not surprising in that blacks and mulattoes were barred from filing complaints or giving testimony against whites and had no means to hire lawyers, few of whom were interested in taking on their cases. The rare cases that did arise were initiated because of disputes by whites over ownership or sympathetic assistance to slaves by whites. They were resolved on narrow grounds that posed no threat to the system, a system from which many members of the courts themselves were benefiting.[18]

The first case to reach the Illinois Supreme Court was *Cornelius v. Cohen*, decided in December 1825 on appeal from the circuit court of St. Clair County. Joseph Cornelius, who had been involved in several litigations in St. Clair County, sued to recover the services of Betsey, a daughter born in 1805 while her mother, Rachel, was his indentured servant. The supreme court ruling was a narrow technical one, but the facts of the case are illustrative of the state of indenture law and masters' attitudes concerning the treatment of servants.[19]

Betsey was born to Rachel when Illinois was still part of the Indiana Territory. The 1807 territory law, later incorporated in Illinois state law, stated that children born to an indentured servant during her term of bondage would themselves be bound to serve the master until age thirty for males and twenty-eight for females. Because of this hereditary bondage, Cornelius claimed that Betsey was his servant; he made the same claim—not directly involved in this case—for four other children of Rachel. When Betsey was fifteen, in August 1821, she sued Cornelius for assault and battery and false imprisonment, claiming, in the words of the trial court record, that Cornelius had "seized and laid hold of the said Betsey and with great force and violence tied her with a rope and dragged her through the streets of Belleville many miles tied as aforesaid and struck her many great and violent blows and then imprisoned her and kept her detained."[20]

Cornelius, in his court response, admitted that he had committed the violence but claimed he was justified in doing so because he was "using no more force than was necessary to restrain the said Betsey and commit her to labour for him."[21] Cornelius was apparently not abashed in asserting his claimed rights, and nothing in any court record or in commentary on the case suggests that this was unusual, let alone shocking, behavior on the part of a master toward his property.

The supreme court ruled that indenture contracts were to be made in strict compliance with the laws or they would be voided. Because the indenture contract between Cornelius and Rachel had not been witnessed by the county clerk or signed by the owner, Cornelius, as the law required, it was void and Betsey was free.[22]

The court's ruling in *Cornelius v. Cohen*, requiring strict compliance with the provisions of law, was reinforced in 1836 in *Choisser v. Hargrave*. The slave, Barney Hargrave, had been brought to Illinois before 1816 but was not indentured until August 15, 1818, just before the delegates approved the Illinois constitution. Because the law required an indenture to be made within thirty days of bringing a slave into the territory, the court ruled that the claimed servitude of Barney was void.[23]

The right of a master to whip an indentured servant to compel her to work for him was also asserted by William Jay in *Phoebe v. Jay*, a case that reached the Illinois Supreme Court in December 1828. William's father, Joseph Jay, had signed an indenture contract in November 1814 for Phoebe to serve him for a term of forty years. After Joseph Jay's death, William, his only son, heir, and administrator of his estate, claimed ownership of Phoebe to serve out the remaining term of her contract. William acknowledged in his court papers that "he had necessarily to use a little force and beating" to compel her service. Phoebe sued William Jay in Randolph County in 1827 for assault, battery, wounding, and false imprisonment, claiming that her indenture had "ceased to have any operation" upon Joseph Jay's death.[24]

Justice Samuel D. Lockwood, who had been one of the leaders in the campaign against a slavery constitutional convention in 1824 and who served on the supreme court for twenty-four years, wrote the opinion for the court in December 1828. In a long and eloquent essay, he explained why there never could be a truly voluntary contract between a black and a master. He and the court ruled nevertheless that the 1818 constitution had validated such contracting that "was in effect an involuntary servitude for a period of years." The court confirmed that the service contract was property but ruled that it could not be passed to an heir but was one of the assets of the estate to be sold at auction by executors or administrators. The result was that Phoebe was not free but was to be sold at an auction arranged by the estate's administrator, William Jay, the man she sought to escape. She could only hope that some more charitable person might buy her contract and either set her free or provide a more benevolent existence.[25]

In the same December 1828 term, the court ruled in another case that the ostensibly voluntary contractual relationship between master and indentured servants in fact transformed the registered servants into goods and chattels that could be sold on execution. After observing that the territorial and state legislatures had considered registered servants to be personal property, and that they had always been taxed by their value as property, the court ruled that indenture contracts were transferrable like other goods and chattels.[26]

In other cases into the 1840s, the Illinois Supreme Court ruled on narrow grounds while upholding the general validity of involuntary servitude through the use of indentures. It was not until 1845 that the court began to rule that indentured service contracts were invalid.

Servitude of Children; The Value of Human Capital

When Governor Coles in his farewell address urged Illinois to abolish the constitutional provision holding children born of indentured servants in hereditary bondage until adulthood, he would have known that he was striking at one of the most important economic pillars of slavery. Growing up among large slaveholders, and inheriting slaves himself, he would have understood what slave owners had realized for centuries: the production of babies by childbearing slaves added capital to their assets at a profitable rate.[27]

Thomas Jefferson at Monticello had a workforce numbering at times as many as 140 slaves, a large number of them children. Jefferson for decades was careful to measure his manufacturing and agricultural sales and costs. As was his analytical custom, he had calculated that he was making a 4 percent profit every year on the birth of black children, a perpetual human dividend at compound interest. In a letter to George Washington in 1792, he described the phenomenon: "I allow nothing for losses by death, but, on the contrary, shall presently take credit for four per cent per annum for their increase over and above their own numbers."[28]

Of the value of children, he wrote to one of his plantation managers, "A child raised every two years is of more profit then [*sic*] the crop of the best laboring man. In this as in all other cases providence has made our duties and our interests coincide perfectly.... [W]ith respect therefore to our women and their children I must pray you to inculcate upon the overseers that it is not their labor, but their increase which is the first consideration with us."[29] In the 1790s he advised a friend that slavery presented an investment strategy for the future; if he had any extra cash, "every farthing of it [should be] laid out in land and negroes, which besides being a present support bring a silent profit of from 5 to 10 percent in this country by the increase in their value."[30]

In Illinois also, masters understood that there was economic value in children born to indentured servants. They were kept for service by their mother's owner, sold as an additional asset with their mother, or sold separately apart from their mother or other members of the family.

The case of Joseph Cornelius is illustrative. He lost his supreme court case, discussed earlier, on a technicality because the indenture of his servant, Rachel, had not been timely signed and properly witnessed. The facts of the case, however, are illustrative of the value of slave children. In the trial court, Cornelius claimed that Rachel's daughter, Betsey, had a value of $500 as a servant, and Rachel's four other children, Louisa, Jerry, Tempey, and Henry, had an aggregate value of $1,000—significant sums at the time.[31]

Servants' value depended in large part on the length of their remaining terms of service. In the 1820s the prices of boys and girls varied from $300 to $600, depending on their physical qualifications and the period of servitude remaining. They were used as security for notes and contracts. If their owners did not have immediate use for their services, they rented the children to others on a yearly basis.[32]

Many of the iconic portrayals of slavery in paintings, sculpture, and literature that show children and young people being torn from their families to be sold separately at slave markets dramatize the economic value of slave children. While such images were widely used by antislavery advocates to show the personal, emotional, and spiritual evils of slavery, they rested on the recognized economic values of slave reproduction.

Apprenticeships in Illinois: Bondage of the Young

Just as it had employed the euphemism of indentured servitude to cloak slavery under another name, Illinois held numerous children and adults in bonded servitude under the euphemism of "apprenticeship." The apprenticeship label not only provided the legal justification for child slavery, it offered a cloak of beneficence until the eve of the Civil War for respectable families to hold bonded servants for periods of up to two decades, even as owning slaves and indentured servants became less respectable and even unlawful.

Illinois recorded indentures that referred to the servants as apprentices both before and after the constitution of 1818. The 1818 constitution conferred exceptional status to the apprenticeship of blacks and mulattoes, with no discussion and seemingly little thought to what the exception would mean in practice.[33]

The words "apprentice" or "apprenticeship," of course, mean learning a skill or trade from a skilled employer. Many of the early "apprenticeship" indentures in Illinois that used the term "apprentice" to characterize the servant or that entitled the indenture as one for "apprenticeship" did not spell out any trade or skills to be taught or learned. In time, it became typical to state that boys would be taught "farming" and girls "housewifery." That learning and those duties, of course, did not distinguish these "apprentices" from hundreds of thousands if not millions of slave children who had been taught those same "skills" as their regular work for two centuries in the slave states. Household slaves, whether male or female, learned housewifery—to sew, cook, and clean house. Farm and field workers, male or female, learned the "skills" of farming. Boys and sometimes girls were employed in manufacturing, foundries, smithing, or other service.

In the years after 1818, their mothers' masters entered many young black and mulatto children in Illinois into service contracts called apprenticeships that bound them to serve into adulthood. The beneficent gloss of apprenticeship on the indentures of children, made without their consent, did not alter the nature of their work or the lack of freedom of their bound service.

The apprenticeship status was defined in detail in December 1826, when the Illinois General Assembly passed the state's first "Act Respecting Apprentices."[34] The act specified that a child could be "bound by an indenture *of his or her own free will and accord*" (emphasis added), and with the consent of a parent or guardian, "to serve as a clerk, apprentice, or servant in any art or mystery, service, trade, employment, manual occupation or labor" until age twenty-one for males or eighteen for females. The act set out in sixteen detailed sections rules to govern the behavior of such servants and the conduct of county officials and courts in dealing with them.[35]

While the act applied to white children as well as to blacks, it made a significant distinction between them. The law stated that all indentures made for binding out any child were to include a clause specifying what they would be taught, which was to state, "That the master or mistress, to whom such child shall be bound as aforesaid, shall cause such child to be taught to read and write, and the ground rules of arithmetic; and shall also give unto such apprentice, a new bible, and two new suits of clothes, suitable to his or her condition, at the expiration of his or her term of service."[36]

Significantly, however, the teaching requirement specified that indentures for black or mulatto children need not say that they should be taught to write or to do arithmetic. These skills were considered dangerous for young blacks or mulattos; freed from indentures at age eighteen or twenty-one without knowing how to write or to add and subtract left them less independent.[37]

From the 1820s until well into the 1840s, many masters were able to procure the services of their female servants' children as apprentices for decades into the future, even as the mothers were freed by emancipation or their terms of servitude were fulfilled. On June 24, 1839, for example, Henry Cook emancipated his black slave Hariot and her seven slave children, whom he had brought to Pope County from Alabama. The same day Cook indentured to himself as apprentices, with Hariot's consent, all seven children, the males until they reached twenty-one and the females until age eighteen. Ranging in age from a boy of fifteen down to a one-year-old girl, the children faced bonded servitude that in some cases would last until the late 1850s. Cook then freed Hariot "as a reward for faithful service."[38] The effect of this practice was to bind minor children to serve, potentially for decades, on the enticement or promise of freedom for their mother.

The practice of bonding young children to years of service under the beneficent label of apprenticeship was widespread among well-to-do and prominent citizens even as limitations of court cases and growing public sentiment against bonded servitude eroded the extent and use of indentures. Nowhere was this demonstrated more than among the leading citizens of Sangamon County. Locus of the capital at Springfield from 1839, and described as one of the more enlightened counties in the state, Sangamon sat in the growing mid-center belt of counties being settled by northerners and immigrants with antislavery sentiments. The 1845 state census reported, however, that Sangamon County, with seventy-five slaves and servants, was second in numbers of slaves only to the eighty slaves of Randolph County, locus of Kaskaskia and many of the early settlers and political leaders and their families. These two were far ahead of all other counties in numbers of slaves and bound servants.[39]

The passage from infant slave to lengthy bondage as an "apprentice" was exemplified by one black house servant who came to be celebrated in the press because of her service to the Ninian Edwards and Ninian Wirt Edwards families, and to Mary Todd and Abraham Lincoln. In 1827, a black child named Epsy Smith, born on the plantation of Arnold Spear in Kentucky, was brought by Mrs. Spear to Illinois as a maid when she visited old friends, Governor Ninian Edwards's family. The governor apparently took a liking to Epsy, said to be a bright and active child seven or eight years old. Before Mrs. Spear returned to Kentucky, she made a gift to the governor of the child, who remained in the Edwards household as a maid.[40]

Espy's legal status in Governor Edwards's household is not clear. There is no evidence that she was registered as an indentured servant or apprentice, as required by the Act on Apprentices that went into force on June 1, 1827, while Edwards was governor. From the time Edwards completed his term in December 1830, he resided in Belleville until his death in 1833. There is no inventory of servants or apprentices in his probate file. However, by the fall of 1835, it appears Espy was a servant living in the Springfield household of the governor's son, Ninian Wirt Edwards, and his wife, Elizabeth Todd Edwards. On October 19, 1835, Ninian W. Edwards signed an indenture of apprenticeship for "a mulatto girl aged eleven years" named Hepsey Smith to serve as an apprentice for seven years, until her eighteenth birthday.[41]

By her accounts to her own family later in life, Espy Smith, born a slave in Kentucky, was the black servant girl in the Springfield home of Ninian W. Edwards. There she met Mary Todd, sister of Elizabeth Edwards, when Mary visited for several months in 1837. There, Espy related, she also knew Abraham Lincoln, opening the door for him during his courtship of Mary, working in the household the evening of November 4, 1842, when Lincoln wed Mary Todd in the Edwards home, and, later, loaned out for a period of time to work in the Lincoln home. The spelling of Hepsey in the contract may have been a phonetic spelling or a common misusage of her name. Describing her age as eleven, when she likely was fourteen or fifteen, was a misjudgment or, perhaps, an intentional misstatement. Children born in slavery often had no idea of their birth dates, and masters signing indenture contracts often lied or "misjudged" the child's age.[42]

The Edwards family was only one of many Springfield families that held indentured blacks and mulattoes as household help, often under apprenticeship indentures made in the period 1835 to 1845 that bound blacks to service to the late 1850s. Mary Todd Lincoln's uncle, Dr. John Todd, listed in the 1830 census as owning five slaves, entered into an indenture on April 18, 1836, binding Elizabeth, an eight-year-old black girl, to serve until she reached age eighteen in 1846, with the consent of her mother, one of Todd's slaves. The Rev. Charles Dresser, who moved to Springfield in April 1838, entered into an indenture a month later for the labor of Rhoda Jane, a fifteen-year-old black girl. In 1839 Dresser constructed the house at Eighth and Jackson Streets that Lincoln purchased six years later. Meanwhile, in 1842 Dresser performed the Lincoln/Todd marriage ceremony.[43]

Ninian W. Edwards signed another black child to an indenture on March 19, 1840. Sidney McInstry, an eight-year-old mulatto girl, was bound to serve ten years as an apprentice, until age eighteen. Edwards executed the indenture before a justice of the peace of Sangamon County, who signed on behalf of the girl, indicating that she could not read or sign her own mark or name and that she did not have a parent to consent. Edwards apparently transferred ownership of McInstry in less than a year. On March 3, 1841, she was indentured to Nathaniel A. Rankin, again in Sangamon County.[44]

Years later, in 1884, Ninian Wirt Edwards, editing his father's papers, offered a description of Illinois in the 1820s that applies also to his own ownership of "apprentices" in the 1840s. Thus, he referred to "strange times in Illinois, when colored persons were held to service, and those services subject to transfer. It was a qualified condition of slavery, which was put an end to in 1845 by a decision of the Supreme court in the case of Jarrot v. Jarrot."[45]

Kidnapping, Bounty Hunters, Abolitionists

While the public was not much troubled by the forms of quasi-slavery in the late 1820s through the 1830s, the search by bounty hunters for runaway slaves and its barbarous twin, the nefarious business of kidnapping free blacks to spirit them out of the state into slavery, did become a concern. An act to prevent kidnapping was passed in Illinois in 1825; however, no serious attempt was made to enforce it. Instead, kidnapping assumed proportions of an established enterprise.

Although Illinoisans generally claimed to be opposed to the practice of kidnapping, great numbers of people, especially in the southern part of the state, sympathized with slave owners and those who assisted them in seeking to recover their property by capturing runaway slaves. Reflecting those attitudes, the "apprentices" law passed in 1826 made it a crime with a penalty of $500 to advise a servant to run away or to secrete, harbor, or assist a runaway. These laws, along with restrictive codes against immigration of free blacks and laws directing officials to sell out for service blacks without freedom papers, all made life precarious for blacks.[46]

As the years passed, the state's population increased significantly, filling in the central and northern areas with immigration from northeastern states and Europe. Many new settlers were people of strong antislavery principles who favored stopping the spread of slavery and aiding blacks in Illinois to escape bondage. Southern sympathizers at the same time became more vocal in protecting the institution of slavery, not only in Illinois but also in the South and the District of Columbia.

Antagonism grew between people holding these opposing views. Where antislavery sentiments evolved into promotion of abolition and into practices to aid blacks to escape to safety, known later as the Underground Railroad, hostility was so great in some areas of the state that activists' lives were threatened. The romantic depiction of the Underground Railroad in the century and a half since the Civil War makes it difficult to comprehend the bitter animosity proslavery inhabitants of Illinois felt toward the conductors of this escape system. The highest degree of secrecy was important to the security of Underground Railroad promoters.

Reflecting widespread public sentiment, the state legislature in January 1837 adopted resolutions denouncing abolitionism. Approved unanimously by the senate and by a vote of 77 to 6 in the house, they stated,

> *Resolved* by the General Assembly of the State of Illinois. That we highly disapprove of the formation of abolition societies, and of the doctrines promulgated by them.
>
> *Resolved*, That the right of property in slaves is secured to the slaveholding States by the Federal constitution, and that they cannot be deprived of that right without their consent.
>
> *Resolved*, That the General government cannot abolish slavery in the District of Columbia, against the consent of the citizens of said District without a manifest breach of good faith.
>
> *Resolved*, That the Governor be requested to transmit to the States of Virginia, Mississippi, Alabama, New York and Connecticut, a copy of the foregoing resolutions.[47]

Twenty-eight-year-old Abraham Lincoln, in his second term in the Illinois legislature, was one of the six votes in the house against the resolution. Six weeks later, on March 3, 1837, he and Daniel Stone, a Whig colleague from Sangamon County, took the courageous step of filing a protest in the official journal. They raised a moral point by condemning slavery as "founded on both injustice and bad policy," but stated that they agreed that "the promulgation of abolition doctrines tends rather to increase than to abate its evils."[48]

Lincoln's votes were recorded a few times on slavery issues in his eight years in the state legislature. The year before the resolution to which he and Stone filed a protest, Lincoln had voted for a resolution dealing in part with the rights of blacks to vote, which stated, "*Resolved*, That the elective franchise should be kept pure from contamination by the admission of colored votes."[49]

Lincoln did not explain his motivation for filing the protest voting as he did in January 1837. It may have been to go on record firmly against slavery. It also may have been to make clear that in voting against the resolution, he and Stone were not aligning themselves as abolitionists, whom they did not favor at the time and with whom it would have been political suicide to be allied. Nevertheless, delayed and qualified as it was, the protest did show political courage. Thomas Ford, who became governor in 1842, the year Lincoln retired from the legislature, made the point in his memoirs that it was "dangerous" for a politician to be sympathetic to the negro cause.[50]

The Disappeared Indians

In the first years following statehood, a few isolated farms and small communities were settled in northern Illinois. Indian culture and presence persisted. The so-called Winnebago War foreshadowed a change. The trouble began when the Winnebago, angry over sexual liberties by white men against Indian women and fearing they were being crowded out of hunting grounds, killed two whites on a boat near Fort Crawford at Prairie du Chien, now Wisconsin. Galena miners, a regiment of volunteers, and regular soldiers mobilized. Winnebago chief Red Bird yielded, sacrificing valor for prudence. In the next year, Winnebago chiefs signed the customary treaties, trading away areas in southern Wisconsin and northern Illinois for cash payments and other promises, and moving to eastern Iowa.

The Winnebago skirmish and concessions were a prelude to the 1832 Black Hawk War, which achieved legendary status in Illinois as the last Indian war in the state and the last "Indian trouble" in the old Northwest. It began with disputes over summer cultivation by Sauk and Fox Indian families of eight hundred to a thousand acres of land east of the Mississippi and north of Rock Island. The Indians came across the river from Iowa in summer to raise their year's corn and other crops, as they had for generations and were entitled to do under an 1804 St. Louis treaty and other agreements.

White squatters occupied the Indian farms, destroyed the natives' crops, and burned their lodges, precipitating the trouble. In the spring of 1831, Black Hawk, an elderly, dissident Sauk headman, who for decades had complained about the 1804 treaty, attempted to force squatters to leave, igniting small skirmishes.

The conflict that followed in 1831, with seven hundred Illinois state volunteers who mobilized but saw no action, consisted of sporadic fights with no result. Resuming in 1832, militia and army regulars fought with Indians along the Wisconsin River near what is now Madison. Pursuit of the Indians to the Mississippi culminated on August 2, 1832, in the Battle of Bad Axe, a massacre at the Mississippi River between Prairie du Chien and La Crosse. There, in an hours-long slaughter, U.S. soldiers killed some Indian fighters and hundreds of women and children as they struggled in the water attempting to reach the west bank. Only one hundred and fifty of the nearly one thousand Indians who had crossed the Mississippi in April lived to return to Iowa.

The massacre was celebrated in Illinois for decades as a great victory. Many men who later rose to prominence in Illinois and the nation recounted their war service in political campaigns and in their professional careers, although very few ever saw any Indians.[51]

Chicago was far removed from the war, but the war spurred its growth. Glowing reports from soldiers about the fertile Illinois prairies and the legend of the conquest sparked immigration to the Chicago region. The population more than doubled by the spring of 1833, half a year after the war's end. Within a short time, newly arrived immigrants, primarily from the East, outnumbered the early settlers. Soon Chicago and neighboring lands were occupied by a predominantly Yankee community.

The U.S. government moved promptly to consolidate its control of remaining Illinois territory and ease the new settlers' anxieties. In September 1833 the government summoned Indians for negotiations to remove them from their lands. More than five thousand Potawatomi, Ojibwa, and Ottawa from Illinois and neighboring territories came to Chicago for the occasion, arriving early to enjoy food provided by the government and drink supplied in abundance by traders who knew that alcohol would lubricate their paths to profits.

Large numbers of speculators, agents, traders, and others attended, as had become the custom, in order to be present when government payments to the Indians would enable them to pay existing debts. These assorted participants connived in various ways to cheat the Indians out of the money and goods they would receive.

Three U.S. commissioners assembled the chiefs in mid-September. The Indians were led by Shabbona, an Ottawa warrior who had married into the Potawatomi and become an influential chief, and the métis traders Billy Caldwell and Alexander Robinson. They protested that they did not want to sell their lands and refused for days to attend any negotiating sessions. At length, however, urged on by the many traders in attendance, the chiefs joined in talks. On September 26, seventy-seven chiefs signed a set of agreements that promised them five million acres of land west of the Mississippi in Missouri and Iowa in exchange for the same total acreage in northeastern Illinois and southeastern Wisconsin, as well as large sums of money to be paid to them and their creditors and assignees.[52]

The treaty was extraordinary, both in the great size of the tracts of Indian land that were being traded away to the United States and in the amount of money involved, which far exceeded any precedent. The payout by the United States exceeded $1 million, with annuities to be paid to the tribes over twenty years. Cash was paid to a long list of individuals who the Indians agreed had claims against them; funds were allotted to the construction of mills, blacksmith shops, farms and Indian houses, and other improvements in new villages in the west; $70,000 was designated to foster "education and the encouragement of the domestic arts"; and $100,000 to pay individuals in lieu of awarding them reservation lands, a practice the federal government no longer permitted. Prominent métis families in the region were paid money, with the negotiating métis Robinson and Caldwell each awarded $10,000 and an annual annuity.

The treaty furnished the last and greatest opportunity in the old Northwest for individuals to enrich themselves at the expense of the Indians or the U.S. government. Hundreds took advantage. In far greater numbers than for any other Indian treaty, more than five hundred persons with no Indian heritage received payments. The families of traders John Kinzie and Thomas Forsyth each received more than $50,000.

Many historians and commentators have described the 1833 treaty as a scandal. "Dishonest claimants absorbed [much of] the fund," wrote prominent historian

Milo Quaife in 1913. "The impropriety of many of the claims allowed is patent even today."[53] The federal government accomplished its objective in calling the conclave, however. By 1836, most of the Potawatomi and their allies were removed to Missouri. There local militias and settlers took hostile action against them, causing the government to move them to Iowa. In Iowa they faced Dakota Indians, who likewise were unhappy with their arrival, leading many of the Potawatomi to relocate to Kansas. In Illinois, however, the Indians were gone. The Northwest Ordinance admonished in 1787 that "the utmost good faith shall always be observed toward the Indians; their lands and property shall never be taken from them without their consent; and in their property, rights, and liberty, they shall never be invaded or disturbed, except in just and lawful wars authorized by Congress."[54] In spirit, if not always in word, that provision was forgotten, ignored, or trampled on for decades.

Burgeoning Population of the North

After stretching to count enough people to meet the required forty thousand for statehood in 1818, Illinois became one of the fastest growing states in the nation in the next half-century. In the 1820s, the decade of the fight over calling a slavery convention, the state's population tripled to 157,575 in 1830. Remarkably, the pace accelerated over the next five years, bringing the state's population in 1835 to 269,924 and shifting the center of population after a century from the vicinity of Kaskaskia to a point considerably north of Vandalia. Another two hundred thousand in the ensuing five years brought the 1840 population to 476,183. The 1840 federal census for the first time recorded Illinois cities, but enumerated only four: Chicago (4,476 inhabitants), Springfield (2,571), Alton (2,340), and Quincy (2,311). By 1850, the state's population nearly doubled again, to 851,470, exceeding the size of its earlier-settled neighbor Indiana.[55]

The nineteen counties of 1819 had been trebled to fifty-eight in 1831 and increased to eighty-seven in 1839. Most of the new counties were in a broad swath across the center third of the state, with a half-dozen newly organized in the southern third. When Cook County was created in 1831, named after Daniel Pope Cook, it and Jo Daviess, the two organized counties extending along the Wisconsin border from Lake Michigan to the Mississippi River, had a population that likely was no more than six thousand to seven thousand in an area covering more than eight thousand square miles.[56]

The shifts in population brought a decrease in the political and cultural domination of the state by southerners. Increasingly large numbers of people came to

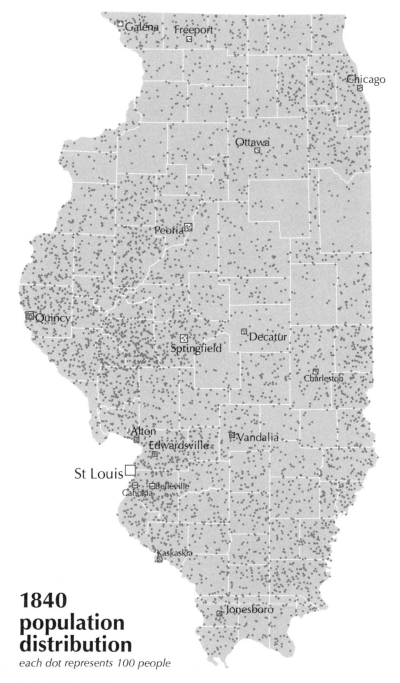

Galena
Freeport
Chicago
Ottawa
Peoria
Quincy
Decatur
Springfield
Charleston
Alton
Edwardsville
Vandalia
St Louis
Cahokia
Belleville
Kaskaskia
Jonesboro

1840
population
distribution
each dot represents 100 people

Map 5. 1840 Population Distribution

Illinois from the Northeast and from Europe, numbers that grew rapidly with the opening of the Erie Canal in 1825 and the arrival of Great Lakes steamships at Chicago in 1832.

Land sales reflected population growth. The mid-1830s saw the most frenzied speculation in land in American history. Public land sales in Illinois increased 600 percent in 1835. Sales in Galena, Chicago, and central and western Illinois led the way. Speculation in the Military Tract, wedged between the Illinois and Mississippi Rivers, boosted sales.[57]

The Military Tract

Congress created the Military Bounty Tract in 1812 on federal land, reserving it for payment of 160-acre parcels to soldiers of the War of 1812. The tract covered a large portion of the huge triangle of land between the Mississippi and Illinois Rivers. Extending north 160 miles from the mouth of the Illinois River at the Mississippi, it contained 3.5 million acres that in time were formed into fourteen counties and parts of four others. Surveys were completed and land distribution began in 1817. In a short time, more than seventeen thousand nontransferrable warrants entitling a veteran or his heirs to 160 acres were registered at the land office in Washington and exchanged for transferrable patents that covered almost three million acres. Relatively few of the original patent holders exercised their ownership by moving to Illinois. The far greater number were content to gain immediately what they could by selling their patents to large-scale speculators, primarily easterners, many of whom had agents working to purchase patents for as little as ten cents per acre. While speculators accumulated rights to land and held out for high prices, in the late 1820s the population grew, first close to the two great rivers, which provided connections to older settlements of the south. Peoria, on the Illinois River, was established in 1819. Adams County, bordered on the west by the Mississippi, was organized in 1825, with its county seat at Quincy. By 1830, the tract had a population of more than twelve thousand people. Between 1831 and 1840, another 83,500 people settled there.[58]

Numerous settlers, in the tradition of the frontier, obtained valuable farms by moving on to the land as "squatters," with no title other than occupation. Eastern investors and titleholders, and their spokesmen in Congress, scorned such occupiers. Westerners, however, defended frontier traditions, which recognized the value in furthering the country's development through cultivation and improvements made by the settlers.[59]

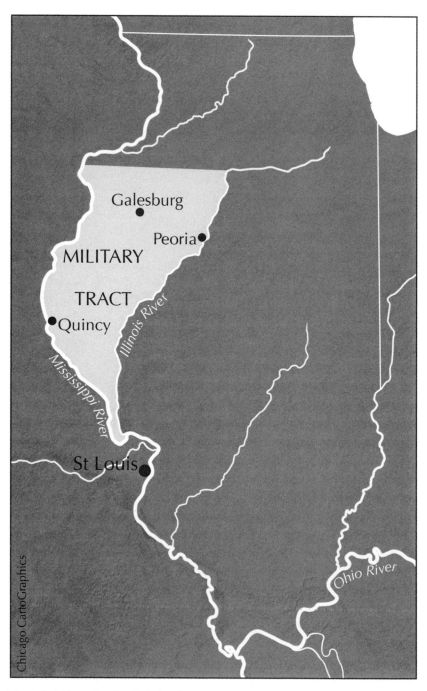

Map 6. The Military Tract (established 1812)

Disputes and litigation between squatters, who claimed compensation for improvement of their properties, and those who claimed ownership rights by acquisition of patents became commonplace, augmented by the arrival of many whose patents were forged. The business of Nathaniel Pope's federal court was enlarged considerably by litigation over claims to land in the Military Tract.[60]

Public Works Spur Settlement

Transportation advancement spurred Illinois development in the three decades before the mid-nineteenth century. The opening of the Erie Canal in 1825 slashed shipping costs across New York State. Great Lakes cargo vessels linked the canal's terminus at Buffalo to Chicago, forging commercial and migratory connections between Illinois and the Northeast in the 1830s and 1840s.[61]

The National Road eased migration for thousands. Pushing from Cumberland, Maryland, to Wheeling, Virginia, in 1818, thence on to Columbus, Ohio, and Indianapolis, people used it to reach Illinois even before construction of the road concluded in Vandalia in 1836. By 1833, Chicago had intercity stagecoach service

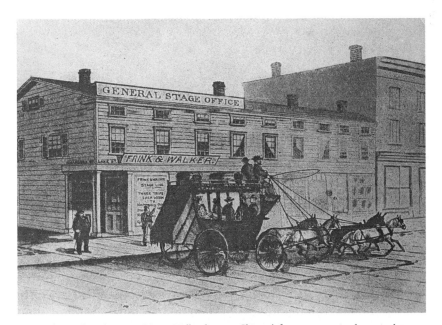

Fig. 4. John Frink, with partner Martin Walker, became Chicago's first transportation baron in the 1830s with multistate commercial and passenger stagecoach service. Courtesy of the Abraham Lincoln Presidential Library and Museum.

east to Detroit, and by mid-decade stagecoach lines served cities in several mid-western states.[62]

On July 4, 1836, construction of the Illinois and Michigan Canal began formally with imposing ceremonies at a place newly named Canalport, the eastern origin of the canal, on the south branch of the Chicago River. The canal, to connect Lake Michigan to the Illinois River and open ship traffic to the Mississippi River and Gulf of Mexico, had been dreamed of for more than a century. Surveying the canal route had begun in the 1820s, stimulating wild speculation in Chicago real estate in the 1830s. After collapse in 1825 of the first companies to attempt to construct it, federal assistance with grants of land along the route obtained by congressman Daniel Pope Cook and state efforts finally got construction under-way in 1838.[63]

Construction of the canal was a massive project in difficult conditions. When completed, it extended ninety-seven miles from the Chicago River to a turning basin at the junction with the Illinois River at LaSalle. Six feet deep, sixty feet wide at the surface to thirty-six feet at the bottom, it descended 141 feet through fifteen locks from its highest point near Chicago.[64]

Fig. 5. Canal barges at LaSalle junction with Illinois River awaiting opening of navigation. Courtesy of the Abraham Lincoln Presidential Library and Museum.

To satisfy the need for manpower, contractors began importing large numbers of Irish laborers. By 1838, hundreds of men lived in hastily built shantytowns along the canal route and worked sixteen-hour days for a dollar a day in low, wet ground and stagnant water. Cholera or the less deadly malaria frequently devastated the camps. Paid partly in scrip usable only to purchase land along the canal, these workers settled and created new towns, contributing to the robust economic development in the north.[65]

Despite the seemingly hopeless condition of the state's finances by 1842, there was confidence that a completed canal would be of significant economic benefit. With the assistance of European creditors, the legislature adopted a financing plan in 1843, allowing construction to proceed and setting deadlines for its completion, which did occur in the allotted time. On April 23, 1848, a gala was held at the terminus in Chicago to celebrate the canal's opening to traffic.[66]

Constructed primarily to carry freight, the canal also benefited from passenger traffic in its early years. Travel times decreased markedly between Chicago and downriver communities served by the canal and river system. Toll revenues increased each year as more canal boats went into service. Traffic was seasonal, however. While canal boats were more reliable and comfortable than stagecoaches, especially in the mud or rainy seasons, they offered no service in ice-bound winter months.[67]

Chicago's remarkable growth during the canal's construction soon was far surpassed. The city's population more than tripled in the six years from 1848 to 1854, increasing from 20,035 to 74,500. The population of the four canal counties more than doubled in the five years from 1850 to 1855. By 1855, the state's most densely populated areas lay in the region of the waterway.[68]

Even as the canal was being completed, railroad construction was underway. Construction of the Galena and Chicago Union Railroad began in Chicago in 1848 and moved in stages west: to the Des Plaines River that year, then on to Elgin in 1850, Rockford in 1852, and Freeport, its western terminus, in 1853. Access to its namesake, Galena, occurred in 1854 when it agreed to joint service with the Illinois Central to that city on the Mississippi. The coming of the railroads saw a boom in development in counties and cities all along the canal route and north to the Wisconsin line.[69]

With interstate railroads from the east reaching Chicago in 1852, lumber from the Great Lakes and merchandise from the East passed westward down the canal for distribution to the interior. Farm products from the canal region and from farther down the Illinois River, and sugar, molasses, coffee, and tropical products

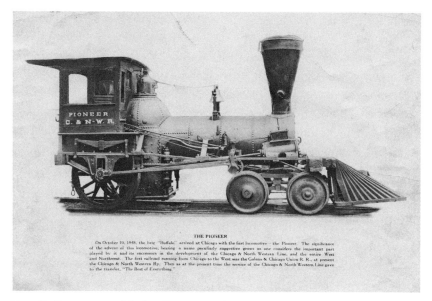

THE PIONEER

On October 10, 1848, the brig "Buffalo" arrived at Chicago with the first locomotive — the Pioneer. The significance of the advent of this locomotive, bearing a name peculiarly suggestive grows as one considers the important part played by it and its successors in the development of the Chicago & North Western Line, and the entire West and Northwest. The first railroad running from Chicago to the West was the Galena & Chicago Union R. R., at present the Chicago & North Western Ry. Then as at the present time the service of the Chicago & North Western Line gave to the traveler, "The Best of Everything."

Fig. 6. The Pioneer powered the first Chicago-area rail trip on the Galena and Chicago Union Railroad. Chicago History Museum, ICHi-037010.

from New Orleans and St. Louis markets were carried to Chicago on their way east. Freight rates from the Illinois River to eastern cities by way of Chicago, the Great Lakes, and Buffalo were lower than those on the Mississippi to the Gulf of Mexico and east.[70]

General Assembly Follies

In the first two decades of statehood, the general assembly rashly put the state into the banking business, with disastrous consequences. In 1820 the Second General Assembly, almost entirely composed of novices to the legislative process and to the realities of finance, ignored the failings of banks formed in Shawneetown and Edwardsville late in the territorial period and an abortive attempt by the First General Assembly to open a state bank. Determined that the state should have money, the general assembly in 1821 chartered a State Bank of Illinois without capital of any kind but based entirely on the state's credit. With a main bank in Vandalia and four branches, it put in circulation $300,000 in bank notes with denominations of one, three, five, ten, and twenty dollars. The bill passed the legislature over the strenuous objection of the speaker, John McLean, who resigned his position in order to speak from the floor of the house against the proposal. The council of revision rejected the bill as inexpedient and unconstitutional. The governor, a member of the revision council, had no separate veto. The legislature promptly passed the measure again. Briefly stated, the bank failed. Payments of loans by borrowers of the specie were slow. By 1825, the currency fell in value as much as 70 percent. In 1830 the legislature conceded failure and the bank was liquidated. Governor Ford estimated the total loss to the state at $400,000.[71]

Legislative dominance influenced personnel in every level of government. Every two years each new general assembly elected numbers of officials, including as many as eight or more statewide officeholders and supreme court judges. Judicial offices were created and later discontinued by the legislature, which also named state bank officers. The general assembly each year passed numerous private bills, including divorces, and created new corporations.[72]

The most egregious and costly undertaking, which pushed the state to the brink of bankruptcy, was the massive internal-improvements program enacted by the Tenth General Assembly. In 1836, Illinois voters and the legislature still had the attitudes of the frontier. Every member of the legislature who gathered in Vandalia for its first session in December 1836 was born outside the state. Some had grown up in poverty. Others were born into families of wealth and position. Several had political careers in the states they left. A large majority, however, were new members who had no legislative experience.[73]

They were also men of ambition. Perhaps the most illustrious group of legislators in the state's history, they included two future presidential candidates, one of whom would become president, six future U.S. senators, three governors, a presidential cabinet member, eight congressmen, and several generals. Others later were elected or appointed to important state government positions, including supreme court justice, secretary of state, auditor, attorney general, and other posts.

Serving in his first elective office only since December 5, twenty-three-year-old Stephen A. Douglas, a brilliant and charismatic five-foot-four-inch Yankee with a massive head, a booming baritone voice, and boundless energy and ambition, demonstrated his precocity within a few days after the session began. Assuming leadership of the Democrats, he introduced in the house of representatives a plan for the construction of railroads running the length and breadth of Illinois, financed and underwritten by the state.

Douglas's action reflected the public mood. In July 1836, before the August legislative elections, the *Illinois State Register* of Vandalia had urged, "Let's elect representatives who will borrow money to make internal improvements."[74] The voters did just that. As the general assembly session approached, public meetings at several points in the state pressed for legislative action. They culminated in a convention on internal improvements in Vandalia attended by delegates from all parts of the state during the first two days of the legislative session in December 1836. The delegates urged the legislature to act without delay in constructing an elaborate system of canals and railroads.

Douglas's legislative initiative was not surprising. Born in Vermont in 1813, son of a doctor who died when Douglas was two months old, raised by a single mother for seventeen years in Vermont and for three years in upstate New York, enrolled in an exclusive private academy, hired to study law in a small firm, but impatient with the years required to attain the New York bar, Douglas moved west in June 1833. After short stops in Cleveland and St. Louis, he moved to Illinois later in 1833. That winter, he studied law, made speeches supporting President Jackson's policies at evening lyceums in Pekin, and decided he could prosper in larger Jacksonville, the seat of Morgan County. In March 1834, before his twenty-first birthday, he moved to Jacksonville and soon was examined for a law license by supreme court justice Samuel Lockwood, whose background in New York State was similar to Douglas's. Although Lockwood thought Douglas was not as prepared as he should have been, the justice nevertheless licensed him to practice law in Illinois.[75]

From his earliest days in Illinois, Douglas had shown himself to be a masterful political organizer. On the first day of the special legislative session in 1835, twenty-two years old and not a member of the legislature, Douglas organized a statewide meeting of Democrats in Vandalia to decide on support of candidates and issues. Such a political convention was new to the state; its opponents denounced the endeavor as an un-American "scheme." Abraham Lincoln was among the legislators who passed a resolution stating that such a convention was "dangerous to the liberties of the people" and "ought not to be tolerated in a republican government."[76]

Soon thereafter, with one of the representatives he had helped elect, Douglas drafted and promoted passage of a law changing the power to appoint state's attorneys from the governor to the legislature. Rewarding him promptly for his effort, the legislature appointed Douglas in February 1835 to serve as one of the new state's attorneys in an eight-county judicial district. He did not finish his term.

In August 1836 Douglas quit that position and attained election to the legislature. He would not serve out his term. After attending only the first session of the Tenth General Assembly, from December 1836 to March 1837, he resigned his seat to accept an appointment by President Martin Van Buren as the register of the federal land office in Springfield. That position gave him authority over a large territory covering much the same area as the Third Congressional District. Eight months later, he ran for Congress from that district even though he had not yet reached the constitutional age of twenty-five to serve in the House of Representatives. Douglas narrowly lost the general election in the predominantly Whig district to John Stuart, Lincoln's law partner, who won by only thirty-five votes out of a total 36,495 cast.[77]

Soon after Douglas's loss, on the initiative and with the advice and consent of the legislature, the governor appointed him to the statewide office of secretary of state. He served only three months. In February 1841 he resigned to accept another legislative appointment, to be a justice of the state supreme court. The Democrat-controlled legislature, unhappy with the court's Whig-dominated membership, had enlarged the court from four justices to nine, effectively making it a Democratic court. Twenty-seven-year-old Douglas had masterminded the controversial legislation—known to many as the "Douglas bill"—from his office as secretary of state.[78]

Douglas continued his ambitious push upward and onward in politics two years later, engineering the creation by the legislature of a new congressional district following the 1840 census. The boundaries of the new Fifth Congressional District corresponded closely to the judicial district he served as a supreme court justice. At the Democratic convention in June 1843 Douglas gained the nomination to run for the seat. He promptly resigned from the supreme court, declared himself a new resident of Quincy, the seat of the largest county in the new district, and carried the district in the August 7 election by a margin of 461 votes out of more than 17,000 cast. Thirty years old, he took his place in the U.S. House of Representatives in December 1843. Reelected to the House in 1845, Douglas took the final step in his legislature-aided political ascension in December 1846 when the Democrat-controlled Illinois General Assembly elected him at age thirty-three to his first six-year term in the U.S. Senate. Election to a second six-year Senate term by the overwhelmingly Democratic general assembly followed the 1852 elections. In January 1859 after the arduous 1858 contest with Lincoln that featured the Lincoln-Douglas debates, the gerrymandered legislature elected Douglas over Lincoln to a third Senate term despite the fact the voters narrowly voted Republican in the elections.[79]

Back in Illinois, the railroad proposals that Douglas introduced in December 1836 were sent to committee. The committee enlarged them into a comprehensive system of internal improvements to be constructed and owned by the state. The committee's report, sent to the full house on January 9, recommended the construction of railroads, canals, and river-improvement projects. The railroad network was to connect population clusters in southern Illinois. No lines were to serve Chicago, or north of a line running from Danville to Decatur to Bloomington in the central north regions of the state. The projects altogether required borrowing of $8 million, a huge sum several times the taxable value of property in the state. Making only general cost estimates, with no surveys or expert consultation or any outside advice, the committee gave assurances that the system was entirely practicable, that it would result in the population of large land areas and thereby increase the state's taxable property, and that tolls on the roads would yield sufficient monies to pay the interest on the cost.[80]

Douglas's ambitions and his zeal for internal improvements were matched by those of Abraham Lincoln. Twenty-seven years old and serving in his second term, Lincoln in December 1836 was among the leaders of the small Whig delegation in the house of representatives. He had made his first bid for elective office at age twenty-two. After moving to Illinois in 1831 and residing only a few months in the small village of New Salem, in March 1832 Lincoln sought election as a representative in the Eighth General Assembly. In a lengthy announcement of his candidacy, he wrote candidly of his aims: "Every man is said to have his peculiar ambition. I have no other so great as that of being truly esteemed of my fellow men, by rendering myself worthy of their esteem." On policy matters, Lincoln stated his support for internal improvements, such as railroads, roads, bridges, canals, and clearing of rivers, to enable rural farmers to escape poverty. "That the poorest and most thinly populated countries would be greatly benefitted by the opening of good roads, and in the clearing of navigable streams within their limits, is what no person will deny," he asserted.[81]

Lincoln lost that first election but was gratified by winning 270 of 300 votes cast in New Salem. Two years later, in 1834, Lincoln again ran for the house seat. He won easily, finishing a close second among four men elected from Sangamon County.[82]

In August 1836, running for a second term from New Salem, Lincoln was the leading vote getter among the seventeen candidates in the race in Sangamon County. Following a reapportionment in 1835, the election sent seven house members and two senators from the county to the Tenth General Assembly in Vandalia. Six of the house members and both senators were Whigs. The legislators, all more than six feet tall, were quickly dubbed "the Long Nine" when they arrived at the capital. Lincoln, at age twenty-seven, was the second-youngest of the group, two months older than the governor's son and his future brother-in-law, Ninian Wirt Edwards. A third house member was Vermont native Daniel Stone, a college-educated lawyer and former Ohio state legislator who became known for signing the antislavery protest with Lincoln and later, as a judge, for deciding a controversial voting eligibility case in favor of the Whigs.[83]

During the frenzy over internal improvements in the Tenth General Assembly, the primary objective of Lincoln and the others of the Long Nine was focused on the next issue to be taken up by the legislature, the location of the new capital. The Long Nine assiduously cultivated votes for Springfield as the new capital by pledging support for others' internal improvement projects.[84]

When the already-expanded committee report on the Douglas proposals was debated in the full house, additional railroad projects were proposed to overcome local opposition to the scheme and gain the votes of representatives from dissatisfied areas. The amendments generally were supported by representatives interested in the additions, by all the members from Sangamon County, and by some who wished to kill the bill by overloading it. The total projected cost for the entire plan increased in the house to more than $9 million, all to be borrowed by the state. The bill passed the house on January 31 by a vote of 61 to 25.[85]

Two weeks later, the senate committee reported the bill with amendments. One added a railroad project from Bloomington to Mackinaw to cost $350,000. For good measure, the second amendment added another $200,000 to be divided among unfortunate counties that did not receive any railroad or canal projects. The overall bill, now with a price tag of $10.2 million in debt, passed the senate on February 23 by a vote of 25 to 15.[86]

The council of revision returned the bill two days later with objections. Justices Browne and Lockwood objected to certain technical provisions that were easily altered. Justice Smith concurred. Governor Duncan objected to the bill on the fundamental ground that only citizens or corporations, not the government, could undertake such projects. The house remedied the matters raised by Browne and Lockwood and passed the bill, over the governor's objections, by a vote of 53 to 20. On February 27 the senate adopted the house amendments and passed the bill into law, voting 23 to 13.[87]

Vandalia erupted in a great celebration the night of the bill's passage. The *Sangamon Journal* reported, "The huzzas and acclamations of the people were unprecedented. . . . All Vandalia was illuminated. Bonfires were built, and fire balls were thrown in every direction. . . . The name of those who have been conspicuous in bringing forward and sustaining this law will go down in the future as great benefactors."[88] Instead, of course, they are remembered as a profligate assemblage that in 1837 legislated the state into the most disastrous financial crisis in its history.

A New Capital at Springfield

On February 28, 1837, the day after the final vote concluded the debate on internal improvements, the general assembly met in joint session of the two houses to vote on the permanent location of the state capital. The Vandalia capital had been established out of the wilderness in 1819 to serve for two decades, until 1839. Within a few years, dissatisfaction with it had become widespread. Roads serving the town were in poor condition and frequently impassable. Critics complained that the climate was swampy and unhealthy. The government structures were inadequate. The anticipation that a new town would grow and prosper as residential development followed the seat of government was never realized.

In the early 1830s the legislature began to consider relocating the state capital. The general assembly in 1833 voted to hold a statewide referendum the next year, giving voters six choices for the location of a new seat of government. In light and inconclusive balloting, Alton with 7,511 votes received about one-third of the total count, followed closely by Vandalia with 7,148 and Springfield with 7,044. No further action was taken on the matter at that time.[89]

On February 28 the Long Nine succeeded in carrying the vote in favor of Springfield to be the new capital. Before the voting, the legislature adopted a Lincoln-inspired requirement that the city selected as the capital must donate $50,000 and two acres of land for the new state buildings. Although this requirement caused some smaller contenders to drop out of the competition, more than twenty Illinois communities received votes on at least one ballot. Springfield led the first ballot with 35 votes. On the fourth ballot, Springfield was selected with a clear majority of 73 out of 108 votes. The next-highest vote was 16 for Vandalia.[90]

Following the March adjournment of the general assembly session, Lincoln crammed his worldly possessions into two saddlebags, mounted a borrowed horse, and moved on April 15, 1837, from the log cabin village of New Salem to

Fig. 7. The Old State Capitol. Courtesy of the Abraham Lincoln Presidential Library and Museum.

Springfield, which had reached the frame-house stage and had a population of some eleven hundred persons. Newly licensed to practice law, he wanted to live in the state's political and governmental center. If another town had been selected as the state capital, Lincoln would have moved there.

The citizens of Springfield fulfilled their commitment to contribute a town square and $50,000 toward construction of a new seat of government. The cornerstone for the imposing two-story Greek Renaissance capitol building, with dome, porticos, and rotunda, was laid July 4, 1837, exactly one year after the ceremony initiating construction of the Illinois and Michigan Canal. The building was the most impressive capitol in the new West. Occupied two years later, it became the historic site of momentous events in state and national history.

Almost a Deadbeat State

The legislature's adjournment in early March 1837 was followed by an era of speculation unprecedented in the state's history. The north saw its future assured by the capital move, the development of the Illinois and Michigan Canal, the railroads, and other projects. The south saw in the railroads and canals promised for their area the means to regain the ground lost in the preceding fifteen years by the tide of immigration flowing to the north of the state along the Great Lakes or through Indiana.[91]

The elements of the system's failure were inherent in the law itself, which specified that construction of eight railroads, river and canal improvements, and roads should all proceed simultaneously and in proportionate amounts. Every principal town and area was to be treated equally; none was to be disadvantaged by having its project delayed. Nor would one project be completed and put into operation to earn revenue ahead of any other project. No one faced up to the practical impossibilities of this politically inspired mandate. The state had neither the financial resources nor the engineering and construction capabilities to carry out this requirement.[92]

Additionally, ignoring lessons they should have learned by the demise of a state bank in 1821, and caught up in the belief that internal improvements would foster a great era of expansion, the general assembly chartered a second State Bank of Illinois with a capital of $1.5 million. The bank's main office was to be Springfield, not yet the capital, with branches in nine towns across the length and breadth of the state. The optimistic assumption was that this new bank would be so profitable that it would pay for the railroads and other major projects. The inherent obstacles to success were augmented, even before the Tenth General Assembly adjourned, by the Panic of 1837, which spread economic ruin across the United States and devastated banking systems. By 1839, the state bank went bankrupt. The state assumed the bank's debt obligations.[93]

After only two years, the internal-improvements projects were a hopeless failure, with the state full of equipment and digging but no results. Railroad technology proved too new to support the state's ambitious plans. The only completed construction was a fifty-mile portion of the Northern Cross Railroad that was originally planned to run from Quincy, on the Mississippi, to Danville in the east, and on to the Indiana state line. Laying of rail on a fifty-nine-mile section from Meredosia on the Illinois River east to Springfield had begun in 1838. The primitive construction, its wooden rails topped by English-made wrought-iron strips five-eighths of an inch thick, was hazardous, with rails occasionally catching on carriage wheels and piercing the floor of a car. Traffic also was erratic due to locomotive failures and other problems. Mules were substituted for the worn-out locomotive in 1844. In 1847 the railroad was sold at auction for one-fortieth of its original cost. Thus ended the lone "successful" project of the internal-improvements system.[94]

The original projected debt of $10 million had grown to exceed $15 million by 1842. Political leaders freely traded assessments of blame. Finally, the election of Democratic governor Thomas Ford in 1842 resulted in a solution. Although many were urging repudiation of the debt, default on the state's obligations, and a declaration of bankruptcy, Ford refused. He believed the state had a moral and political obligation to pay its debts and that the state's honor had to be preserved. He secured adoption of a plan that increased taxes and gradually paid off the debt as financial conditions improved. Over the objections of southern counties, whose representatives had frequently tried to hold the Illinois and Michigan Canal hostage to force work on their projects, he also made completion of the canal a Democratic priority. The state slowly achieved fiscal solvency and in 1880 paid in full the last of the bonds.

Erosion of Legal Bondage, 1837–1847

In the late 1830s, and for years after, blacks had no legal status in Illinois. They were not allowed to vote, to sue for their liberty in the courts, to serve as witnesses, to own property, to serve in the state militia, to seek or hold public office, or to reside in the state without showing a certificate of freedom to a court official and giving a $1,000 bond as proof they would not become a county charge. They were forbidden to marry whites or to have white indentured or contract servants. They were allowed to exist free, but the people of Illinois granted them little else.

Sympathy for blacks expanded as advocates for abolition, equality, citizenship, education, and training increasingly agitated for their views. As such antislavery sentiment grew stronger in the late 1830s and into the 1840s, the supreme court and some lower courts became less protective of the indentured service system. Even then, however, from 1836 until 1845, court rulings on liberty questions varied with the biases of jurists. Under the constitution, the legislature chose judges of courts at all levels. They reflected the views of the electorate, which in the majority did not much care to see the condition of blacks changed.

In its 1836 term the Illinois Supreme Court decided two cases in favor of servants asserting their liberty. As discussed earlier, the court in *Choisser v. Hargrave* invalidated an indenture of a slave brought into Illinois and not signed to a contract within the required thirty-day period. In *Boon v. Juliet* the court ruled more broadly that children born to indentured servants who had been registered under the territorial laws were "unquestionably free"; their services did not belong to the parents' master, unlike slave children in slave states. They could, however, be apprenticed with parental permission until age twenty-one or eighteen, respectively, for males or females.[95]

Although the *Boon* ruling was potentially of broad application because many younger slaves were the offspring of blacks indentured under the territorial laws, it is not clear how significant the decision was in practice. Masters still had leverage over the "voluntary" actions of servant parents to sign their children to indenture contracts lasting as long as two decades. This was exemplified by the conduct of Henry Cook, discussed earlier, who, in June 1839, three years after the *Boon* opinion, freed his slave Hariot and, the same day, bound all seven of her children to apprenticeship indenture contracts with her consent, consent that appears to have been bought by her own freedom.[96]

In the early 1840s a number of court rulings showed a more favorable attitude toward runaways or free blacks. The supreme court in 1840 and 1841 ruled in two cases that the presumption of the law in Illinois was in favor of liberty and that every person was presumed free regardless of color. Expression of this principle was important, especially given that blacks were not permitted to testify in court on their own behalf.[97]

In the first of the two cases, Thomas Cook, a black who claimed to be a free man, sued William Kinney for payment for several years of work. Kinney acknowledged the work but claimed that Cook was a slave, therefore not entitled to be paid. Cook was represented by Lyman Trumbull, the most active and prominent lawyer handling cases on behalf of blacks. The supreme court held that in Illinois the presumption of the law was in favor of liberty, and it was not the obligation of the alleged slave to prove his freedom. Instead, the burden was on the claiming owner to show records, an indenture contract, or other proof that the black was a slave or servant. The rule, the court stated, is "drawn from the principles of natural justice." The court added that the principle had been "inverted" in slave states, requiring the person who claimed to be free to prove his freedom. That inverted rule, the court stated, "is founded in injustice."[98]

The supreme court reiterated this principle the next July in *Bailey v. Cromwell*, confirming freedom of a black woman in a dispute between two white slave owners over her services. According to the court's summary, Cromwell had sold to Bailey "a certain black or negro girl or woman named Nance." Bailey had given a promissory note in payment, and the girl had gone to live with and work for him. She had remained for six months and then departed, claiming she was free. In the interim, Cromwell, the seller, had died. His estate sued Bailey to collect on the note. Bailey, represented by Abraham Lincoln, defended against payment on the grounds that Cromwell had promised to give Bailey papers proving that Nance was a slave and had never done so. The supreme court reversed a lower court ruling in favor of Cromwell, reiterating the proposition that "the presumption of law was, in this state, that every person was free, without regard to color." The court ruled that the presumption that Nance was free was never disproved. She was free, the sale of a free person was illegal, the consideration for the note had therefore failed, and there could be no recovery by Cromwell.[99]

The supreme court's enunciation of the broad presumption of freedom of every person for the second time in a few months was significant. At the same time, however, the court did not deny that with proper proof, a claim to ownership and the labor of a black slave or indentured servant might be upheld.

Lower courts also reflected changing attitudes, although not consistently throughout the state. The circuit court of the Sangamon District (Springfield) in 1842 decided two cases that reflected the increasing sentiment of the people of central and northern Illinois to afford blacks legal protection. The *Daniel* case involved a black who had been arrested, was committed to jail under the 1829 law for not having freedom papers, and was to be hired out by the sheriff for labor. The judge declared that the act of 1829 was unconstitutional and freed Daniel.[100]

The second Sangamon District case was that of James Foster. Foster, a black man, had been living in Springfield for more than two years when an Arkansas citizen appeared, claimed Foster as his slave, and demanded possession of him in accordance with the act of Congress regarding fugitive slaves. The trial judge required the slaveholder to prove "by disinterested witnesses" that Foster was his property—a requirement greater than the federal act, which only required an affidavit—and freed Foster when that requirement was not met.[101]

The next year, in 1843, the lower courts and supreme court reached differing results in several notable cases involving slave owners' rights regarding runaway slaves. The appellate court in Bureau County (Princeton) overturned the judgment of a trial court that had found Owen Lovejoy liable for harboring and assisting two runaway women. In the same year, however, Dr. Richard Eels of Quincy was arrested and charged with harboring a runaway slave. The judgment of the circuit court was adverse to Eels, and Judge Stephen A. Douglas fined him

$400. The Illinois Supreme Court on review confirmed the lower court opinion and upheld the Eels conviction and fine.[102]

The supreme court in the same 1843 term similarly affirmed the lower court conviction of Julius Willard for harboring a runaway black woman brought to Illinois from Louisiana on her way to Missouri. The court ruled that slaveholders had the right to pass through Illinois with their slaves, and comity between the states would protect their property rights while doing so.[103]

In another highly emotional case involving harsh facts, the supreme court in the 1843 term also ruled in favor of a master, rejecting a black servant's claim to be free from an indenture. Sarah had been a slave in Kentucky. She was brought by her master to St. Clair County in December 1815 and signed to an indenture for forty years. Less than a year later, she was transferred to a new owner, and then sold again to Elias Kent Kane on July 30, 1818, four days before he began his service as a leader of the 1818 constitutional convention. Sarah was Kane's bound servant through his time as secretary of state and until he was elected U.S. senator and left for Washington in 1825. Kane sold her services to Andrew Borders, "a man well known for his cruelty and rapacity."[104]

Seventeen years later, in 1842, Sarah and another woman, two of Borders's several black servants, escaped with Sarah's three children and fled northward. In Peoria County, however, they were seized by a justice of the peace, held for sale at auction as runaway slaves, and claimed by Borders. Aided by antislavery friends, Sarah, represented by Lyman Trumbull and Gustave Koerner, claimed her freedom and sued Borders for assault, battery, and back wages. Borders countered that he had been entitled to use force and beating to compel Sarah to continue in his service.[105]

The Illinois Supreme Court affirmed the verdicts of a circuit court jury in Borders's favor. A two-justice majority of the court followed the 1828 decision in *Phoebe v. Jay*, holding that the 1818 constitution authorized the indenture system. The court rejected the arguments of Sarah's lawyers that the territorial indenture laws as well as the provisions of the 1818 constitution legalizing such indentures were void. The court also held that Borders asserted a good defense to the assault and battery charges when he stated that he had beaten Sarah to compel her to work for him as required by her contract.[106]

The furor in antislavery circles over the supreme court's decisions in the *Eels*, *Willard*, and *Borders* cases was allayed somewhat two years later. The court's 1845 decision in *Jarrot v. Jarrot* is generally cited as the decisive case ending the indentured service system, although its ruling was more narrow, applying only to descendants of "French slaves" who had been brought into the Illinois country before U.S. possession of the territory. Joseph (alias Pete) Jarrot, whose grandmother was a French slave, sued his mistress, claiming he was entitled to be paid for his past services because he was a free man. The circuit court of St. Clair County (Belleville) in 1843 ruled after a jury verdict that a slave could not sue his master for wages. The supreme court reversed the lower court in 1845, holding that "the descendants of the slaves of the old French settlers, born since the Ordinance of 1787, and before or since the Constitution of Illinois, cannot be held in slavery in this State."[107]

The press and public generally interpreted this decision to mean that no person choosing to live in Illinois could legally hold indentured servants in bondage. The case, on that reasoning, was celebrated in antislavery circles as a great triumph.

Two years later, in the case of General Robert Matson, two of the supreme court justices who were riding circuit and sitting in the court of Coles County expressed a similar opinion. Abraham Lincoln represented Matson at the Charleston hearing in the fall of 1847, shortly before departing for Washington to take his seat in the House of Representatives. Matson, a Kentucky resident, had lived for several years on a farm in Coles County. He had brought with him and kept there a number of black slaves. Jane, one of his servants, fled with her children and took refuge in a nearby settlement of antislavery Presbyterians after she learned that Matson was planning to return with his slaves to Kentucky. Jane and the others were arrested as fugitive slaves. With the help of interested abolitionists, her case reached the circuit court. In October 1847, the two supreme court judges joined the holding that Jane and her children were free by reason of their residence in a free state. The participation of the justices in that case was understood as leaving no doubt that the supreme court opinion in the *Jarrot* case would not be changed.[108]

Growing public dissatisfaction with the constitutional indentured service system combined with the abuses of legislative dominance and the lessons of legislative financial profligacy were not forgotten. By the early 1840s, calls began for a constitutional convention to modify the 1818 constitution and adopt measures to prevent recurrence of the injustices and excesses of the present government structure.

CHAPTER 4

The Constitution of 1848

Reconstructing Government, Balancing Powers, Oppressing Free Blacks

Dissatisfaction with the frontier-era 1818 constitution became widespread within two decades. Criticism grew over the weakness of the governor and the dominance of the legislature over all levels of state and local government, its profligate spending, and its excesses in financing internal improvements, creating banks, and writing laws for private and special interests.[1]

Newspapers, popular opinion, and activists in both the Whig and Democratic political parties urged modification of the 1818 constitution. Efforts in the 1830s to have the legislature call for a constitutional convention failed, however. Finally, in 1841, the general assembly submitted the question of holding a convention to the voters at the next general election, in August 1842. The proposal failed by a narrow margin.[2]

In 1845 the general assembly voted again to submit to the electorate a new proposition to call a convention at the general election, on August 3, 1846. This time, convention backers' increased efforts to inform the public of the need for a new constitution carried the day. The call was approved by a substantial majority of 72 percent of the vote on the question at the general election. The general assembly designated April 3, 1847, as the date for electing delegates to the convention, and June 7, 1847, as the date for the convention to meet in Springfield.[3]

Even before the August 1846 vote that approved holding delegate elections and a convention in 1847, the state entered into one of the most turbulent half-decades in its history. On May 13, 1846, Congress declared war against Mexico. Patriotic excitement was fired by Congress's request for fifty thousand volunteers nationwide. Governor Thomas Ford issued a call for Illinois volunteers on May 25. Illinois responded promptly and enthusiastically, with a greater number of volunteers than any other state except Missouri. Abraham Lincoln's two preceding Whig rivals for election to the U.S. House of Representatives volunteered. The charismatic politician and militia general John J. Hardin of Jacksonville was among the first to do so. Hardin had been elected to Congress after a contest for the nomination with Edward D. Baker and Abraham Lincoln in the district Whig convention in 1843. By agreement at the convention, he served one term, from 1843 to 1845, and was succeeded by Baker, who was serving the 1845 to 1847 term when the war began. Baker quit his seat in January 1847 to volunteer for the war. Lincoln remained in Springfield to win the house seat in the general election on August 3, 1846. Once in Washington, in contrast, he spoke out against the war, criticizing President Polk over which nation was the aggressor and objecting to western expansion as opening the way to slavery.[4]

The summer of 1846 was consumed with the frenetic activity of marshaling volunteers and sending them off to war. Gathered in Alton in June and July, men, materiel, horses, and vehicles composed a grand scene. Each state had a uniform designated by the U.S. Army. The Illinois volunteers were resplendent in dark blue coats trimmed in yellow, light blue pants, and blue cloth caps with glazed covers. Officers brought their own horses and other materiel. Many also brought servants, most of whom were African American. Thousands of family members and others journeyed to Alton to see the troops off to war. Hardin's first regiment departed by steamboat on July 10, 1846. They disembarked August 3 on the gulf coast of Texas. The other Illinois regiments soon followed.[5]

August 3 was also Election Day in Illinois, a fact Hardin noted in a letter that evening to his wife in Jacksonville. Back in Illinois, Whigs celebrated the large majority Abraham Lincoln won in the race for Congress. Democrats statewide hailed the election of the other six congressmen and Augustus French as governor. Proponents of a constitutional convention celebrated the substantial majority vote to hold a constitutional convention in 1847.[6]

The Mexican War dominated the news in the early months of 1847, especially after word of the war's heavy casualties reached Illinois. Among many others, John

Fig. 8. The first known photograph of Abraham
Lincoln, taken in 1846 when he was a candidate
for Congress. Courtesy of the Abraham Lincoln
Presidential Library and Museum.

Hardin was killed at Buena Vista on February 23 leading a valiant—many later
said foolhardy—charge against the much more numerous forces of Santa Anna.
William Bissell, who in 1856 would become Illinois's first Republican governor,
was also seriously wounded at the Battle of Cerro Gordo.[7]

The war intruded directly into the convention after its beginning in June 1847,
interrupting substantive debate on three occasions in July and August for the
adoption of resolutions mourning the deaths of Hardin and other Illinois volunteers. In mid-July, the convention also adjourned for two days to enable delegates
to attend funeral ceremonies for Hardin in nearby Jacksonville.[8]

Democrats Prevail in the Delegate Elections

Political parties played no role in the 1818 constitutional convention. By the 1840s,
however, the Democratic Party dominated the legislature. In the run-up to the
election of delegates, Democrats sought to benefit by appealing to obligations of
party loyalty and emphasizing issues important to the party. Whigs campaigned
openly in favor of the demand for economy and reform, but adopted a "no party"
posture on issues.[9]

The Democrats' superiority prevailed in election of convention delegates on April 3, 1847. One hundred sixty-two delegates were elected, the unwieldy number in accord with the 1818 constitutional requirement that a convention equal the general assembly in number. A substantial majority of ninety-one were Democrats. Seventy-one Whigs made up a large enough minority to prevent a strictly partisan convention. The delegates reflected the huge gains in the state's population that came through immigration from other states. Only seven delegates were native Illinoisans. The delegates also reflected the agrarian character of the state: seventy-five were farmers, and, contrary to custom, there were only fifty-four lawyers. The remainder were twelve physicians, nine merchants, five mechanics, and seven others.[10]

The delegate body was composed of younger men, nearer in age to the two youngest, at twenty-six, than to the oldest, at sixty-two. Among their number were several veteran politicians. Five delegates were current state senators; six were state representatives. One current and another recent supreme court judge also were delegates.[11]

As in most constitutional conventions, there were young men who later would have distinguished public careers. The most eminent future leader was Whig David Davis. Thirty-two years old at the time of the convention, he was born in Maryland, educated at Kenyon College in Ohio and in law at Yale, settled in Bloomington in 1836, where he met Lincoln and many others, and served one term from 1844 to 1846 in the Illinois House of Representatives. Although dubious about the wisdom of an elected judiciary in the 1847 convention, the next year he was elected judge of the new Eighth Judicial Circuit, serving in that position until 1862. Davis and Lincoln became close friends riding that circuit together six months of every year. He was Lincoln's campaign manager in 1860. In 1862, Lincoln appointed him to the U.S. Supreme Court, where he served until 1877, when he resigned to become U.S. senator from Illinois until 1883.[12]

The Convention Organizes for Business

The convention was called to order on Monday, June 7, 1847. The first order of business, election of a permanent president as presiding officer, revealed the diversity and lack of partisan discipline, particularly among the Democratic members. When Democrats could not unite behind a candidate for president, Whigs, who did not offer a candidate of their own, joined with conservative Democrats on the first ballot to elect Newton Cloud. Cloud was among those Democrats who were acceptable to the Whigs because they were not totally opposed to banks but rather advocated a regulated banking system. The vote was a precursor of other key votes: a loose Whig/conservative Democrat alliance would prevail on several important issues in the convention.[13]

Resetting Power of the Three Branches

The convention changed very substantially the allocation of government power among the three departments of state government. Under the 1818 constitution, the general assembly had broad appointing powers, at the expense of the other branches of government. Only two executive officers were elected, the governor and lieutenant governor. Supreme court justices were appointed by a joint session of the legislature, as were the judges of all other courts that might be formed by the legislature. The legislature created numerous other offices and appointed their occupants.

Governor Thomas Ford, who had lived in Illinois for more than forty years and had attended every legislative session from 1825 to 1847, described, in his memoir, the harm of excessive legislative power:

> Sometimes one legislature, feeling pleased with the governor, would give him some appointing power, which their successors would take away, if they happened to quarrel with him. This constant changing and shifting of powers, from one co-ordinate branch of government to another, which rendered it impossible for the people to foresee exactly for what purpose either the governor or legislature were elected, was one of the worst features of the government. It led to innumerable intrigues and corruptions, and for a long time destroyed the harmony between the executive and legislative departments.[14]

The convention greatly enlarged the number of executive and judicial officers to be elected by the people and diminished substantially the appointing powers of the legislature.

The Legislative Department

The striving of the constitution drafters to correct the mistakes of the past was reflected most dramatically in the legislative article. New limitations in the article began with the eligibility requirements, although there was no claim that the decades of legislative abuses were due to excesses of youth. The age to serve as a representative was raised from twenty-one to twenty-five and senator from twenty-five to thirty. U.S. citizenship was required for service in both the senate and house of representatives. The required period of residency in the state to hold office was increased to three years minimum for representatives, five for senators.[15]

The size of the general assembly was decreased from the 162 that had been reached under the 1818 constitution as the population increased. The senate was set at twenty-five members. The house of representatives consisted of seventy-five members initially, with five-person increases to a limit of one hundred as the state's population grew by specified amounts.[16]

With respect to the substance and timing of the general assembly's work, the legislative article contained many more prohibitions than it did permissions. Although elected for two-year terms, the body was permitted to meet only the January after election and no other time. The duration of the single session was not specifically limited. However, the compensation for service—which was fixed constitutionally at the extremely low figure of two dollars per day for the first forty-two days' service and one dollar per day thereafter—was intended to provide an incentive not to remain in Springfield for longer sessions. In practice, the paltry fixed salaries led to disastrous effects. Members used subterfuges to get around the restrictions or supplemented their pay by introducing for compensation hundreds of private bills, which became a major problem in following decades.[17]

Despite the low-pay, part-time nature of service in the general assembly, members were prohibited during their terms from receiving any civil appointment in the state or from being elected to the U.S. Senate. They were barred also from having any interest in any contract with the state or county that was authorized during their term of service or a year thereafter.[18]

The Executive

The convention increased substantially the authority and independence of the executive. Nonetheless, Whig delegates joined by enough conservative southern Democrats prevented Democrats from achieving all the changes to executive power that they would have liked.[19]

The convention agreed with little difficulty on the structure of the executive branch. Five constitutional officers were to be elected by the state's voters. The governor and lieutenant governor were to be elected at the same time for four-year terms. The governor could serve no more than four out of eight years, as in 1818. Thus a governor could not run for immediate reelection but was required to sit out at least one term, something that never occurred under the 1848 constitution. The lieutenant governor served in the absence or death of the governor. He also was speaker of the senate, presided over its sessions, and voted in the event of a tie. The office of secretary of state and the new office of auditor of public accounts were to be filled by election for four-year terms at the same time as the governor. The state treasurer was also made a constitutional office, to be elected statewide for a two-year term. Previously that position was appointed by joint session of the legislature, with no fixed term limit.[20]

Much of the time that the convention spent on consideration of the executive article was consumed in vigorous and occasionally emotional debate over three issues relating to the governor: his eligibility, his salary, and his veto power over legislative acts. Debate on July 10 on the first issue, whether citizenship should be a requirement to serve, presaged the later argument over the right to vote. The majority report of the committee on the executive proposed that only "a natural born citizen" and any person who was "a citizen at the time of the adoption of this constitution" would be eligible to be governor, thus precluding from office any person who became a citizen in the future. Heated protests were made to injecting "Native Americanism" into the constitution by preventing naturalized immigrants from holding the office in the future. At the end of the first day's debate, an amendment that required citizenship only before assuming the office was adopted by a vote of 74 to 49. The same requirement as the governor applied to the lieutenant governor. The other executive officers had no specified citizenship requirement.[21]

The committee report also increased the age requirement for the governor from thirty to thirty-five years and required ten years' residence in the state, in contrast to the two years required by the 1818 constitution. The committee's recommended age of thirty-five survived amendments to make it greater. The residence requirement remained at ten years, although a variety of other numbers were debated.[22]

Although the 1818 constitution left it to the legislature to set the salary of officers, the 1847 convention was not willing to do so. Instead, it determined to fix the salaries for constitutional officers in the constitution. Debate over amounts between $1,000 and $1,500 for the governor's salary consumed more than two days in July and again in mid-August. The committee on the executive had recommended a salary for the governor of $1,250 per year. Amendments substituting $1,000 or $1,500 were discussed at some length before finally settling where the committee had recommended. Salaries for the other constitutional offices ranged downward from that of the governor: the auditor of public accounts at $1,000, and only $800 each for the secretary of state and state treasurer. Salaries of supreme court judges were set at $1,200, a number that made a small point concerning the judges' ranking compared with that of the governor in the eyes of the convention. All of these salaries were parsimonious at the outset and became even more inadequate over time.[23]

The governor's veto power was one of the most important issues to both parties. Democrats, with faith in an elected governor, wanted a strong and effective veto power. Their preference was carried in the report of the committee on the executive article, which required two-thirds of the members present and voting in each house to pass a bill over a governor's veto. After two days of debate in mid-July, a Whig-promoted motion to make a majority sufficient to override failed by one vote, 60 to 61. Debate on the issue continued for another day. In the end, on July 17, a majority of eighty-five delegates compromised, requiring a vote of three-fifths of the members elected.[24]

Thus, on two issues about which the parties felt strongly, votes in July had left the Democrats with less than they wanted on the matter of eligibility of resident immigrants to gain the offices of governor and lieutenant governor, as well as on the governor's veto power, which, though more than a simple majority, they thought too low. None of those results held through the final days of the convention. By that time, a working majority composed of fifty-six Whigs, 80 percent of their number, and fourteen Democrats, mostly conservatives from the southern half of the state, had coalesced on most major issues. On August 11 the convention undertook a final section-by-section review of the executive article. An amendment to the citizenship qualification for the governor, requiring that he have been a citizen fourteen years, was adopted by a vote of 70 to 68. Only four Whigs defected to vote with sixty-four Democrats for the provision that had been adopted in July, which required citizenship only at the time of assuming office. Similarly, another vote in July increased the salary of the governor from the $1,250 voted to $1,500. Later in the day, a predominately Whig vote, augmented

by a sufficient number of Democrats, reduced to a majority the number necessary to override a veto, thus permitting the same majority that passed the law in
the first instance to enact it over a governor's veto.[25]

The executive article was a substantial improvement over the 1818 constitution. It restored balance to the separation of powers between the executive and
legislature. It gave the governor a veto, although a weak one, and eliminated from
the executive article the council of revision that had been imported in 1818 from
the state of New York, thereby removing the supreme court from the legislative
process and sharpening the separation of powers of the other two departments
from the judicial branch.

The Judiciary

The 1847 convention provided for popular election of judges at every level of the
judiciary. In doing so, it put Illinois at the forefront of a growing pattern in state
constitutions, turning away from appointment of all or some judicial officers by
the governor or legislature. Between 1832 and 1846, Georgia, New York, and Iowa
had moved from all appointive or mixed systems to provide for election of all
judges by the people. In a relatively short time thereafter, twenty-seven states followed with constitutional revisions that adopted elected systems for all judges.[26]

By 1847 both political parties in Illinois were unhappy with the legislature-
dominated court system. As their strength and control of the legislature had
grown in the 1830s, Democrats seethed at the Whig-controlled supreme court,
with justices holding "lifetime" legislative appointments and also presiding in
the circuit courts. Under the 1818 constitution, only eight men had served in the
four supreme court justice seats. Three Whigs and one Democrat made up the
court in 1840.[27]

Two decisions by the Whig-dominated supreme court had stimulated Democrats' ire. Their legislative solution, expanding the court from four to nine members and appointing five new Democratic justices in 1841, had in turn aroused
the Whigs, who denounced the "court packing."

The first supreme court ruling, in 1838, involved the office of secretary of
state. Alexander Field, a former Democrat turned Whig, had held the appointment to that office since 1828. After Democratic governor Thomas Carlin was
elected in 1838, he appointed a replacement for Field. Field refused to surrender the office. Democratic circuit court judge Sidney Breese ruled that Field's

replacement was entitled to take office. On appeal the supreme court, by a two-to-one vote with one recusal, reversed Breese, holding that there was no power of removal under the 1818 constitution and that when the legislature created an office without a defined tenure, the incumbent held it for life, during good behavior.[28]

The second supreme court action that infuriated Democrats concerned the right to vote under the 1818 constitution, which stated that "all white male inhabitants above the age of twenty-one years, having resided in the state six months next preceding the election," shall enjoy the right to vote.[29] Democrats strongly believed that the provision was clear and that the term "inhabitants" included resident aliens and not only citizens. Whigs contended that the right to vote was limited to American citizens.[30]

A Whig-inspired test case was filed in Galena before Judge Daniel Stone, a former Whig legislative colleague of Abraham Lincoln in the famous Sangamon County "Long Nine" and co-author with Lincoln of the protest filed in 1837 of the resolutions denouncing abolitionism. Although Stone presumably would have known that both the 1818 constitutional convention in its debates and the Northwest Ordinance of 1787, in providing for elections in territories, made distinctions between citizens, on the one hand, and noncitizen residents or "inhabitants," on the other, he decided against the right of aliens to vote. The case was appealed to the supreme court, which heard argument in December 1839, well before the 1840 presidential and state elections. The court delayed ruling, however, continuing the matter first to the June term in 1840, and then postponing it again to the December term. The elections of 1840 thus were held as Stone had ruled, without the alien vote.[31]

To prevent such political decisions against them in the future, the Democratic-controlled general assembly passed a law in December 1840, abolishing the circuit courts and creating five more supreme court seats, to be filled under the 1818 constitution by the legislature. The council of revision, with its majority of Whig supreme court justices, vetoed the measure. The general assembly overrode the veto and proceeded to elect five new Democratic justices in February 1841 to join the four incumbents. The five included Sidney Breese, whose ruling three years earlier as a circuit judge upholding the governor's removal power was overturned by the Whig-dominated supreme court; Thomas Ford, who resigned in August 1842 when he was elected governor; Stephen A. Douglas, who resigned in 1843 upon election to the U.S. House of Representatives; and Walter

Scates, who resigned in January 1847 and was elected in April to be a delegate to the constitutional convention.[32]

This saga motivated both parties in the 1847 constitutional convention. Democrats wanted popular elections of supreme court judges, believing that their electoral majority in the state would enable implementation of their views in the men selected. Whigs wanted to prevent a recurrence of legislative court packing. The convention fixed the number of supreme court judges at three, a figure that could not be changed by the legislature. They were to be elected by the people to serve nine-year terms. Additionally, they were severed from serving on the circuit courts, as justices had done under the 1818 constitution and over which they exercised considerable influence.[33]

While most Whigs were resigned to an elected supreme court, the manner of election was sharply disputed. Democrats, comfortable in their numerical superiority in the state overall, wanted to elect the members of the court at large. Whigs wanted election from three districts. A long verbal battle continued over an entire week in July and again over six meeting days in August. In the end, a compromise was arranged, but not discussed in the convention record. A three-justice supreme court was to be elected from three large districts for nine-year terms, with the voters in each district electing a judge. In consolation to Democrats, it was agreed that after the first judicial election, the general assembly, if it wished, could "provide by law for their election by the whole state, or by divisions, as they may deem most expedient."[34]

In addition to the supreme court, the convention added numerous courts and judges and considerable detail to the judicial article. Three levels of courts were created below the supreme court, all to be filled by election. Nine circuit court districts covered the state, with a circuit judge elected in each for a term of six years. A county court was created in every county, with a judge in each elected for a four-year term. Justices of the peace were to be elected in each circuit district and county for four-year terms. They would have such jurisdiction and perform such duties as prescribed by law. The constitution also specified that inferior local courts might be created in cities. The clerks for each district of the supreme court, clerks of the circuit court, and clerks of each county court also were to be elected. A state's attorney was to be elected in each judicial circuit. The legislature was authorized to provide for the election of a county attorney in each county.[35]

Burdensome restrictions were added in the judicial article: very low specified salaries for the judges of the supreme and circuit courts, and the judges of those courts were also declared ineligible to hold "any other office or public trust of profit in this state, or the United States, during the term for which they were elected, nor for one year thereafter."[36]

Curtailing Government Powers

The convention curtailed powers of the general assembly by specific subject matter prohibitions in the legislative article and the article on corporations. Intended to prevent abuses of the past, they included forbidding granting divorces, authorizing lotteries, paying extra compensation to public officers or contractors, enacting private or special laws to authorize the sale of any real estate belonging to any individual, chartering a state bank, or extending the charter of other banks. In a significant change motivated by the internal-improvements mania, the legislature was prohibited from creating debt that in the aggregate exceeded $50,000 unless approved by the voters at a general election.[37]

Article X on corporations stated that they "shall not be created by special acts." That clear dictate was undermined by the next clause, which allowed special legislation "in cases where, in the judgment of the General Assembly, the objects of the corporation cannot be attained under general laws." Numerous times thereafter, the legislature invoked this last clause and authorized the formation of private corporations.[38]

Expanding Voters' Power; Restricting Who Can Vote

The 1847 convention thus provided for election by the people of all state, county, and local officers, supreme court justices and judges of the lower courts, and all court clerks and circuit, county, and local attorneys. In providing for a plethora of popular elections, the convention went much further than had been anticipated. Even as it vastly enlarged the number of offices to be filled by voters' elections, however, it significantly decreased the number of persons eligible to vote.

The Right to Vote

One of the longest and most heated debates in the convention raged over the question whether the right to vote should be restricted to white male citizens or be extended to white male inhabitants of the state who were not citizens. That question had divided the body politic in Illinois from earliest days. It continued to be one of the dominant issues between the two major parties throughout the nineteenth century.

Democrats, the beneficiaries of widespread support among immigrants, wanted to retain the provision of the 1818 constitution that gave the vote to "all white male inhabitants" above age twenty-one. For most Whigs, restricting the vote to "every white male citizen" above age twenty-one was the most important thing to be accomplished in the convention.[39]

The committee on elections and the right of suffrage adopted the preferred Whig language requiring citizenship, filing its report to the convention on July 19. When the report came to the floor for debate on Friday, July 23, former supreme court justice Walter B. Scates immediately framed the issue by moving to substitute the word "inhabitant" for "citizen."

More than 10 percent of the convention's time allotted to substantive discussion of issues—more than three full days—was consumed by the debate over suffrage. The arguments ranged from intense exchanges about history and political philosophy to invective against immigrants, charges of vote fraud, and offensive personal remarks.[40]

Whig proponents argued that the founders of the American republic, the Continental Congress, and the U.S. Congress reserved for citizens the privilege. They maintained, "in any society whatever, members alone have a right to a voice in the management of the affairs of that society. This is true of civil society as well as of all others."[41]

Advocates of the broader franchise accused the Whigs of "nativism." They contended that immigrants had built Illinois, that the state's prosperity depended on immigrants, and that "a state burdened with debt and sparsely settled" should not restrict the right of suffrage and penalize immigration. They also invoked the founding fathers, observing that one of the subjects of complaint against Great Britain in the Declaration of Independence was that she restricted emigration. Additionally, they cited precedents by the Continental Congress in the territorial laws of Ohio, Indiana, and Illinois that gave noncitizen inhabitants who were residents for a specified time the right to vote.[42]

A nasty personal squabble on July 28 between two feuding Democratic delegates from Jo Daviess County (Galena) dramatized the emotion the issue generated. The dispute ended in a challenge to decide the matter by a duel. Thompson Campbell and O. C. Pratt had campaigned together in the county before the delegate election. When Pratt contended in convention debate that immigrants should not be able to vote until after many years of learning American values, and included in his remarks invidious references to the motives of "foreigners" and their "execrable and detestable" participation in riots, Campbell charged him with breaking a pledge that Pratt had made in his presence to immigrant miners during the campaign. Campbell asserted that Pratt had told the miners that he favored voting by foreigners who had resided in the state one year and had filed a declaration of intention to become citizens. The two traded additional personal insults, including the charge by Pratt that "a barrel of beer and a keg of whiskey on the ground" impaired Campbell's recollection of what occurred. In the end, police intervention prevented the duel to which the two men had agreed.[43]

In a vote on July 29, Whig defenders of "true Americanism" prevailed when a sufficient number of Democratic defectors joined them on the issue. Section 1 concerning the right to vote narrowed the franchise from the 1818 constitution. Exactly as the committee had originally reported to the full convention, it restricted the vote to "every white male citizen" above age twenty-one who had resided in the state for a year.[44]

The question of allowing African Americans to vote was raised once, early in the convention. On June 22, when committees had just begun their work, prominent Whig delegate James Knox, a New York native and founder of Knox College at Galesburg, introduced a resolution calling on the committee on elections "to limit the right of suffrage to *all white male citizens*" (emphasis in original). Before reference was made to committee, Whig delegate Dr. Daniel Whitney, recently come to Illinois from New York, moved to strike out the word "white." His motion allowing negro suffrage lost 137 to 7. Like Whitney, the other six voting for the amendment were all Whigs from far-northern Illinois counties, natives of New York and New England.[45]

In Section 2 of the suffrage article the convention also settled the recurrent dispute in the legislature about the manner of voting in elections. It specified that all voting must be by ballot only. Thus ended the venerable tradition of *viva voce* voting—a boon to biographers, historians, and gossips—which required an announcement and public record of each voter's choices. The legislature had changed the viva voce provision of the 1818 constitution to ballot in 1819, to viva voce in 1821, to ballot in 1823, and to viva voce in 1829.[46]

Section 9 of the elections article accomplished a welcome reform by establishing a single date on which biennial general elections could be held. Previously, several statewide elections might be held in a year. In 1848 there were four general elections. Since the ratification of the 1848 constitution, all general, state, and presidential elections have been held biennially at the same time, the Tuesday after the first Monday of November of even-numbered years.[47]

Issues Ardent beyond Significance

BANKING

Each party had an issue that it considered paramount to raise in a constitutional convention. For Democrats it was the question of banks or no banks. Democrats for years had insisted that bank charters were inconsistent with democracy, had served to crush the state's prosperity and hurt the common man. They had campaigned against any banking system. Whigs had sought to downplay the issue in the campaigns, fearing its strong emotional pull, but maintained hopes of a properly regulated banking system.[48]

The issue did not await adoption of an orderly procedure in the convention. On June 14, even as the body debated a resolution establishing a procedural order, Democrat William Kinney moved to instruct the committee on corporations to write a provision preventing the creation of banks or the issuance of paper money. That motion was withdrawn at the president's request, and the orderly procedure adopted. Later the same afternoon, however, two Democrats introduced antibank resolutions, contrary to the schedule that had just been adopted. The body suspended the rules to permit their introduction. From that time forward, the bank question consumed more of the convention's time than any other issue; it was before the convention on fourteen days as the subject of debate and on many days was linked with other questions.[49]

Three days later, the opposing partisan positions on banks were put to test votes. A Whig delegate's proposal that the constitution "provide for a system of general banking laws" was defeated 99 to 60. The question then was put on the opposite proposition, to prohibit the incorporation in the state of any banking company or the circulation of any banknote or paper money. That motion was defeated by a larger margin, 102 to 58. The early votes thus established that neither side could prevail in its absolute position on banking.[50]

On July 6 the committee on incorporation submitted its report. The majority report prohibited the state from creating or owning a state bank but proposed allowing banking corporations with conditions and restrictions on their operations. The minority report prohibited any banking operations in the state. The banking question was contested to a decision over several days in the first half of August. Delegates who opposed banks cited past failures and misdeeds. Supporters argued the need for a regulated banking system to assist in developing the resources and economy of the state. The final result was a compromise. It prohibited the state from creating, owning, or being liable for any banking enterprise and from circulating any bank paper or money. However, it did provide that the general assembly could enact laws to establish corporations with banking powers, but such laws would go into effect only if approved by the voters at the next general election.[51]

POLL TAX

Two days after Democrats put the banking issue before the convention, on Wednesday, June 16, Whigs went on the offensive with their pet issue. Joseph Eccles, a member of the revenue committee, moved "that the new constitution shall provide for a poll tax," a tax to be levied on every person regardless of income or wealth. Arguments on the issue consumed the remainder of that day and continued until a decisive vote the next. Proponents of the poll tax contended that all residents, poor and rich, benefit from government and should bear equally its burdens, including paying off the huge state debt. Opponents, primarily Democrats, argued that a poll tax was unjust in principle, that the poor were obligated to serve in the militia and provide road labor in lieu of taxes, that the tax would be a burden on the poor and do little to defray the debt, and that the debt was incurred by the schemes of bankers, speculators, and the well-off, and it was unfair to call on the poor to pay for others' misdeeds. They also argued that nonresidents owned a huge amount of the state's land; accordingly, taxes on property were a fairer way to raise revenue.[52]

The proposal was amended during the debate. Rather than placing a poll tax in the constitution, it authorized the legislature, at its discretion, to levy such a tax to be not less than fifty cents nor more than one dollar on free white males above age twenty-one. The provision was approved 109 to 49. Democrats who joined almost all the Whigs in the majority vote came largely from southern Illinois.[53]

Treatment of Blacks: No Slavery, No Tolerance

Issues relating to African Americans were not significant factors in the call for a convention. They were important in the minds of the delegates, however, and inevitably became strongly and emotionally contested during the convention.

In contrast to the 1818 convention, no effort was made to adopt euphemistic forms of slavery or bondage by indenture. To the contrary, slavery was prohibited in no uncertain terms. The influx of population from New England and free states in the East and from foreign immigration had peopled the north of the state with residents opposed to slavery. In the last week of the convention, the full body took up the report of the bill of rights committee, which made no reference to a slavery prohibition. On August 23 Democratic delegate Curtis Harvey, a native of Vermont who had relocated to Knox County in 1836, moved to add the same broad prohibitory language as in 1818, with the same customary proviso. The provision became section 16 of the bill of rights. The section states in its entirety, "There shall be neither slavery nor involuntary servitude in this state, except as punishment for crime, whereof the party shall have been duly convicted." The convention record reflects simply that the motion "was adopted," with no indication that there was any discussion or controversy about it.[54]

The most heated issue related to blacks' immigration into the state. Early in the convention, on June 24, Benjamin Bond, a Whig delegate from Clinton County in southern Illinois, introduced a proposal "prohibiting free negroes from hereafter emigrating to and settling within the bounds of this state" and preventing "owners of slaves in other states from bringing them into and setting them free in this state." The matter provoked emotional debate and ill feeling between many of the delegates from northern and southern Illinois. The arguments raised nearly every issue that would divide the nation in later years.[55]

Members from northern Illinois argued that the proposal violated the plain dictates of humanity and the principles of the Declaration of Independence and were a direct infringement of the Constitution of the United States. They maintained that some of the laws concerning the treatment of all blacks were already "a disgrace to the state" and that adding this proposal "would be a disgrace to any people claiming to be free, enlightened, and humane."[56]

Delegates from southern Illinois asserted that members from the north "do not understand our position in the south." Said delegate Alexander Jenkins, "[W]e have [negroes] in large numbers, whole settlements of them, who do nothing, idle away their time, and are as trifling, worthless filthy and degraded as in any part of the union." Delegate William Kinney, Democrat from St. Clair County, across the Mississippi from St. Louis, asserted that his county "had already nearly 500 free colored persons collected there from Missouri. . . . [M]embers from the northern part of the state," he said, "did not know how lazy, and good for nothing these people were." Others echoed Kinney: "Free negroes amongst our people was a great evil," said Democratic delegate Edward West of Madison County. "These people were, mostly, idle and worthless persons, and his people were very anxious to get rid of them."[57]

Delegate George Lemon of far south Marion reached an extreme. The debates record,

> he did not believe they were altogether human beings. If any gentleman thought they were, he would ask him to look at a negro's foot! (Laughter.) What was his leg doing in the middle of it? If that was not sufficient, let him go and examine their nose: (roars of laughter) then look at their lips. Why, their skulls [sic] were three inches thicker than white peoples.[58]

So went the debate for two days in June. Several delegates cautioned that adding any provision to the constitution might offend people in some portion of the state and might become a topic that would influence voters against adoption of the constitution. They favored keeping the subject out of the constitution and leaving the matter to the legislature. Finally, at the end of the day on Friday, June 25, a motion to postpone indefinitely the whole subject was adopted by a vote of 80 to 55.[59]

The convention took up the matter again during its last week. In the final review of the bill of rights, on August 23, Benjamin Bond moved to end the matter by referring it to the legislature. Bond's proposal, later adopted as a separate article, stated, "The General Assembly shall at its first session under the amended constitution pass such laws as will effectually prohibit free persons of color from immigrating to and settling in this state, and to effectually prevent the owners of slaves from bringing them into the state for the purpose of setting them free." Bond added the proviso that the section would be submitted to the voters as a separate proposition, to be accepted or rejected apart from the rest of the constitution.[60]

Debate on the motion lasted only half a day, but its tenor was even angrier than in June. Dr. Daniel Whitney, the Whig delegate from Boone County, spoke at great length, saying that he "was surprised that such an abhorrent proposition should be introduced into a constitutional Convention in the state of Illinois, in this enlightened age of civilization, humanity, and Christianity." The section, he said, "would disgrace the constitution of the State of Illinois."[61]

Delegate Andrew McCallen, Whig of Shawneetown on the Ohio River in far south Gallatin County, sarcastically derided Whitney's remarks as stating that the stars would be blotted out, revolutions of the globes would be stopped in their orbits, and all would be darkness and deep obscurity. "What an awful state of affairs!" he said. Then he added apocalyptic warnings of his own: "[T]he people of the south would not suffer the evils and vices attendant on a negro population any longer. . . . [T]he south had borne with them long enough." McCallen added a threat: "[U]nless [the delegates] now came forward and permitted adequate protection to the south from being overrun by these swarms of free negroes from every state in the Union . . . the people of the south would take the matter into their own hands, and commence a war of extermination."[62]

After similar comments from others, as well as expressions of disappointment from some southern members that the section was to be submitted to the voters as a separate proposition, the debate ended. The vote was divided along sectional lines. With heavy support from southern delegates, it passed 87 to 56.[63]

Disqualification by Dueling

During final consideration of the bill of rights late in the convention, the body adopted without debate two sections relating to dueling. The first disqualified from holding office any person who had fought in or aided or abetted a duel or challenge after the new constitution was adopted. The second section required that anyone elected or appointed to any office take an oath that he had not fought a duel or seconded, assisted, or aided any duel after the constitution.[64]

These provisions became the subject of political debate eight years later when William Bissell was elected in 1856 as the first Republican governor. Bissell, an Illinois hero wounded in the Mexican War, famously had accepted a duel challenge relating to the war from Jefferson Davis in 1850 when both were members of the U.S. House of Representatives. Surprised at the acceptance and choice of weapons, Davis backed down. Bissell maintained that the Illinois provisions did not apply to a duel challenge in the District of Columbia, took the oath, and served until he died in office in March 1860.[65]

Public Education: Failure of Foresight

The most forward-looking discussion, in a convention focused on correcting past mistakes, was initiated by proponents of a statewide system of common schools. Joseph Duncan, later a Whig governor from 1834 to 1838, had introduced the state's first school law in the senate in 1825. It provided that "there shall be established a common school or schools in each of the counties of this state, which shall be open and free to every class of white citizens between the ages of 5 and 21." It contained provisions for creating school districts, training teachers, selecting local schoolhouse sites, and financing the system by taxation. In advance of its time, the Duncan bill embodied the common school law of later in the century and beyond. It also preceded public appreciation of the benefits of education and the need for a tax to pay for it. The bill was amended to leave the question of education to the voters in local districts. For almost three decades thereafter, only local and individual effort promoted public schools.[66]

In the 1840s, public-spirited citizens had begun efforts to overcome the belief that economy was more important than education. In 1844 a school convention in Peoria adopted a memorial asking the state legislature to recognize the problem and create a new office, state superintendent of public instruction. The general assembly did not go that far, compromising instead by passing a law in 1845 that gave the title ex officio to the secretary of state. The law had exemplary features, including educational requirements for teachers to be versed in reading, writing, arithmetic, geography, grammar, and history. In a busy office, however, secretaries of state had little ability to collect information and promote the ends of the law.[67]

Against that background the 1847 convention created an education committee, chaired by Thompson Campbell of Jo Daviess County. Campbell, a Democrat, held the office of secretary of state from March 1843 until December 1846. In that position, he also had served as the state's first superintendent of public instruction, ex officio, and wrote the state's first public-school report. Campbell had left state office to return to his law practice in Galena, where he was elected delegate to the convention.[68]

On June 23, apparently in Campbell's absence from the convention, Cyrus Edwards, the Whig vice chairman, reported the resolutions the education committee was contemplating. The full day was spent discussing the report. The greater part of the proposals related to funds already available for school uses. These funds were derived from the terms Nathaniel Pope had negotiated as part of the enabling act for statehood in 1818. That act dictated that the money from the sale of section 16 in every township would be made available for the use of schools. Further, the enabling act specified that a portion of the 5 percent proceeds from the sale by Congress of public lands within the state would be used "for the encouragement of learning," with one-sixth of the amount "exclusively bestowed on a college or university." Although such sources had contributed substantial monies, the members of the committee believed that the state had not been prudent in the use of the funds and in realizing values for the lands it sold.[69]

Edwards reported that the education committee was devising specifications for the use of the funds and also "looks to the appointment of a State Superintendant of Instruction." Knowing that there would be objections to the expense, he described the successes of such an office in other states. Many delegates voiced approval of the committee's report and objectives. Others opposed every aspect of the project. At the end of a full day's debate, the matter was left with the committee to go forward.[70]

The convention did not return to any matter from the education committee for two months. On Thursday, August 26, the next-to-last day the convention considered substantive matters, the committee presented its proposed article. The first two sections of the concise, six-section article dealt with the school funds, specifying procedures for their safeguarding, use, and investment. Section 3 obligated the general assembly to provide for "a system of common schools which shall be as nearly uniform as may be, throughout the state; and such common schools shall be equally free to all the children in the state, and no sectarian instruction shall be permitted in any of them."[71]

Section 4 vested the supervision of public instruction in "the superintendent of common schools" and county or local superintendents as may be established by law. Section 5 provided for the governor to appoint the superintendent for a two-year term at a salary to be specified by the legislature. Section 6 stated that Section 5 would be in force for only six years, and no longer, "after which the General Assembly may provide for the continuance of said office, or for the election of such officer by the people."[72]

Instead of supporting his committee's report, chairman Thompson Campbell immediately moved to amend it by providing for election of the superintendent by the voters of the state instead of appointment by the governor. Speaking on his motion, Campbell acknowledged the impatience of the convention to adjourn and that it was "but little disposed to hear discussion upon any subject." Nevertheless, he proceeded with a very long discourse explaining the importance of the position, describing in great detail what he saw as the seven principal duties of the office, and extolling the benefits that had accrued to other states from such a position. He continued with a lengthy argument for election, not appointment, and appealed to "the friends of economy and retrenchment" to vote for this great "cause of education and enlightenment of the people."[73]

Campbell had established himself as the most publicly cantankerous delegate in the convention. In June, the convention's record marked as "Personal" remarks he made when he asked the full convention to relieve him of further service on the education committee, of which he was chairman, a request that was denied. On that occasion, he apparently was piqued by committee vice chairman Cyrus Edwards's presentation on education to the convention three days earlier during Campbell's absence. On July 26, during debate over suffrage provisions, he made the duel challenge concerning the truth of remarks by O. C. Pratt, his fellow Democratic delegate from Jo Daviess County. Now, at convention's end, Campbell's refusal to support his own committee's proposal for the method of selecting the superintendent of education opened up the education proposal to a welter of motions and amendments.[74]

The short time remaining on August 26 and the morning of the following day was occupied by substitute motions for appointment of the officer by the governor, another for appointment by the legislature, and another simply urging the legislature to act on the matter. Other motions were made to amend details regarding the use and security of the funds. Judge Scates announced that he opposed the whole system. As other remarks and revisions followed from the impatient delegates, Cyrus Edwards's motion to end the debate and lay the whole subject on the table with no action taken on it carried, 73 to 58. Thus concluded the involvement of the 1847 convention with the subject of education. Campbell's ill-timed personal adventure terminated whatever good or slim chance the pioneering education proposal had to carry the convention.[75]

The Amending Process: Don't Tread on Our Work

Constitutional convention delegates in Illinois, as in other states, consistently have expressed distrust of legislatures and been jealous to protect their work product from being undone. They have written into constitutions requirements of extraordinary majority votes by legislators and the public to alter "their" constitutions. With justification, they have been criticized from within their own ranks for manifesting an attitude that they are superior in wisdom and judgment to the legislature and others in government and even at times to the voting public.

These attitudes were clearly expressed in the 1847 convention. In the first half of the nineteenth century, a convention was the accepted device for revising a state's fundamental document. The 1818 Illinois constitution was typical in providing that the only way "to alter or amend" the constitution was for the legislature by a two-thirds vote to recommend to the electorate that they vote "for or against" a constitutional convention. By the time of the 1847 convention, a second method of revision, changing constitutions by legislative-initiated amendments approved by the state's voters, without conventions, came into common use.[76]

Reflecting distrust of the legislature and the electorate, the process adopted in the constitution for submission to the voters of proposed amendments was a difficult one. Putting an amendment before the voters required, first, a two-thirds vote of each house of the general assembly. After the next general election, a majority vote of the new general assembly had to approve the same proposal. Amendments could be proposed to only one article of the constitution at a session. Finally, at the next general election the proposal required the approval of a majority of the number of voters casting votes for members of the house of representatives.[77]

The difficult process of amendment was never utilized. In the twenty-two years until the adoption of the 1870 constitution, the 1848 constitution was never amended.

Special Debt Tax and Wrapping Up

In the closing days of the convention, members took a significant step in confronting the huge state debt that internal-improvements schemes had created. On August 25 Cyrus Edwards introduced a proposal to collect annually a property tax of two mills, in addition to all other taxes; the funds would apply exclusively to payment of state indebtedness. In support of his proposal, Edwards supplied a calculation showing how it would extinguish the debt within twenty-five years. Although many in the convention and public believed the state should honorably liquidate the debt, an active minority favored repudiation. Edwards argued that the matter should be a constitutional requirement and thus beyond legislative tinkering. To that end, he specified as part of the proposal that the provision would be submitted as a separate proposition for approval by a majority of voters. Thus, the new tax would not jeopardize approval of the rest of the constitution, and approval would cement the matter as one favored by the greater part of the voters.[78]

The convention debated the proposal over portions of two days. Many offered objections and amendments to defeat or dilute the tax or prevent its consideration. When finally called for votes on August 28, the special tax was approved 97 to 23, to be submitted to the voters as a separate question.[79]

In its final days, the convention ordered that the proposed constitution be printed in German and Norwegian as well as in English and asked the delegates to report the number of copies of those texts needed in their districts. The convention also set a schedule for submission of the constitution to the voters for ratification six months later, on March 6, 1848. The convention included a sample poll book in the schedule to show how the constitution as a whole was to be submitted for adoption or rejection, with the exception of Article XIV, concerning negro immigration, and Article XV, which provided for the two-mill tax to pay debt. Those articles were to be voted for or against separately.[80]

The constitution was adopted and signed on August 31, 1847, by 131 delegates. Seven Democrats refused to sign. Twenty-four delegates were absent.[81]

Ratification by the Voters

In the six months leading to the vote on ratification of the new document, newspapers generally favored approval. Some Democratic leaders derided it as a "mongrel affair" and grumbled about the success of the convention's Whigs in carrying important points with Democratic support. Whigs were exultant. The night before the convention finished its substantive work, David Davis wrote to his wife: "The Convention will adjourn tomorrow night. . . . [T]he Whigs are in a great State of Excitement for fear they will lose tomorrow what they have gained in the last three months. . . . We have been in the majority (although in an actual political minority of 20) at least 9 times out of every ten on the Journal. Altho the Constitution is in a great many respects worse than we would like, yet it is better than we had any reason to expect and why the party will be in the main satisfied with it."[82]

Generally, activists in both parties valued their gains from the new document more than their losses and were careful not to alienate voter support. Gustave Koerner, leader of the German community, fought against adoption because noncitizens would lose the right to vote, but the immigrant community's opposition was muted because of other beneficial articles.[83]

On balance, most people agreed that the new constitution was a considerable improvement upon the old. In the ratification election on March 6, 1848, the constitution was adopted by a majority of almost four to one, 60,585 favorable and 15,903 opposed. Article XIV, prohibiting free persons of color from immigrating to and settling in the state, also was approved by a large majority, 50,261 to 21,297. Article XV, levying the special debt tax, received the smallest majority, 41,349 to 30, 945, but also passed with 57 percent of voters approving the extra tax burden. The new constitution went into effect on April 1, 1848.[84]

With the adoption of this new constitution, Illinois became the first state created from the Northwest Territory to revise and amend its fundamental law. The first statehood constitutions of Ohio (1802), Indiana (1816), and Michigan (1838) remained in force. In Wisconsin, the territory's voters had rejected the draft of a first constitution in 1846; a second constitutional convention was called in 1847. A new constitution was approved by the convention on February 1, 1848, and ratified by the voters on March 13, 1848, a week after Illinois voters ratified their new constitution.[85]

Wisconsin Concedes the Illinois Boundary

Signally, events in Wisconsin relating to its failed constitution of 1846 and the approved constitution of 1848 were significant to Illinois in finally putting to rest controversy over Nathaniel Pope's 1818 boundary amendment. Several attempts had been made in the 1830s and 1840s to restore Illinois's northern boundary line to the southern tip of Lake Michigan. In 1838, Wisconsin territorial officials petitioned Congress, claiming, without success, that the amendment adding that territory violated the Northwest Ordinance of 1787. In 1842, instigated by Wisconsin governor James Doty, delegates from nine of the fourteen Illinois counties in the Pope amendment area held a convention in Rockford and asserted that they legally and by right belonged in Wisconsin. In the referendum that followed, in which Cook County refused to participate, the vote was one-sided in favor of leaving Illinois. The effort to gain support included the offer of a U.S. Senate seat to a prominent Chicagoan.[86]

Governor Thomas Carlin of Illinois ignored a notice from Governor Doty that the fourteen counties were not within the constitutional boundaries of Illinois and that Illinois's jurisdiction was "accidental and temporary." Governor Doty on his own issued proclamations in 1842 and 1843 to all the people within the "ancient limits of Wisconsin" to vote, on a date he named, to form a state government, but people paid little attention to his pleas. The Wisconsin territorial legislature of 1843–44 sent to Congress an elaborate petition on the subject, which Congress ignored. In 1846, however, the act of Congress enabling the people of Wisconsin to adopt a constitution made acceptance of the existing boundary a condition of admission as a state. Wisconsin voters rejected that first constitution. An effort was made to revive the boundary question in the 1848 Wisconsin constitutional convention leading to statehood, but instead the 1848 constitution confirmed the previously established boundary line with Illinois, settling the question once and for all.[87]

CHAPTER 5

Two Transformative Decades

1848–1868

The two decades between ratification of the 1848 constitution and the voters' call in 1868 for the post–Civil War convention saw a transformation of the nation and the state of Illinois. Population, transportation, technology, manufacturing, and trade and commerce all changed markedly. By almost every measure, the greatest part of these changes in Illinois was in the north, on the land area added to the state in 1818 by the Pope amendment, fulfilling the promise Pope articulated in advocating for it in the Congress.

The relationship of the state to its people, particularly its black persons, changed as well. Black bondage was gone, but issues relating to their civil rights and treatment remained. Divisions between the north and south of the state sharpened, leading to unique voting provisions adopted in the 1869 constitutional convention.

State and national politics changed markedly as the amendment-added area supplied the votes for the new Republican Party to win state elections in the 1850s and 1860s, enabling Abraham Lincoln to win the party nomination and the presidency in 1860. The Lincoln-era Thirteenth, Fourteenth, and Fifteenth Amendments to the United States Constitution reinforced movement in the 1869 Illinois constitutional convention toward progressive civil rights provisions.

Nathaniel Pope lived long enough to see a glimpse of the changes his foresight enabled. In 1848 he traveled to Chicago to preside over the first U.S. federal court to sit in that city. With the growth in multistate commercial activity and Board of Trade contracts, federal court business in northern Illinois had grown to the point that the U.S. Congress had specified that one term of the district and circuit courts should be held at Chicago on the first Monday of July each year.[1]

Pope had served as U.S. judge for Illinois for nearly three decades, from the time his appointment was confirmed in 1819. After a brief initial federal court session in Kaskaskia in December 1819, Pope moved the court to the new capital at Vandalia. For the next eighteen years he traveled from his home in Kaskaskia to Vandalia twice a year, normally needing at most three days in Vandalia to complete the little business that came before the court. When the state capital was transferred to Springfield in 1839, Pope's federal court also moved its base to Springfield. By the late 1830s, Pope's court experienced increases in work from throughout the state.[2]

In the summer of 1849 Pope again held court in Springfield and Chicago. These sessions, which would be his last, were the busiest ever for the federal courts in Illinois. Pope presided alone in Springfield, clearing a trial docket of some seventy cases. He then proceeded to Chicago for the annual session, which

CHICAGO HARBOR, 1849

Fig. 9. Shipping crowded into Chicago Harbor on March 12, 1849, due to flooding in Des Plaines River near I&M Canal.*

* Fort Dearborn is shown at the right. Putnam, *Illinois and Michigan Canal*, 109.

lasted five weeks, during which he disposed of more than twenty-five important cases.[3]

Pope relished what he saw in his Chicago visits. During the 1849 Chicago term, Pope described the excitement and importance of the city and the sight of the ships that carried commerce and passengers across the Great Lakes and through the canal and Illinois waterway. In a letter to one of his granddaughters he wrote,

> This is a very improving city of about 24,000 inhabitants . . . situated on Lake Michigan and on both sides of the Chicago River, that is always full of ships, steam boats and canal boats—some of the steam boats are more magnificent than any I have ever seen. They carry passengers from here to Buffalo, passing through Lakes Michigan, Huron, the Detroit river & Lake Erie a thousand miles for five Dollars and give fine accommodations. The Ships carry produce such as beef, pork & wheat &c &c and among other things bring lumber in great quantity such as plank, shingles, and scantling—much of which goes down the Illinois River through the Canal.[4]

Toward the end of the Chicago term, on August 1, 1849, Pope was stricken during the night with a cerebral attack that affected his memory. The incident passed. He finished the court session and returned to Springfield, where four months later he held the winter term of court. In early January 1850, he was stricken again, at his daughter Elizabeth's home in Alton. He rallied briefly, traveled to another daughter's home in St. Louis, and died there on the morning of January 23, 1850.[5]

Nathanial Pope had served Illinois with distinction for more than forty years. While not well known to many, he deserves recognition among the greatest of the state's founding fathers.

Development of the North

Illinois's population doubled, from 851,470 in 1850 to 1,711,951 in 1860, making it the fourth-largest state, and increased almost 50 percent to 2,539,891 in 1870. Increases in the northern part of the state greatly outpaced those in the south. Chicago's population almost quadrupled, from 29,964 in 1850 to 112,172 in 1860, and more than doubled by 1870, to just less than 300,000, with most of its residents foreign born. Other cities in the state grew rapidly as well. Springfield's

Galena
Freeport
Rockford
Chicago
Rock
Island
Ottawa
Galesburg
Peoria
Bloomington
Quincy
Decatur
Springfield
Charleston
Alton
Vandalia
Edwardsville
St Louis
Cahokia
Kaskaskia
Jonesboro
Cairo

**1860
population
distribution**
each dot represents 100 people

Map 7. 1860 Population Distribution

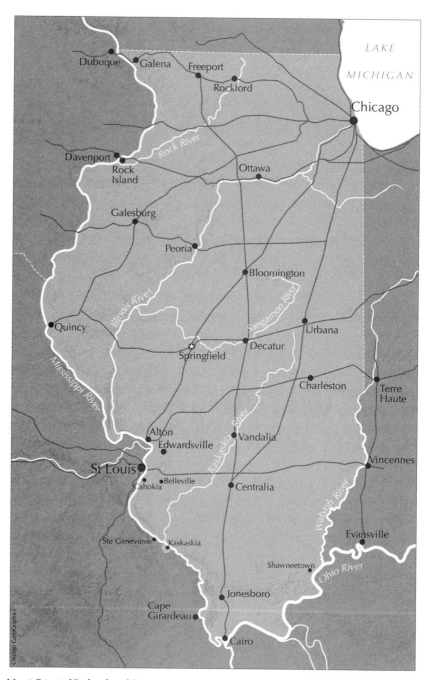

Map 8. Principal Railroads and Rivers, 1860

Fig. 10. The American class 4-4-0 locomotive was the mainstay of power on U.S. railroads until after the Civil War.* Courtesy of the Abraham Lincoln Presidential Library and Museum.
* Young, *Chicago Transit*, 27.

population doubled, from 4,533 to 9,320; the travel time between it and Chicago was cut from three days to a few hours.[6]

The state's railway network exploded, hugely increasing the movement of goods and slashing travel times. In the 1850s, railroads in Illinois constructed 2,867 miles of track, more than any other state except Ohio. Among them, the Illinois Central built a "Y" embracing the entire state, linking Cairo in the far south to Galena and Chicago. Chicago became the largest and most important rail center in the nation by 1854, serving as the terminal for ten different lines stretching for three thousand miles in almost every direction.[7]

Discussion continued surrounding the aspiration of constructing a Pacific railroad linking Illinois to the west. In the late 1840s, Douglas began pushing in Congress for such a railroad to advance his vision of opening Kansas and Nebraska Territories to settlement. His dream continued to be discussed through the 1850s. Not realized during Douglas's lifetime, it was finally undertaken during Lincoln's presidency.[8]

Slavery

The 1848 constitution altered the course of slavery law in Illinois. The emotional debates over free blacks in the constitutional convention, reflecting public opinion, especially in the south of the state, and the provision directing the general assembly to pass laws prohibiting free blacks from entering or settling in the state or owners of slaves from bringing them into the state, kept the issue before the public.[9]

Census figures help explain the transition. The 1820 federal census recorded 957 slave and 457 free African Americans in the state, equaling in total 2.5 percent of the state's population. By 1830 the number of slaves had decreased and free blacks quadrupled, to 747 and 1,637, respectively (1.5 percent). The 1840 federal census, the last to record free and enslaved African Americans in Illinois, reported 330 slaves and 3,598 free blacks, the total constituting 0.8 percent of the state population of 476,183. Almost all resided in the southern thirty-four counties of state.[10]

A Prewar Decade of Diverging Antiblack Attitudes

Article XIV of the 1848 constitution was ratified by a majority of the voters by more than two to one. It directed the general assembly to "pass such laws as will effectually prohibit free persons of color from immigrating to and settling in this state, and to effectually prevent the owners of slaves from bringing them into this state, for the purpose of setting them free."[11]

The article reflected public attitudes toward blacks that would prevail for almost two decades. None of the strict provisions of the black codes were rescinded or amended. At the same time, however, efforts to pass laws to prohibit the immigration of free blacks were unsuccessful. Bills on the subject failed to become law in the 1849 and 1851 general assemblies.[12]

Even as the general assembly in 1849 was considering legislation to implement new restrictions on negroes, the reorganized Illinois Supreme Court, composed of three justices elected by the people rather than nine appointed by the legislature, decided the first of two cases that changed Illinois law from acquiescence in the system of slavery to erosion of fundamental aspects of that system.

The first, *Thornton's* case, in 1849, challenged provisions of the 1829 code, reenacted in 1845, that said fugitive slaves could not sue for their freedom and that sheriffs were obligated to arrest them in order to send them back to their masters or sell them for service. The court held the provisions unconstitutional because they conflicted with federal law concerning the capture and return of runaway slaves.[13]

The court's second holding three years later in *Hone v. Ammons* has been widely hailed for its language about a presumption of freedom for blacks, but the case did not in itself involve freedom for anyone. It was another dispute between two white men who both claimed entitlement to ownership of a black slave. David Hone had sold to Godfrey Ammons the ownership of a person he claimed was his slave but who was at large somewhere in Illinois. Ammons gave Hone a promissory note in payment for the slave, who could not be found. Nonetheless, Hone sued on the note to collect his money.[14]

In a ruling that evokes little sympathy for either side, the supreme court by a 2–1 vote affirmed a judgment of the lower court in favor of the debtor defendant, Ammons. The justices filed three separate opinions reflecting very different attitudes toward slavery. In that, they can be said to mirror public opinion in the state.

Justice John D. Caton, in the lead opinion, wrote much of the oft-cited expansive language. On the facts, he first observed that the black man in question was seen walking abroad as a free man in Clinton County the day the note was given. "[B]eing in this State, the presumption of the law was that he was a free man," he wrote. To overcome that presumption and sustain his claim, Caton said, Hone needed more than the bare assertion that the man was a slave and that he owned title to him. Lacking affirmative proof, Hone could not maintain his case. Far from being revolutionary, Caton's opinion thus implied that, with proper proof of ownership, a black could have been obligated to return to his claimed master.

Justice Lyman Trumbull—soon to leave for a seat in the U.S. Senate—concurred in the judgment but wrote a long opinion against slavery and the sale of slaves. He asserted that the state's public policy opposed the sale of a person as a slave. Accordingly, a contract made in Illinois to sell a slave was illegal and void. Chief Justice Samuel Treat filed a one-sentence dissent, saying he believed Hone was entitled to judgment on the note and that he differed with the others' conclusions.

The *Thornton* and *Hone* cases together were taken to mean that the court would not allow state officials to help in the capture of fugitive slaves and that the presumption of freedom would allow many blacks to be freed. Those conclusions were unacceptable to the legislature and aroused it to act on the mandate of the 1848 constitution.

In February 1853 the Democratic-controlled legislature passed a law barring the immigration of free blacks. To overrule the implications of the *Hone* case, the legislature added a proviso declaring that slaves in transit through the state were not entitled to claim their freedom. The legislature also included a long section setting forth procedures by which an owner of an arrested slave could claim him, prove his ownership, and pay the balance of any fines and costs that had been assessed after the sheriff's capture of the slave.[15]

All the legislators from districts south of Springfield voted for the legislation, which was said to allay fears that Illinois would become a depository for emancipated slaves. Notwithstanding the act, the supreme court in 1857 reasserted that Illinois officials would have no part in the rendition of fugitive slaves. In *Rodney v. Illinois Central Railroad*, the court rebuffed a Missouri slave owner's attempt to recover the value of a slave who had escaped by boarding an Illinois Central train at Cairo, the southernmost town in Illinois. The court ruled that the laws recognizing slavery in another state from which a fugitive had fled did not affect the condition of a fugitive as free in Illinois or give a claiming owner any property right or control over him.[16]

The general assembly was unwilling to acquiesce in the court's rulings on these issues. Although the court had ruled in 1849 that Illinois's fugitive slave act was unconstitutional, the legislature nevertheless included it in adopting its 1858 revision of the laws. Public attitudes continued to support the exclusionary legislation. In March 1862 the Democratic-dominated constitutional convention, in the first article it approved, imported into the draft constitution the restrictive provisions of the 1853 Black Laws. The convention went further, prohibiting negroes from voting or holding office. The voters on the proposed constitution approved the restrictive clauses on negroes overwhelmingly, even as the constitution itself failed of passage.

National Issues Pervade State Politics

The decades of the 1850s and 1860s saw Illinois politicians attain prominence on national issues that reverberated and influenced political and constitutional issues in their home state. By 1850 Stephen Douglas exceeded all in influence in Washington and effects in Illinois. From the time he began his service in the House of Representatives in 1843, he was an ardent proponent of expansion of the Union. He advocated extension of railroads, including unsuccessful efforts in the 1850s to initiate a Pacific railroad. He wrote the laws that organized five territories and admitted five states. On questions of slavery, which became the major issue of his political life, he maintained that he held no moral position. It was a matter for the people of a state to decide—a matter of "popular sovereignty"—he asserted.[17]

In 1850 Abraham Lincoln was back in Illinois after serving one term, from 1847 to 1849, in the U.S. House of Representatives. He was dismayed with the state of the Whig party, and many in Illinois were dismayed over his criticism of President Polk and opposition to the Mexican War in which his two predecessors had become heroes and one of them, John Hardin, had died. Further, Lincoln had become a backer of General Zachary Taylor, the greatest hero of the Mexican War, to be the Whig nominee for president in 1848, despite the fact that Taylor had neither political experience nor views on the issues. Many Whig loyalists deplored Lincoln's support of Taylor for the presidency over venerable leader Henry Clay. Others were dismayed that he was opposing the war and at the same time supporting a nominee celebrated for his leadership in winning it.[18]

Believing that his career had reached the limits possible for a Whig in Illinois, from 1849 through 1854 he concentrated on developing a successful law practice, riding the Eighth Judicial Circuit twice a year, spending time at home and with his children, enjoying his books and private life.[19]

Political Turmoil, Party Realignment

Illinois politics changed in 1854. On January 4 Stephen Douglas introduced the Kansas-Nebraska Act in the United States Senate. The bill proposed creating a government for the huge Nebraska Territory, which embraced the present states of Kansas and Nebraska and extended north to the Canadian boundary. The bill included Douglas's "popular sovereignty" principle, providing that any states created in the territory would be slave or free depending on what their people decided in their constitutions when they became states. The provision opened huge areas west of Missouri to the possibility of becoming slave states. These territories had been declared to be forever free of slavery under the terms of the Missouri Compromise of 1820 and the Compromise of 1850, both of which Douglas had claimed to support. Pressed by proslavery senators, Douglas agreed to include in the act an explicit repeal of the Missouri Compromise, although he knew it would "raise a hell of a storm."[20]

It did. The Kansas-Nebraska Act fomented intense controversy in the nation and the state. The dispute did not succeed in slowing the bill in Congress.

Douglas, "with brilliant parliamentary management and unrelenting ferocity toward his opponents," forced the bill through both houses of Congress to final passage and President Franklin Pierce's signature on May 30, 1854.[21]

The "Nebraska Act" stirred Illinois politics. Abraham Lincoln wrote later that he was losing interest in politics when the repeal of the Missouri Compromise aroused him to action by creating the possibility that slavery might be entering new areas where it never had existed and from which it had explicitly been banned.[22]

Many others felt the same. Lyman Trumbull was among them. Trumbull held a secure position as a Democrat on the Illinois Supreme Court when Douglas introduced the Kansas-Nebraska Bill. The act so angered him that he resigned from the court to fight against it. He ran for the U.S. House of Representatives in 1854 as an anti-Nebraska Democrat, winning handily.[23]

The outrage over the Nebraska Act focused in the late months of 1854 on the second Illinois Senate seat, held by Douglas's ally, Democrat James Shields, another Mexican War hero. That seat was up for election by the legislature in February 1855. As Trumbull took his seat in the U.S. House in January 1855, he also became a candidate for election to the Senate by the Illinois legislature when it would meet early in February 1855.[24]

Lincoln set out on a more complicated route. Not holding any office in 1854, he came to believe that an anti-Nebraska coalition might be elected to the state legislature that would choose the senator—and that he would be a strong Senate candidate. With friends urging him to run for the state legislature to further his strong views on the issue, Lincoln agreed to run as a Whig for the state house of representatives. Ostensibly, the plan was to elect a favorable general assembly majority to instruct Douglas to repeal the bill and to elect a favorable senator.[25]

Lincoln's popularity showed in the election results. He led the vote for state representative in his district. Anti-Nebraska men gained a majority in the general assembly. More Whigs than expected were elected, as well as eighteen anti-Nebraska Democrats. At the same 1854 elections, Trumbull, in addition to four others running as anti-Nebraska candidates, succeeded in winning five of the nine Illinois seats in the U.S. House of Representatives.[26]

The 1854 results confirmed for Lincoln the possibility that he might win the office of U.S. senator when the new general assembly voted the next February. At some point, however, Lincoln also realized that under a reform instituted in the 1848 Illinois constitution, a sitting member of the state legislature could not be a candidate for election by the legislature to the Senate. To avoid the bar that membership in the legislature posed for his candidacy, Lincoln wrote the county clerk declining to accept election to that office.[27]

Lincoln, Trumbull, and incumbent Shields were the leading candidates when the legislature met in joint session February 8, 1855, to elect the senator. With a majority of fifty votes needed to elect, Lincoln received forty-five on the first ballot, Shields received forty votes, and Trumbull five, with eight votes scattered. After nine ballots, during which Lincoln's vote was decreasing while Trumbull's increased, it was clear that Shields could not prevail and that a compromise choice might be the Democratic governor, Joel Matteson, whom Lincoln and others believed might side with the Nebraska men on the slavery issue. To avoid that result, Lincoln directed his support to Trumbull, who then won election on the tenth ballot.[28]

The outcome was a sharp rebuke to Douglas and his popular sovereignty credo. Although he was disappointed, Lincoln liked Trumbull, stood with him philosophically, and knew that his strong personality and sharp tongue would

Fig. 11. Senators Stephen Douglas and Lyman Trumbull. Courtesy of the Library of Congress.

make life difficult for Douglas. The way was cleared also for Lincoln himself to run against Douglas in 1858 with the support of anti-Nebraska Democrats in the legislature as well as the new Senator Trumbull, who pledged to support him in the next Senate contest.[29]

Lincoln nevertheless was discouraged. Some time later, likely in 1856, he expressed his feelings in a note fragment found in his papers:

> Twenty-two years ago Judge Douglas and I first became acquainted. We were both young then; he a trifle younger than I. Even then, we were both ambitious; I, perhaps, quite as much so as he. With *me*, the race of ambition has been a failure—a flat failure; with *him* it has been one of splendid success. His name fills the nation; and is not unknown, even, in foreign lands.[30]

In time, of course, the awakening of a new political party and the drive of Lincoln's unsatisfied ambition had his name celebrated in the nation and world well beyond that of most mortals.

The Republican Party Emerges

The early 1850s were a time of political fragmentation in Illinois, as elsewhere in the nation. Democrats in Illinois were split sharply between those who favored and those who opposed westward expansion that might lead to the extension of slavery, and also on the issue of internal improvements in the north. Although the Democratic split over Nebraska reduced them to a legislative minority in 1854, the Whig Party was dying. Internal differences over slavery, nativism, and immigration, as well as opposition to opportunity for negroes, foreigners, and Catholics were alienating many.[31]

The new Republican Party emerged as an amalgam of diverse elements united primarily in opposition to the extension of slavery. In 1854, Republicans held statewide meetings in Ripon, Wisconsin, and elsewhere. The Republican name was first used in Illinois that year by a group of abolitionists from northern counties who held a convention in October 1854 and were active in elections in congressional districts. Lincoln as a Senate aspirant did not want to be classified as an extremist and avoided public association with the groups.[32]

By 1856, however, Lincoln was ready to cast his lot with the Republicans. On May 29, some 270 delegates from seventy counties met in convention in Bloomington to organize the Illinois Republican Party and select candidates for office. Lincoln refused to run for governor. He strongly believed that the Republican candidate should be a former Democrat. He convinced Republican leaders that William H. Bissell, a lawyer, former physician, and hero of the Battle of Buena Vista, who had served three terms as a Democrat in Congress and had broken with Douglas and the Democrats over the Kansas-Nebraska Act, was the only former Democrat with a chance of winning. Bissell was nominated at the convention without opposition.[33]

Bissell had become a folk hero in Illinois in 1850 when Jefferson Davis challenged him to a duel after Bissell made a telling response on the floor of the House of Representatives to southern accusations of cowardice by northern troops at Buena Vista. The southerners contended that the day was saved only by Davis's Mississippi troops. In a powerful oration in reply, Bissell forcefully corrected the record, saying that he was there, the northerners fought valiantly and did not give way, the Davis regiment was a mile and a half away, and "not yet had it fired a gun or pulled a trigger." Surprised that Bissell accepted the challenge and chose devastating military muskets at close range as the weapons, Davis backed down.[34]

During the campaign and following the election, Democrats argued that Bissell was disqualified from holding office by the anti-dueling prohibitions of the 1848 constitution. They contended also that he would perjure himself if he took the constitutional oath that he had never participated in a duel. Bissell was unfazed, proceeding on the theory that the Illinois constitution did not apply because the duel challenge was in the District of Columbia.[35]

In a momentous shift of the political landscape, in the 1856 fall elections Republicans gained victories with Bissell and their other statewide candidates, as well as four of the nine congressional seats, losing the seat Trumbull had won in 1854. Bissell's election began a string of Republican governors that continued for thirty-six years.[36]

After the election, Bissell, who was an invalid and unable to walk without the use of crutches or wheelchair, transacted all business from the executive mansion and never entered the state capitol. Bissell's health deteriorated. He died on March 18, 1860, ten months before his term ended. Lieutenant Governor John Wood succeeded him.[37]

The 1856 election showed how essential Nathaniel Pope's boundary amendment was to the Republican Party and revealed the Republican base for Lincoln's successful campaign four years later. It was the popular vote in the fourteen northern counties that made up the area added by the 1818 boundary extension that

Fig. 12. Famous "tousled hair" photograph of Lincoln taken by Alexander Hesler in February 1857, in Chicago.* Courtesy of the Library of Congress.

* Lincoln, who said Hesler mussed his hair to make him look more natural, claimed the photo was "a very true one" that he liked, "though my wife, and many others, do not. My impression is that their objection arises from the disordered condition of the hair. My judgment is worth nothing in these matters." CW 4:114.

provided the Republican margin of victory statewide in the election for governor. Without the vote in those counties, the Democratic candidate carried the rest of the state by 19,228 votes. Republican Bissell, however, carried the fourteen northern counties by 23,925, for a winning margin of 4,697 votes statewide.[38]

The 1858 Senate Campaign

In 1858 Lincoln, as expected, opposed Douglas, who was seeking election to a third term in the Senate. Their debates in Illinois in the late summer and autumn caught the nation's attention. The campaign, grandly described at the time as "one of the most exciting political contests that has ever occurred," has continued to hold the public imagination for a century and a half.

The issues expounded were national and monumental, but also of consequence to the state. The election turned on local battles in fifty-eight state house of representative districts and twenty-five senate districts that provided the one hundred state legislators who would vote to elect the senator.[39]

Douglas was nominated for the Senate in April 1858 in a routine Democratic state convention in the house of representatives chamber in Springfield. On June 16 the Republican state convention met in the same chamber. Lincoln was nominated by a resolution adopted unanimously.[40]

Fig. 13. The historic House of Representatives Chamber in the Old State Capitol. Courtesy of the Abraham Lincoln Presidential Library and Museum.

That evening Lincoln made his historic House Divided speech in the same chamber. Using the biblical theme, "A house divided against itself cannot stand," he said, "I believe this government cannot endure permanently half slave and half free. I do not expect the union to be dissolved. I do not expect the house to fall. But I do expect it will cease to be divided. It will become all one thing, or all the other." Lincoln thus set the stage for the second part of his address, which was a vigorous attack on Douglas, the Kansas-Nebraska Act, and the Supreme Court's Dred Scott decision.[41]

The speech is celebrated for the house-divided language. The most important part substantively, however, was Lincoln's reference to and warnings about the Dred Scott decision. In Dred Scott, Chief Justice Roger B. Taney, speaking for a 7–2 Supreme Court majority on March 6, 1857, reached out beyond the technical posture of issues framed by the pleadings to hold that blacks had no right to file suit as citizens of a state and, second, that Congress had no power to prohibit slavery in the territories; by implication no territorial legislature could ban slavery. The latter ruling, of course, undermined Douglas's concept of "popular sovereignty."[42]

Lincoln warned that the people of Illinois might "awake to the *reality* . . . that the *Supreme* Court has made *Illinois* a *slave* state." Lincoln's admonition rested on the fact that the court by its holding implicitly had ruled on the meaning of the Illinois constitution. Before living in the Minnesota Territory when he filed suit, Scott had lived in Illinois. Scott claimed that he was free because of his Illinois residency. The court brushed aside Scott's contention, ruling in effect against the Illinois Supreme Court holdings that presence in Illinois freed a slave.[43]

The House Divided speech attracted attention. It also sounded radical to many. Some of Lincoln's closest advisers were alarmed, fearing that the speech had an abolitionist tinge that implied a pledge to make war upon the institution of slavery and abolish it where it existed. Douglas thought so too, and referred to it repeatedly.[44]

The campaign began formally on July 9 in Chicago, where Douglas addressed a huge outdoor audience from a balcony of the Tremont House hotel. Lincoln attended, sitting behind Douglas, who had called him up from the audience, and replied the next night from the same balcony. That exchange set a pattern for the next six weeks. As the better-known Douglas traveled the state attracting large crowds, Lincoln followed, making a speech the next night, often after rising at the end of Douglas's speech and announcing when he would reply. This tactic was not uncommon in Illinois politics at the time, but the practice greatly irritated Douglas, was criticized by Democrats, and concerned Lincoln's friends, who felt he was drawn too much into the Douglas pageantry and feared the public would dislike the shadowing.[45]

Lincoln argued that it was useful to rebut Douglas when his remarks were fresh, but gave in to his advisers' concerns about following Douglas. Instead he challenged Douglas to "divide time and address the same audiences." Douglas felt he could not refuse. Thus were born the famous Lincoln-Douglas debates. The candidates agreed to one debate at locations Douglas chose in each of the seven congressional districts in which the two candidates had not yet spoken. They agreed that the organization of the debates would be formal: each would speak for an hour and a half, with one opening for an hour, the other responding for an hour and a half, and the first allowed a half-hour rebuttal. Douglas as the one being challenged took four openings and Lincoln three.[46]

The debates, which attracted large crowds in most of the locations, were held outdoors on open platforms. Early-arriving spectators often crowded onto the speakers' platforms, leaving little room for luminaries or reporters. "They have a wretched way in Illinois of leaving the platform unguarded and exposed to forcible entry of the mob," wrote one frustrated New York correspondent.[47] As was customary, questioners and hecklers, at times members of the platform party, often challenged the speakers.

The debates were held in seven cities that ranged from Freeport in the far north to Jonesboro in the deep south. The first two were held a week apart in August, the third and fourth over a four-day period in mid-September, and the last three between October 7 and 15. At other times in the long campaign, the candidates appeared separately.[48]

In the first debate, at Ottawa, situated along the Illinois River in north-central Illinois, some ninety miles southwest of Chicago, Douglas led off with a ferocious opening statement in which he charged Republicans with fomenting sectional strife over slavery and Lincoln with being an abolitionist who favored equality for the negro, a serious charge that would undermine popular support. Lincoln was caught off balance by Douglas's attacks and responded weakly. He did not argue for equality, but asserted that blacks had the same natural rights as white men and described Douglas as favoring the extension of slavery.[49]

In the second debate, at Freeport, a heavily Republican town in far northern Illinois, Lincoln attempted to take the offensive by posing questions that would present Douglas with a dilemma. The most famous question asked whether the people of a United States territory had power to exclude slavery from its limits prior to the formation of a state constitution. Lyman Trumbull had put essentially the same question to Douglas on the Senate floor in 1856.[50]

Douglas responded, affirming, "The people of a Territory can . . . exclude slavery from their limits prior to the formation of a State Constitution." The reply, which became known as Douglas's Freeport Doctrine, was politically disarming in Illinois but would cost Douglas in the presidential election two years later.[51]

In concluding his responses to the questions Lincoln posed, Douglas sarcastically mocked him for exhausting himself devising the questions with the aid of radical advisers, including blacks. Antiblack prejudice was strong throughout the state, even in the north. Douglas played to that prejudice. He used an anecdotal recollection in Freeport that he also used on other occasions. Referring to prominent black supporters of Lincoln, he singled out abolitionist Frederick Douglass for an earlier appearance in the town when he was seated with a white woman in a carriage driven by her white husband. Douglas derided Republicans for thinking "that the negro ought to be on a social equality with your wives and

daughters and ride in a carriage with your wife whilst you drive the team." He
continued, "you who believe that the nigger is your equal and ought to be on an
equality with you socially, politically, and legally . . . of course will vote for Mr.
Lincoln."[52]

The candidates made essentially the same arguments in the five later debates.
Lincoln asserted that he was strongly opposed to slavery, that he considered it
morally wrong, and that its reach should not be extended. He supported that
view with reference to the Declaration of Independence. "All men are created
equal," he argued, applied to blacks as well as whites; all had certain fundamental and inalienable rights. Explaining his position on equality, he said, "I am not,
nor ever have been, in favor of bringing about in any way the social and political
equality of the white and black races. . . . I am not, nor ever have been, in favor
of making voters or jurors of negroes, nor of qualifying them to hold office, nor
to intermarry with white people." Further, he added, "There is a physical difference between the white and black races which I believe will forever forbid the
two races living together on terms of social and political equality. [W]hile they
do remain together there must be the position of superior and inferior, and I as
much as any other man am in favor of having the superior position assigned to
the white race."[53]

These were the politically expedient things to say. They also were paradoxical;
a fundamental right to self-government is difficult to exercise without the right
to vote, for example. But they also represented deeply held personal views that
Lincoln had expressed before. Opposed to slavery throughout his life, he was
not personally hostile to blacks. He believed in their basic human rights but had
doubts that free blacks could fit into a free society.[54]

Douglas attacked the House Divided speech and accused Lincoln of being an
abolitionist and favoring full social and political equality. He argued for popular
sovereignty to decide the question of slavery in the territories and maintained
that "the signers of the Declaration of Independence had no reference to negroes at all when they declared all men to be created equal. They did not mean
negro, nor the savage Indians, nor the Fejee islanders, nor any other barbarous
race. They were speaking of white men. . . . [T]his government was established
on the white basis. It was established by white men for the benefit of white men
and their posterity forever, and should be administered by white men, and none
others."[55]

The debates made journalism history. Reporters from major newspapers in Illinois, St. Louis, Philadelphia, and New York attended. Lincoln acquired a national reputation as a worthy opponent of the famed Douglas. The debates also were significant politically. Forced into saying that the voters of a territory could decide whether it would be slave or free, Douglas was maneuvered into a position that made him unacceptable to the South and cost him the 1860 presidential election.

The debates are important also in that the positions argued by the two men reflect widely held attitudes in Illinois on black freedom and civil rights that would be important in the 1862 and 1869 constitutional conventions. Lincoln's positions against black voting, jury service, and other civil rights, while remarkable today, prevailed in 1862 and were heatedly disputed in the 1869 convention, even after the adoption of the three Lincoln/Johnson–era amendments to the U.S. Constitution.

It can fairly be said that it was Stephen Douglas who gave Abraham Lincoln the stature to be elected president two years later, in 1860. Douglas's brilliant national reputation provided the foil for Lincoln to shine as a national figure.

The 1858 elections

On November 2, 1858, more than 250,000 men cast votes in Illinois. No separate vote was recorded for the office of U.S. senator; the election to that office would occur in the state legislature in January. The other contests showed that the popular vote favored Lincoln. Republicans won the two statewide offices on the ballot, for state treasurer and state superintendent of public instruction. The popular vote in the treasurer election was 125,430 Republican, 121,609 Democratic, and 5,071 for the Buchanan ticket. The vote total in the nine U.S. House of Representatives races was almost identical, with Republican candidates receiving 125,668 votes, Democrats 122,181, and the Buchanan ticket 4,110. Douglas's Democratic Party controlled the gerrymandered legislative districts, however, and in January 1859 the legislature reelected Douglas to the Senate by a vote of 54 to 46.[56]

The popular vote in Illinois was sharply divided regionally. The Democrats carried all but three of the counties in southern Illinois and the counties along the Illinois River where the Irish vote was strong. Republicans won all of the northern counties, many by heavy majorities. As in 1856, the popular vote in the fourteen northern counties that made up the area added by the 1818 boundary extension provided the Republican winning total statewide. In the elections for the U.S. House of Representatives, for example, Republicans carried the northern counties by 16,913, while Democrats won the rest of the state by 13,426 votes, giving Republicans a winning margin statewide of 3,497.[57]

Lincoln was not surprised by the outcome, but he was bitterly disappointed. Another defeat had been added to his record despite his personal exertions. On the January day the legislature elected Douglas in the house of representatives chamber that Lincoln knew so well, he was sure his political career had ended.[58]

Laying the Groundwork for 1860

Once again, Lincoln plunged into his law practice. For a time in 1859 he declined invitations to speak. Soon, however, he rededicated himself to politics, looking toward the 1860 election. As the leading Republican in Illinois, he worked to keep his party's fragile coalition together and to block disruptive disputes. He gave speeches in 1859 in Iowa, Ohio, Indiana, Wisconsin, and Kansas that received a warm reception and gave plausibility to suggestions that he ought to be nominated for high office.[59]

While in Council Bluffs, Iowa, on August 12, 1859, Lincoln was introduced to Grenville Dodge, a twenty-eight-year-old railroad engineer who, he was told, knew more about railroads "than any two men in the country." In a long conversation, Dodge explained what he thought would be the best route for a Pacific railroad to the West out along the forty-second parallel. Later, President Lincoln, who in the 1850s had won two landmark railroad cases, became convinced by others as well that Dodge's was the best route west to meet a railroad coming east over the Rocky Mountains from California. Despite the war, he initiated construction of the railroad, the greatest building project of the nineteenth century.[60]

In December 1859 Lincoln made a move to gain broader recognition by preparing an autobiography for campaign purposes. It was published in Pennsylvania and widely copied in Republican newspapers. He also accepted an invitation to lecture at Henry Ward Beecher's Plymouth Church in Brooklyn in February 1860, an event that evolved into one of his most memorable speeches. To appear before a sophisticated eastern audience, he researched and prepared more than for any other speech in his life. By the time he arrived in the East, a Young Men's

Republican Union had assumed sponsorship of the event, and the lecture had been shifted from Brooklyn to the newly established college in Manhattan that became widely known as the Cooper Union.[61]

The Cooper Union speech, in its first half, was a scholarly and sophisticated discussion of constitutional history, refuting Douglas's "popular sovereignty" contention that the Founding Fathers believed the federal government had no power to exclude slavery from spreading into new territories against the will of settlers who wanted it. Lincoln demonstrated just the opposite: that the Founders did believe the federal government could exclude slavery and had acted on that belief in the Continental Congress, the Philadelphia constitutional convention, and the early Congresses, for example in the Northwest Ordinance's prohibition of slavery.[62]

The second half of the address began with a pugnacious challenge to the South to look at history, listen to reason, and not threaten to dissolve the Union if a Republican was elected and claim it was the fault of the North. Lincoln continued with a vigorous exhortation to Republicans to stand fast and persist in excluding slavery from the territories, confining it to the states where it already existed.[63]

The speech was enthusiastically applauded in the hall, widely reprinted in the newspapers the next day, hailed as exemplary by those who read it, and reprinted in pamphlet form and issued as a Republican tract.[64]

The 1860 Presidential Election

Events leading to the 1860 presidential election began with the Democratic National Convention that opened in Charleston, South Carolina, on April 23, Douglas's forty-seventh birthday. Delegates were in no mood to congratulate him. To the contrary, slave-state delegations were determined to prevent Douglas from getting the nomination and strongly opposed any platform that would suggest that popular opinion in a state or territory could prevent the expansion of slavery. The convention promptly engaged in a week of controversy over a platform. By May 1, eight southern-state delegations had withdrawn, with no accord reached. Balloting for a presidential candidate began that day, with Douglas receiving a majority of votes on the first ballot but failing to reach the required two-thirds. After fifty-six more inconclusive ballots, the Douglas leadership adjourned the convention, to reconvene in Baltimore six weeks later, on June 16.[65]

Douglas's forces controlled the Baltimore convention from the beginning. On June 22, following a week of credentials disputes, Virginia delegates withdrew from the convention, followed by five other slave-state delegations. The next morning, the Kentucky delegates withdrew, followed by delegates from Missouri, Arkansas, and Massachusetts. With the convention in a shambles, and fewer than 200 votes out of an original 303 remaining, the delegates began voting. Douglas received all but eighteen votes on the first ballot and a few more on the second, at which point he was declared to be the nominee. The same day, the seceding southern delegates held their own convention in a nearby hall. They adopted their preferred platform without dissent, nominated John C. Breckinridge for president, and adjourned.[66]

Tradition dictated that Lincoln could not openly campaign for the Republican nomination; the office was to seek the man. Others worked to carry out his planning. The Republican state convention met in Decatur May 9–10, a week before the national convention in Chicago. Richard J. Oglesby, a vigorous young Decatur Republican and future Illinois governor and U.S. senator, with John Hanks, a cousin of Lincoln's mother who had split fence rails with Lincoln in 1830, located two rails that Lincoln allegedly had split. During a lull in the convention, Oglesby introduced Hanks, who carried the rails into the hall decorated with flags and streamers and a banner that proclaimed Lincoln "The Rail Candidate" who had made three thousand rails in Macon County in 1830. An image as "the rail splitter" was born as Lincoln, to deafening applause, acknowledged that he had indeed built a cabin and split rails thirty years earlier near Decatur. The next day, the convention unanimously adopted a resolution stating that Lincoln was the choice of the Republican Party of Illinois for the presidency and that delegates to the national convention were to vote for him as a unit and use all honorable means to secure the nomination.[67]

The second-ever Republican National Convention was held in Chicago May 16–18, 1860. The site was the huge Great Wigwam, specially erected in April for the convention. The rambling two-story wooden shed at Lake and Market Streets had a large open space in front that could accommodate rallies or a large overflow crowd. Dubbed "the largest audience room in the United States," it drew major crowds and created a deluge of enthusiasm.[68]

Lincoln was tempted to attend the convention but was persuaded that he should remain home. The Illinois delegation focused on the presidency. They took no prominent part in the first two days' debates on members' credentials and the party's platform. On Friday, May 18, when voting on the nomination began, Lincoln awaited the results at the Lincoln and Herndon law office. Edward Baker, editor of the *Illinois State Journal*, brought him telegrams as the results came in. As had been predicted, the strongest candidate going into the convention was Senator William H. Seward of New York. With 233 needed to nominate, on the first ballot Seward received 173½ votes, Lincoln 102, with others widely scattered. The second ballot showed 184½ votes for Seward, with Lincoln increasing to 181. Seward retained most of his votes on the third ballot, but others flocked to Lincoln, giving him 231½ votes, 1½ votes short of a majority. Other delegations switched their votes, giving Lincoln 364 out of 466 votes, whereupon the Seward men moved to make the nomination unanimous.[69]

Between his nomination and the election, Lincoln, as was the custom, did not campaign. He remained in Springfield entertaining visitors, working daily in the state capitol governor's office Governor John Wood lent to him, dealing with a large amount of correspondence, posing for photographers, providing answers

Fig. 14. Great Republican Rally, August 8, 1860, Springfield. Courtesy of the Abraham Lincoln Presidential Library and Museum.

to questions about his life, and attempting to put to rest the rumors about his record that his detractors and political enemies circulated.[70]

Initially reluctant, Lincoln voted on Election Day after being persuaded to do so by William Herndon. In the evening, after first joining other Republicans in the capitol to hear returns relayed from the telegraph office, he went to the telegraph office and stayed into the early morning hours, when the news that he had carried New York made his election certain.[71]

The final national tally showed that Lincoln received 1,865,908 votes to 1,380,202 for Douglas, 848,019 for Breckenridge, and 590,901 for Whig senator John Bell of Tennessee, the candidate of the Constitutional Union Party. Although receiving just under 40 percent of the popular vote, the Lincoln ticket won a substantial majority of 180 votes in the Electoral College to 72 for Breckinridge, 39 for Bell, and 12 for Douglas. The Republican ticket won all but one of the free states and divided that one, New Jersey, with Douglas. In ten of the southern states, Lincoln and running mate Hannibal Hamlin did not receive a single recorded vote.[72]

Lincoln led the popular vote in Illinois and thereby won the state's 11 electoral votes. Once again, as in 1856 and 1858, the Republican margin of victory statewide was secured by the popular vote in the fourteen northern counties that composed the area added by the 1818 boundary extension. Lincoln carried those counties handily with 50,114 votes, doubling Douglas's vote of 24,555. Lincoln's winning margin of 25,659 in the north gave him victory by 11,956 votes statewide over Douglas, who won the rest of the state by 13,703.[73]

Republicans swept other key contests. Richard Yates won the governor's seat, and the rest of the Republican state ticket won for the third election in five years. In addition, for the first time, Republicans won majorities in both houses of the general assembly, assuring the reelection of Senator Lyman Trumbull.[74]

The 1860 election was Abraham Lincoln's first statewide victory and his first election success over Stephen Douglas. Among many other factors, including, of course, Lincoln's talents and shrewd cultivation of his stature after 1858, his 1860 election was a direct result of the growth of the north from the Illinois and Michigan Canal to the Wisconsin state line over the previous thirty years.

Lincoln maintained his base in Springfield for three months. Without advance fanfare, he traveled to Chicago two weeks after the election. There he met with vice president–elect Hannibal Hamlin, whom he had never met, Senator Trumbull, and other Republican leaders to discuss selection of the cabinet and other political matters. As word quickly spread of his presence in the city, he held a reception at the Tremont House hotel attended by thousands, was escorted to visits in friends' homes away from the city center, attended religious services joined by many prominent Chicagoans, and fit in additional time for meeting on political and personnel matters before he and Mary quietly left the city.[75]

Springfield was a busy place until Lincoln's departure for Washington on February 11, 1861. Lincoln opened his office daily to visitors and job seekers. He continued to use the governor's office in the state capitol until the inauguration of Governor Yates in mid-January. Because of the press of business in the new governor's office, Lincoln yielded the space in his last weeks in Springfield and worked thereafter in a small room above the store of his brother-in-law, Clark M. Smith, across the street from the capitol. There he drafted the remarks delivered at his departure from Springfield and worked on his first inaugural address.[76]

Lincoln issued no public statements and made no formal addresses. He recognized that his election was not final and he had no legal standing as a public official. Presidential electors chosen in the states in November would not meet to cast their ballots until December 5, and ballots would not be opened and counted in the House of Representatives until February 13, three weeks before the March 4 inauguration date.[77]

At the end of January, Lincoln journeyed out of Springfield to visit his seventy-three-year-old stepmother, Sarah Bush Lincoln, at her home in Coles County. In February, the Lincolns made farewell visits to friends in Springfield and, on February 6, held a reception in their home welcoming seven hundred guests. In the final days, Lincoln made a last visit to Herndon at their law office. As he was leaving after a long conversation, he looked at the law shingle of Lincoln and Herndon. In a low voice he said, "Let it hang there undisturbed. Give our clients to understand that the election of a President makes no change in the firm of Lincoln and Herndon. If I live I'm coming back some time, and then we'll go right on practicing law as if nothing had ever happened."[78]

Early morning on a cold and rainy February 11, 1861, a crowd of Springfield friends gathered at the Great Western Railroad depot to see Lincoln off on a special train chartered for the trip to Washington. From the steps to his private car, Lincoln paused to say a final farewell. "My friends," he said,

> No one not in my situation can appreciate my feeling of sadness at this parting. To this place, and the kindness of these people, I owe everything. Here

I have lived a quarter of a century, and have passed from a young to an old man. Here my children have been born, and one is buried. I now leave, not knowing when, or whether ever, I may return, with a task before me greater than that which rested upon Washington. Without the assistance of that Divine Being, who ever attended him, I cannot succeed. With that assistance, I cannot fail . . . let us confidently hope that all will yet be well. To his care commending you, as I hope in your prayers you will commend me, I bid you an affectionate farewell.[79]

Abraham Lincoln would not again set foot in Illinois.

CHAPTER 6

Civil War, a Partisan Convention, the Decisive Later 1860s

On January 10, 1861, the Illinois General Assembly met in joint session to elect a U.S. senator. Lyman Trumbull was elected on the first ballot to serve a second term. The vote was 54 to 36, an exact reversal of the vote of Douglas over Lincoln two years before. The process was a far cry from the ten-ballot contest in which Trumbull eventually prevailed in February 1855. Trumbull, reelected chairman of the Senate Judiciary Committee, would play a leading role in writing the U.S. constitutional amendments that would remake Illinois constitutional law.[1]

Richard Yates was inaugurated as governor on January 14, 1861. Yates was a close colleague and favorite of Lincoln. He had served three terms in the lower house of the state legislature before winning election as the Whig candidate to the U.S. House of Representatives in the old seventh district that had success-fully elected Whigs Hardin, Baker, and Lincoln to Congress. Ironically, in 1854 Yates, running as a Republican for the first time, and strongly opposed to the Kansas-Nebraska Bill, narrowly lost his bid for a third term in what had become a proslavery district. Lincoln, still a Whig, had campaigned for Yates in 1854 as he conducted his own successful campaign for election to the state house of representatives.[2]

Abraham Lincoln arrived in Washington surreptitiously in the early morn-ing of February 23. He had been spirited off his special train in Harrisburg,

Pennsylvania, by Pinkerton security officials and aides who feared an assassination attempt that was rumored to occur when the train arrived at its destination in Baltimore. Lincoln met that afternoon in his quarters at Willard's Hotel with the Illinois congressional delegation, including Stephen Douglas, whom Lincoln had particularly asked to see. This was their first encounter since their final debate in October. The meeting was described in the press as "peculiarly" or "particularly" pleasant; if there was a substantive discussion, it was not revealed.[3]

Stephen Douglas had finished the 1860 campaign in Mobile, Alabama, after an electioneering swing in the South. He was strained and fatigued. His voice was shattered. Seeking some rest, Douglas and his wife traveled from Mobile to New Orleans, then left to cruise slowly up the Mississippi River on a steamer, stopping on the way to inspect the Mississippi plantation now owned by his children.[4]

From his arrival in Washington on December 1, Douglas was caught up in efforts at a compromise to resolve the looming constitutional crisis, efforts that would continue until the morning of Lincoln's inauguration on March 4, 1861. The Union was coming apart. On December 20 a convention in South Carolina declared that the state had seceded and was no longer part of the United States. Florida, Mississippi, Alabama, Georgia, and Louisiana followed before the end of January 1861, and secession was underway in Texas. In February, emissaries of six Deep South states met in Montgomery, Alabama, and prepared a constitution for the new Confederate States of America.[5]

Douglas, with longtime Whig senator John J. Crittenden of Kentucky, worked to achieve a compromise that would maintain the Union. They, as well as committees in the House and Senate, proposed compromises that varied but generally involved constitutional amendments that would define slave and free territories in the West and prohibit federal or state legislative actions to eliminate slavery in states where it existed.[6]

Unsuccessful efforts at compromise continued through the last days of February, culminating in an all-night Senate session that began before a packed gallery of spectators on the evening before the presidential inauguration. In the early hours of March 4, galleries emptied, senators napped in their seats, and voting on compromise proposals began at five o'clock in the morning. All were quickly defeated. The Senate finally recessed at seven o'clock after a twelve-hour session.[7]

Douglas met with Lincoln several times after inauguration day. He encouraged Lincoln to be firm in pursuing the war effort and assured the president that he stood steadfastly with the Union. Douglas received no support from Lincoln for any of the various compromise proposals, which guaranteed the continued existence of slavery, included the possibility of geographical expansion of slavery, and prohibited legislative power from rolling it back.[8]

Restless Democrats in Illinois

Democrats in Illinois were not happy. They distrusted Lincoln; they believed the oft-made charges by Douglas and others that Lincoln was an abolitionist who favored equality between the races. When war broke out in April 1861, sentiments for joining the Confederacy existed in parts of southern Illinois as well as Indiana and Ohio.[9]

The Illinois legislature convened a special session in April, which Douglas determined to attend in order to rally support for the Union cause. He arrived in Springfield on April 25 and spoke to a joint session of the legislature that evening. A packed crowd of hundreds cheered when he entered the house of representatives chamber. Douglas gave a brief, eloquent speech. He urged Republicans not to make "partisan capital out of the misfortune of your country" and cautioned Democrats not to turn from "patriots into traitors to your native land."[10]

The audience greeted the address with enthusiastic applause; the press complimented it lavishly. Six days later, on May 1, Douglas returned to a hero's welcome in his adopted hometown of Chicago. Both Republicans and Democrats hailed him, and thousands jammed the Wigwam to hear him speak. Douglas roundly criticized the South. The secessionist movement, he said, was a long-planned conspiracy formed well before the last election that used slavery and Lincoln's election as an excuse for its cause. He called for resistance to secession. The man who had professed moral neutrality toward slavery when he campaigned for the Senate declared what he strongly believed about the Union. "There are only two sides to the question," he said. "Every man must be for the United States or against it. There can be no neutrals in this war, only patriots—or traitors."[11]

Douglas's two speeches did much to consolidate the state of Illinois and Democrats in the North for the Union. Nonetheless, there was still skepticism and suspicion about Lincoln among members of Douglas's party in Illinois, particularly as Republicans lavished praise on him. No one knew that, even as Douglas spoke, he was beset by the beginning of his final illness. The strains of the secession winter and the yearlong presidential struggle within his party and with Lincoln took their toll. Douglas abandoned plans to return to Washington in order to rest for a few days with Adele in his usual rooms at Tremont House. His condition, diagnosed as acute rheumatism and described as assuming "a typhoid character," steadily worsened. He died at nine in the morning on June 3, 1861, asking in his last words that his sons "obey the laws and support the Constitution of the United States." He was forty-eight years old.[12]

Boys in Blue Head South

Two days after surrender of Fort Sumter on April 13, Lincoln issued a proclamation calling for the states to provide seventy-five thousand volunteers, supposedly to serve only three months. Illinois's quota was six regiments. The supply immediately surpassed the demand as a great wave of patriotism swept across the state. Many counties, including in the south, exceeded their manpower quotas. The volunteers were mostly young, between ages eighteen and twenty-five, untrained but eager. Many were farm boys, expert in the use of firearms.[13]

On April 19, the secretary of war notified Governor Yates that the federal government was taking possession of the somnolent city of Cairo. At the farthest point south in the state—the junction of the Ohio and Mississippi Rivers—it was an important strategic point and served as a crucial supply post throughout the war. In the south and at other critical places throughout the state almost every building of adequate size became a temporary barracks or supply depot.[14]

The war also wrought a change in the administration of state government. The laws of Congress and regulations of the War Department vested in state governors the power to appoint and commission officers of the volunteer regiments. Governor Yates assumed a key place in the administration of the state's military effort and served with distinction in that role.[15]

Ulysses S. Grant is easily the best remembered of the many generals commissioned by Yates. Grant came to Springfield out of retirement in Galena heading a volunteer company, worked as a quartermaster for several months, was commissioned a general and commander at Cairo because of the intervention of his friend, Congressman Elihu B. Washburne of Galena, and led Union forces from that base to their first important victories.[16]

The first call for volunteers, made in mid-April, was filled and the six regiments sent to Cairo by the first part of May. Under a second call, on May 3, ten more regiments were mustered into service within sixty days. In May, June, and July, seventeen additional infantry and five cavalry regiments were authorized by the secretary of war and speedily raised. On July 22, the day after the unexpected reversal in the first battle of Bull Run, President Lincoln issued a call for an additional five hundred thousand troops. Governor Yates responded by tendering thirteen additional infantry regiments, three of cavalry, and an artillery battalion. By December 3, 1861, Illinois had in the field, in addition to the first six regiments, forty-seven thousand volunteers and another seventeen thousand in training camps.[17]

Official records show that Illinois sent 259,092 men into the war, which was 15.1 percent of its total population and beyond expectations. "Negro" units were organized beginning in 1863. More than eighteen hundred black men from Illinois enlisted directly into them; this at a time when the 1848 Illinois constitution, still in force, barred blacks and mulattos from serving in the militia. The total contribution from the state was greater because some volunteers, black and white, went across state lines to sign up.[18]

Casualty lists showed that 34,834 Illinois volunteers died in the war. Of these, 5,874 were killed in battle and 4,020 died of wounds. The far greater parts of the dead, totaling 22,786, were caused by disease, reflecting the comparatively primitive sanitary facilities of the era.[19]

The 1862 Convention: Civil War in the State Capitol

The Republican majorities at the November 1860 election overwhelmingly voted for the state to hold a constitutional convention that would not occur until well over a year later. In the later months of 1861 and into 1862, the convention created a distraction and sideshow to the swirling events and enthusiasm for the war.[20]

Efforts to revise the 1848 constitution had begun within a few years of its ratification. Population growth and technological development in the decade of the 1850s had transformed Illinois from a frontier state. The rapid population increases and industrial development created demands on government that the constitution did not allow it the flexibility to meet. The low salaries of state officers, fixed by the constitution, resulted in subterfuges and evasions to circumvent the limitations. The restrictions on general legislation resulted in floods of special corporate charters and private bills granting favors to individuals, such as divorces, name changes, changes of venue, or other interference in civil and criminal litigations that consumed the limited time of the legislative sessions and hampered or delayed adequate consideration of public matters.[21]

In 1856, only eight years after the constitution went into effect, the legislature sent to the voters a referendum to call a convention. In a period of political party realignment, it received little attention and failed to receive enough favorable votes. Those who did vote were divided sharply along sectional lines, with Republicans in the north and east favoring a convention and Democrats in the south opposing.[22]

In February 1859 the legislature again asked the voters to approve a convention at the regular election almost two years later, in November 1860. Newspapers urged approval. Republican majorities responded overwhelmingly at the election, with 179,668 favorable and 83,572 opposed. The legislature followed promptly with an enabling act that provided for one delegate to be elected from each of the seventy-five representative districts a year later, on November 5, 1861. The act specified that the convention would begin on January 7, 1862.[23]

In the year between the 1860 call for a convention and the November 1861 delegate elections, events in the nation changed the political climate. Eight months into the intense mobilization for the war, the delegate election drew only about half as many voters as the 1860 general election and produced a sharp reversal for the Republican Party. Democrats elected forty-five delegates, the Republicans twenty-one, while seven classified themselves as fusionists, and two others doubtful. Apathy or distraction by the war was one cause of the shift. In addition, in the delegate campaigns Republicans had urged nonpartisanship while Democrats were outspokenly partisan in favorable districts. Moreover, many of the asserted problems requiring a convention involved banks, corporations, railroads, and corporate special interests; Democrats and their farmer adherents were traditional enemies of those interests and seized the opportunity to act against them.[24]

The delegates, among them some of the state's most prominent men, promptly moved in controversial directions, asserting that they had supreme authority limited only by the federal constitution. On that theory, they began by refusing to take the oath to support the state constitution that had been specified by the enabling act, asserting that it was inconsistent to swear to support the constitution they were elected to change. Instead, they formulated their own oath. They proceeded to assume powers that normally are legislative, and to act in fiercely partisan ways. They voted to ratify an amendment to the United States Constitution that would deny the power of Congress to abolish or interfere with slavery in any state, despite the fact that Congress had sent the amendment specifically for ratification by state legislatures and not by conventions. They adopted a partisan reapportionment scheme for future legislatures in which smaller southern counties, traditionally Democratic, were given equal representation with larger Republican counties in the north, and small Republican counties were attached to large Democratic districts. They acted to redistrict the state for congressional elections into districts favoring Democrats and gave serious consideration to electing a U.S. senator to succeed Republican O. H. Browning. They provided that the governor and other executive officers, all Republicans, would be turned out in midterm for new elections a few months later in November 1862, while circuit and county clerks, mostly Democrats, served out their full four-year terms.[25]

Early in the convention, while substantive work was being carried on principally in committee meetings, Democrats used the convention to investigate the administration of the Republican governor, Richard Yates, and the conduct of the war by his office and the Republican legislature. On January 13 they asked the governor to furnish information about the amount and description of all the state's indebtedness. They also demanded detailed information about all persons he had appointed to office, all contractors and payments, copies of all other contracts, and copious additional correspondence and information. On January 18 they began an investigation into "whether the soldiers sent into the field from this state have been and continue to be provided for in all respects as the troops sent into the field from other states have been provided for, and if the committee find that the Illinois troops have not been thus provided for, they be instructed to inquire further, whether the neglect is justly chargeable to any person or persons holding office under this state." Every state officer was called on for extensive reports, and some were told how they should act in their specified roles.[26]

Governor Yates complied for a time with the convention's requests for a wide variety of information. On February 1, however, the convention went further, directing him and all state officers "to suspend all state action in relation to the claims of the Illinois Central Railroad against the state for transportation of troops or munitions of war, until further investigation of such claims can be had by this Convention, and until further instructions shall be received by said officers of state from this Convention."[27] Prompted by this instruction and the ongoing burden to his administration and the military by the convention's demands, Yates refused to answer such communications thereafter. On February 6 he wrote to the convention, curtly stating that he did not acknowledge the right of the convention to instruct him in the performance of his duties. Several troop commanders also refused to answer communications from the convention. Not surprisingly, relations between the convention and the governor became hostile.[28]

The assumption of powers by the convention, and the antagonism and rhetoric directed at the Republican administration, eventually led to charges of disloyalty. Yates expressed his belief to that effect in a letter to Senator Trumbull on February 14: "Secession is deeper and stronger here [in the convention] than you have any idea—its advocates are numerous and powerful, and respectable. . . . I believe the leaders [of the convention] would like to disarm the state government if they can. They would like civil war in Illinois."[29]

Rhetoric in the convention gave support to the Republicans' suspicions. On January 31 Democratic delegate Austin Brooks of Adams County, a frequent critic of the Republicans, offered a resolution that stated, "*Resolved*, that the committee on federal relations be instructed to inquire and report who, what class, faction, or party is responsible for the present rebellion against the federal government; and whether the odious and treasonable doctrine of secession has not received its vitality and nourishment from the abolition leaders of the north; and whether, in short, the abolitionists of the north and the rebels of the south are not equally alike and traitors." The resolution was tabled that day by vote of the convention; it nevertheless is revealing of the views of some delegates.[30]

When the public reacted adversely to these arrogations of authority, the convention sought to improve its image by voting to raise $500,000 for the care of sick and wounded soldiers. Their proposed method was to sell bonds, which the convention had no authority to do. State officials refused to issue the bonds, and nothing came of the plan.[31]

Once the convention finally moved to action on substantive issues in March, members immediately took up two that were important politically, especially to Democratic delegates. The first, on which they had campaigned ardently and on which many had gained election, imported into the constitution restrictions on black migration and settlement in the state. Even while debate over emancipation of slaves occupied Washington and the North, a convention majority in Illinois, controlled by Democratic delegates from the south of the state, voted overwhelmingly for three antiblack propositions. In early March the first complete article approved by the convention for inclusion in a new constitution incorporated provisions of the Black Laws of 1853. Adopted on March 5, the proposed article consisting of three sections stated,

Sec. 1. No Negro or Mulatto shall migrate or settle in this State,
Sec. 2. No Negro or Mulatto shall have the right of suffrage, or hold any office in this state,
Sec. 3. The General Assembly shall pass all laws necessary to carry into effect the provisions of this article.[32]

The delegates approved Section 1 by a substantial majority, 39 votes to 25. Demonstrating the widespread public sentiment against equality, Section 2 precluding blacks from voting or holding office carried by an overwhelming 57 to 7 vote.[33]

The delegate votes reflected the attitudes of the state's majority toward blacks. At a time when former slaves, liberated by Union armies and coming north as contraband of war, were pouring into Cairo, Quincy, Rock Island, and other river ports, southerners in particular, but others as well, were unwilling to let black migrants remain in the state, had no desire to encourage more to come, and certainly did not want them to vote or hold office.

The convention eventually voted to submit Sections 1 and 2 of this article for separate votes when the draft constitution was sent to the electorate for ratification. Reflecting public attitudes, the voters approved the section to prevent black immigration by a margin of 2.5 to 1. The section prohibiting blacks from voting or holding office was approved by a vote of almost 6 to 1. These sections did not go into effect, however, because the constitution itself was defeated.[34]

The bill of rights article adopted a week later included the same language as the 1848 constitution prohibiting slavery or involuntary servitude. Article II, Section 17 stated, "There shall be neither slavery nor involuntary servitude in this state, except as punishment for a crime, whereof the party shall have been duly convicted."

To the surprise of many, late in the convention the draft bill of rights reported out of committee for adoption by the convention included a section containing a definite denial of a state's right to withdraw or secede. The provision was included in the proposed constitution, Article II, Section 31.[35]

The convention on March 7 took up the recurrent partisan issue of whether citizenship would be required for voting. The proposed suffrage provision granted the vote to all white male citizens over age twenty-one who had lived in the state a year, and also to "white male inhabitants" who were resident in the state at the time of the constitution's adoption. In a departure from past Whig positions, many Republicans joined Democrats in voting for the provision allowing non-citizens to vote, which was approved 57 to 2 on March 11.[36]

The convention took constructive action on other matters to correct defects of the 1848 constitution; many of these provisions were included later in the 1870 constitution. Low salaries fixed by the 1848 constitution for state officials, judges, and legislators had long been a problem in the more modern economy. The proposed constitution provided that "compensation" for executive officers and "salaries" for judges would be specified by legislation, allowing the general assembly to alter them as necessary. For legislators, the constitution fixed a per diem rate of three dollars compensation during the first session under the new constitution, plus payment for mileage necessarily traveled to and from the capital. The legislature was authorized to prescribe its own compensation after the first session.[37]

Legislative domination and abuses had been widely criticized in calls for a convention. The 1862 convention proposed several reforms. Under the 1848 constitution, a majority vote of each house of the general assembly could override a governor's veto, a low threshold to override the governor that had permitted excesses by the legislature. The new constitution required a two-thirds vote of each house to override a veto.[38]

The legislature was instructed for the first time to pass laws providing "liberal" homestead exemptions for families of householders, exempting them from levy and forced sale for debts.[39]

The proposed constitution prohibited the state and towns or other units of local government from issuing credit and mortgaging themselves in aid of any individual, association, or corporation, nor could they subscribe to the stock or raise money in aid of any corporation or association. Many public bodies had succumbed to the lure of such promotions, particularly to finance construction of railroads, and wound up with unsustainable debt burdens.[40]

Despite provisions of the existing constitution intended to curb them, the number of private and special laws had mounted steadily. Often of a trivial character, special-interest bills consumed considerable time, could not be given careful attention, and, because the length of legislative sessions was limited, delayed or prevented a focus on public matters. Among the private laws, scores of new corporations had been created by the legislature in the 1850s, stimulating demands for change by the traditionally anticorporation farmers. The proposed constitution limited the passage of private bills, particularly those creating corporations.[41]

A stringent new measure to curb banks—also particularly irksome to farmers and other Democratic constituencies—was also enacted by the convention. The 1848 constitution allowed the creation of a system of state banks if approved by the voters. In 1851, over the governor's veto, the legislature had submitted and voters approved a law to create such a system. Many of these banks failed in the 1850s, and a great number of those remaining failed in 1861 when their bonds were depreciated significantly by the secession of southern states.[42]

Article XVII of the proposed constitution prohibited creation of banks or other banking enterprises and virtually nullified the charters of existing banks by prohibiting in great detail the circulation of checks or other writings as money. The banking provision, known to be controversial, was designated by the convention for separate submission to the voters for ratification.[43]

Although much public complaint had been voiced about railroad rates, and their regulation was a subject in delegate campaigns for election, the convention did not agree to suggestions concerning their control. The ability of railroads, and in particular the Illinois Central, to influence the legislature in their favor was shown, however, by the convention's adoption of a provision stating that "the general assembly shall have no power" to forgive, alter, or in any way fail to hold the Illinois Central Railroad Company to its obligations to pay monies to the state as set forth in its February 1851 charter.[44]

In a significant symbolic and substantive statement, the 1862 constitution elevated public education to constitutional importance. The previous two decades had seen a shift from education being a matter promoted by public-spirited

citizens in the 1840s to it being the subject of law, first in 1851, allowing townships to levy property taxes, and then in 1855, when state and local educational
tax laws were enacted. Conventions in 1853 organized teachers' associations and
campaigned for school betterment. In 1854 the legislature created the state superintendent of public instruction, culminating ten years of public effort to establish
an office at that level. Governor Joel Matteson appointed Ninian W. Edwards
to the position. Edwards's consultations and surveys of the state resulted in the
1855 law, establishing the principle that the state should use its taxing power to
support schools. By 1860 the superintendent's report showed that four out of
five persons of school age were enrolled in almost nine thousand districts that
maintained public schools.[45]

The proposed education article passed through committee and the convention with little controversy between March 10 and 15. Adopted as Article X by a
bipartisan vote of 49 to 5, it had four significant sections. Section 1 stated, "The
general assembly shall encourage, by all suitable means, the promotion of intel-
lectual, scientific, moral and agricultural improvement." Section 3 added, "The
general assembly shall provide for a uniform, thorough and efficient system of
free schools throughout the state."[46]

Section 2 of Article X took the important step of specifying that funds and
property that came to the state for educational purposes would forever be held
inviolate and the income applied to the support of the common schools. In earlier
decades, the funds derived from the public lands dedicated for public education's
support had not always been so scrupulously held. The fourth section of Article
X established the office of state superintendent of public instruction, to serve
for two-year terms, with the powers, duties, and compensation to be prescribed
by law.

The last matter to occupy the convention's attention was a precursor of home-
rule issues to come, as the state grew more urban and cities pressed for more
power to legislate their own affairs. Delegate John Wentworth, influential Dem-
ocrat-turned-Republican and former mayor of Chicago, gained the votes for a
provision that Chicago could hold a special election in April 1862, on a proposition that the city should elect its own officers. The convention approved the
provision on March 21, three days before the convention adjourned.[47]

Amid the convention's consideration of substantive proposals, on March
13 the chairman of the convention's committee on military affairs shared the

results of the partisan inquiry ordered two months earlier concerning whether troops in the field from Illinois were "provided for" as well as those from other states and, if not, who in the Yates administration was to blame. The chairman reported that regimental officers had been surveyed and that the committee, "with the highest pride and satisfaction," could say that, "with few exceptions, all unite in saying that the troops of Illinois have been, and continue to be, provided for in all respects as well as if not better than the troops sent into the field from other states."[48]

Opposition to the proposed constitution began even before the convention adjourned. Several delegates withdrew in its last days. When the final vote on the constitution's adoption was taken on March 22, only forty-six of the seventy-five members were present. The vote was 42 to 4 for adoption. The four negative votes were Republicans.[49]

Voters Reject the Proposed Constitution

The Republican press in the state, with some of the Democratic papers that favored the administration's war policy, began to assail the document as soon as the convention ended. Republicans attacked the convention for disloyalty because of its investigations into the conduct of the war and its refusal to take the oath specified by the legislature. Most dangerous to many was the apportionment of the legislature, which they saw as guaranteeing rule by a southern minority. They were angered also by the provisions that ended incumbent Republican state officers' terms midway while circuit and county clerks, mostly Democrats, were permitted to serve out their full four-year terms. Many disliked the proposed abolition of the use of grand juries for offenses other than felonies. Business interests objected to a provision that corporate charters could be amended or repealed by later legislatures.[50]

The proposed constitution was rejected, 141,103 to 125,052, at the special election on June 17, 1862. The proposed article on banking was defeated: 126,538 for and 130,339 against. Congressional apportionment was also defeated: 125,732 for, 132,339 against. As noted earlier, the restrictive clauses on blacks, approved overwhelmingly, did not go into effect because of the constitution's defeat.[51]

Generally, matters submitted for a separate vote are those that the convention fears might be disfavored by the voters and could cause the entire proposed constitution to fail. The irony in this case is that the electorate confirmed the delegates' attitudes toward blacks so overwhelmingly that, had the restrictions been included in the principal submission, they might have attracted enough favorable votes to adopt the constitution.

The constitution drafted by the 1862 convention contained constructive changes that would have been improvements on the 1848 constitution. Many were adopted later in the 1870 constitution. In 1862, however, rancorous partisanship in the midst of a divisive war, starting with the delegate elections and continuing in the convention debates, caused public disgust that led to the document's defeat and delay in dealing with some of the existing constitution's defects.[52]

The Tardy End Game for Black Bondage in Illinois

In January 1864, eleven years after the 1853 anti-immigration law was passed and a year after the effective date of the Emancipation Proclamation, the Illinois Supreme Court uttered its final word on the subject of slaveholding and the treatment of fugitive blacks in the state in a case testing the 1853 law. In *Nelson v. The People*, a mulatto, Nelson, was prosecuted criminally for being in the state more than ten days. He was convicted and fined by a justice of the peace and on appeal by a jury.

In an inglorious but perhaps fitting end to a long and checkered history of Illinois court action on slavery issues, the supreme court upheld all the provisions of the 1853 law against a constitutional challenge by Nelson's defense. The court ruled that the sale into short-term service did not make Nelson a slave in violation of the 1848 constitution's prohibition against slavery or involuntary servitude. The legislature, the court said, had the right to make entry into the state a violation of law, and "having declared it an offense, the punishment by involuntary servitude, provided by the act, is not unusual, but is one of the common means resorted to, to punish offenses."[53]

Thus, three years into the Civil War, with more than two hundred thousand Illinois soldiers—including tens of dozens of freed blacks—fighting for the Union, when the Senate Judiciary Committee chaired by Lyman Trumbull was preparing to pass the Thirteenth Amendment outlawing slavery and involuntary servitude, the Illinois Supreme Court upheld a statute originally enacted to keep black and mulatto people out of the state in order to conciliate Illinois's southern neighbors and to strike a blow at abolitionists.

The 1864 Elections

Chicago hosted its second presidential nominating convention in August 1864. Democrats chose the city this time, anticipating that it was their turn to go forth from Chicago to the White House. Emulating further the Republicans of 1860, they met in a temporary wood and canvas "Wigwam" located in Lake Park (today's Grant Park) on the eastern edge of the city center.[54]

The convention, originally called to meet on July 4, was postponed to August 29. The conflict between the "peace at any price" element of the party, led by former congressman C. L. Vallandigham of Ohio, and the conservatives, among whom General George B. McClellan was the front-runner for the nomination, created doubt whether the delegates could choose a candidate and write a platform that would assure a united party.[55]

With some difficulty, over a two-day period, the party finally arrived at a peace platform. Shortly thereafter, however, after demonstrations and fights on the floor caused an overnight recess, the convention overwhelmingly endorsed a war candidate for president, nominating McClellan on the first ballot.[56]

The Illinois Democratic state convention met in Springfield on September 6. The national platform adopted at Chicago was reaffirmed. The convention nominated James C. Robinson for governor and the candidates for the other six offices up for election. Robinson and James Allen, the nominee for congressman at large, both were members of Congress who, as all Democratic members from Illinois, had voted in favor of all propositions for compromise and peace.[57]

Earlier in the summer, on May 25, Illinois Republicans met in Springfield under the new name of the Union Party. They nominated for governor Richard Oglesby, who had been severely wounded serving as a general in the war, and a slate of candidates for other state offices. The body endorsed President Lincoln for reelection and commended "the upright and faithful manner in which he has administered the government in times of peril and perplexity unknown in the history of our Nation."[58] The Union Party national convention renominated Lincoln in Baltimore on June 7, with opposition only from the Missouri delegation, which voted for General Ulysses S. Grant. Andrew Johnson, a Democrat, was nominated for vice president.[59]

In the general election in November, Lincoln carried all but three of the twenty-five states that voted, losing only New Jersey, Delaware, and Kentucky. Lincoln won 212 electoral votes to McClellan's 21 and received 55 percent of the popular vote in those states, with more than 2.2 million votes to McClellan's 1.8 million, 44.9 percent of the total. In addition, twelve states collected the votes of their soldiers; the military vote supported Lincoln over McClellan by an overwhelming 119,754 to 34,291.[60]

Lincoln's coattails were long in his home state. The Republican or Union ticket carried the state with a majority of just under 31,000 votes. Union candidates won eleven of the fourteen congressional races, an increase of five seats. Richard Oglesby was elected governor, gaining 54.5 percent of the vote.[61]

Nationally, the 1864 election also presaged the status of the Democratic Party. Reduced to a minority in nearly every loyal state, it was unable to win the presidency until 1884, even when reinforced by the electoral votes of all the seceding states.

The Crucible of the Civil War

Chicago burgeoned during the Civil War. The city grew from 110,000 population in 1860 to 190,000 in 1865 and multiplied again to just under 300,000 by 1870. The expansion occurred in many ways. Chicago's premier status in the grain markets

Fig. 15. War Eagle steamboat, launched 1854. Drafted into service by the Union army during the Civil War. Courtesy of the Abraham Lincoln Presidential Library and Museum.

continued to ensure the city's prosperity. The giant grain elevators along the Chicago River dominated the skyline. Chicago became the financial heart of the Midwest. The Chicago Board of Trade and the development of futures markets in grain became renowned in the financial world, establishing a reputation that continued through the twentieth century.[62]

The economic boom of the Civil War also nurtured foundries and other industrial cornerstones of nineteenth- and twentieth-century Chicago. George Pullman developed the Pullman sleeping car during the war. Heavier, a foot wider, and several feet taller than other cars, it required railroads to change their rights of way, which they were forced to do as the car became popular. Pullman enterprisingly secured a place for his sleeping car in the 1865 Lincoln funeral train that made its solemn return across the country to Springfield. Railroads were forced to make the necessary alterations to their passageways to accommodate the car. Within two years after the war's end, Pullman created an industrial empire that lasted until 1983. Development of heavy industry in the state was also fostered by the location in Rock Island of a badly needed federal armory.[63]

The Civil War favored Chicago by directing the flow of vital commodities away from its two major urban rivals. The older and larger city of St. Louis watched as trade shifted to Chicago when the war forced closure of the Mississippi and Ohio Rivers. During the 1850s, Chicago emerged as an important market for meatpacking. Although its slaughterhouses led the nation in 1860 in beef cattle killed, other western towns vied for shares of the market, and Cincinnati was overwhelmingly the pork-packing capital. Cincinnati lost its dominant position during the war when it was partly cut off from its supply of southern hogs and lacked the rail network to expand its sources elsewhere. In April 1862 the *Chicago Tribune* claimed that Chicago had taken the title of "Porkopolis." By 1864 Chicago slaughtered three times the number of hogs as did Cincinnati.[64]

Chicago's meatpacking industry in 1864 underwent an important change in the way it conducted business. Operators from Michigan, Indiana, and Wisconsin had moved to Chicago to join the thirty packers already there. By 1864, fifty-eight packers, including several large-scale businesses, were located in various places throughout the city. The industry's growth outstripped the facilities to handle the influx of animals. Drovers herded livestock into the city. Even more arrived by rail. Huge numbers of swine and cattle were herded through the public streets on their way to slaughterhouses. Accidents and property damage were common.

The need for a central corral and slaughterhouse became apparent. Eventually, packers proposed and the railroads helped to provide a central stockyard. The newly formed Union Stock Yard and Transit Company held a competition for the best engineering plan for the novel enterprise. Oscar Chanute, a young civil engineer and later an aviation pioneer, laid out an efficient 345-acre commercial center. Streets sewers, drains, railroad terminals, loading and unloading docks, slaughterhouses, and a pure water system created an orderly, high-capacity yard. When the Union stockyard opened on Christmas Day 1865, it was the biggest in the world. It remained a leading enterprise until the middle of the twentieth century.[65]

Outfitting the military caused its own boom. Chicago cloth and clothing merchants responded to the sudden and overwhelming demand by starting their own manufacturing operations. The introduction of the sewing machine fostered new ready-made clothing businesses that multiplied in volume in each of the early years. Soldiers required a vast amount of leather goods, with cavalry needing even more. For wholesale shoemakers and saddlers, 1861 was a boom year, followed by several more, with round-the-clock manufacturing operations employing twenty-five hundred workers and establishing new businesses that had not before competed with New England producers.[66]

Introduction of a stable banking system greatly spurred industrialization in Chicago and the state. The Lincoln administration in 1862 authorized the creation of national banks, which issued "greenbacks," national banknotes backed by Washington. The First National Bank of Chicago was founded in 1863, initiating a new era of financial confidence. By war's end the city boasted thirteen national banks, more than any other city in America.[67]

The war effort was not sustained only by commerce, manufacturing, and technology. The Sanitary Commission, a volunteer civilian relief enterprise organized and led by philanthropic women and religious leaders, aided, nursed, and comforted wounded at the fronts and families at home and brought to battlefronts. The commission held fairs at home to garner donations of money, goods, and volunteer time, created and inspected hospitals and hospital ships, and in many creative ways aided those in and out of the military.[68]

The industrial revolution that swept across the cities and prairies was accompanied, in the latter half of the decade, by reactions against the railroads and their high rates. Having lost the competition of the Mississippi River water carriers and encouraged by general economic prosperity, railroads steadily increased rates to levels that seemed extortionate to many. Rumors spread of combinations and partnerships between the railroads and warehouse and elevator operators to raise and fix rates. Indignation and efforts to control rates became rampant. As early as 1864, rate regulation was proposed by farmers' organizations. Public officials in Winnebago County and elsewhere in the north proposed rate legislation in 1865 and 1866. In 1867 antimonopoly forces met in Springfield and formed a league demanding rate restrictions and other reforms. The general assembly passed a maximum rate measure in 1869, but Governor John Palmer vetoed the proposal. Challenges to the constitutionality of such measures resulted in deferring the matter to the 1869 constitutional convention, where it became a major and hard-fought issue.[69]

Labor's growing class consciousness and increasing sense of power accompanied the state's industrial revolution. Mass meetings of workers, the formation of trade unions, strikes by labor groups, agitation for an eight-hour law, and efforts to obtain workplace safety regulation all were attempted by employees and resisted by employers. Labor leaders turned to independent political action. At the close of the decade, they looked to the constitutional convention and future political activity to gain their end.[70]

The Dramatic Last Half Decade of the 1860s

In the final five years of the 1860s, events in Illinois and on the national stage changed forever the state of the law in the state and throughout the United States. On January 31, 1865, the U.S. House of Representatives acted, as the Senate had earlier, and passed the Thirteenth Amendment to the U.S. Constitution prohibiting slavery or involuntary servitude in the United States or any place subject to its jurisdiction. The next day, February 1, Illinois became the first state to ratify the amendment. Governor Oglesby, an ardent supporter of President Lincoln and an opponent of slavery, had arranged for Senator Trumbull to notify him as soon as the amendment was adopted. Trumbull, as chairman of the Senate Judiciary Committee, had drafted the amendment and guided it to passage in the Senate on April 8, 1864. After receiving Trumbull's telegram in the morning on February 1, Oglesby urged immediate ratification by the general assembly, which was standing by for that purpose. Later that day, a joint resolution of the two houses voted approval of the amendment, allowing Oglesby promptly to cable the news to Trumbull to pass on to President Lincoln in Washington. Thereafter, Lincoln proudly pointed out to others that Illinois had been the first to ratify

Fig. 16. Old State Capitol, draped
for Lincoln funeral, May 3–4,
1865. Chicago History Museum,
ICHi-029348.

the hard-fought amendment. Also on February 1, in a symbolic act, President
Lincoln added his signature.[71]

Finally, a week later, on February 7, 1865, the Republican majority in the Illinois
legislature repealed the anti-immigration act of 1853. It also repealed all the restrictive and discriminatory Black Laws that had been in effect in the state and
territory for more than fifty-six years.[72]

Abraham Lincoln's Return to Illinois

Abraham Lincoln returned to Chicago on May 1, 1865. His funeral train arrived
at a special reception arena that had been constructed in the city's lakefront park
where the Democratic convention had been held little more than eight months
before. The president's coffin was transferred from the train to a specially built

dais featuring a large structure of three gothic arches draped in black. In a brief ceremony, thirty-six high school girls, in white gowns and black headbands, each placed a wreath representing one of the states around the casket. The casket was then taken from the park to the courthouse. Tens of thousands of people joined the procession or lined the route, viewing from sidewalks, windows, and rooftops. The president's body in an open casket lay in state in the courthouse rotunda, while a stream of Chicagoans filed by to pay their last respects. Newspapers estimated that 125,000 people viewed the remains through the day and night of May 1 and into the next afternoon. The evening of May 2, the casket was escorted to the railroad depot for the final leg of the trip to Springfield.[73]

The funeral train made its way through the night. As it crossed the dark prairie, blazing tar barrels signaled the attendance of mourning farmers and townsfolk. The train arrived in Springfield the morning of May 3, at the railroad depot a few blocks across town from the depot where Lincoln had bid farewell to his neighbors four years earlier. For twenty-four hours, mourners streamed by the casket as it rested in the state capitol's house of representatives chamber. The funeral procession the morning of May 4 detoured a few blocks to pause before the only home Lincoln had ever owned, at Eighth and Jackson Streets, before it proceeded to Oak Ridge Cemetery at the city's edge. There the president's remains were placed in a receiving vault and later laid to rest in an imposing tomb.[74]

The Fourteenth and Fifteenth Amendments

The steady progress of the 1860s toward a transformed nation and state continued despite President Lincoln's murder on April 14, 1865. In the next four years, Illinois approved promptly the Fourteenth and Fifteenth Amendments to the U.S. Constitution. Congress proposed the Fourteenth Amendment to the states on June 13, 1866. On January 15, 1867, Illinois became the tenth state to ratify the amendment, which went into effect on July 9, 1868, after ratification by three-fourths of the states. On February 26, 1869, Congress proposed the Fifteenth Amendment to the states. A week later, on March 5, Illinois became the third state to ratify it. The amendment went into force on February 3, 1870.[75]

The Civil War amendments can legitimately be called Lincoln's legacy. They changed the law in fundamental ways for hundreds of millions of people subject to the jurisdiction of the United States and tens of millions in Illinois. The amendments did not grant to women the right to equal participation in political life or to enjoy equality in other respects, however. That process took another half-century to begin to be achieved.

Nor did the six years of momentous change in the United States and Illinois constitutions and laws quickly transform the attitudes of whites toward blacks in Illinois. In time, people in the center and north of the state became accustomed to the presence of blacks in public schools and in public life. The entitlement of blacks to citizenship and to vote or hold office ceased to be discussed. But in the southern regions of the state, attitudes changed much more slowly. Opposition to immigration of blacks and the full benefits of citizenship was a cardinal principle of the Illinois Democratic Party for years. Among many in the state, the concept of equality was slow to be accepted. For most of a century after the Civil War, in the geographical south as well as in other parts of the state, Illinois continued to have the attitudes toward African Americans of a southern state.[76]

With the beginning of the Fourth Illinois Constitutional Convention on December 13, 1869, the end of the decade saw a step taken toward a changed state. The accomplishments in that convention were in large measure facilitated by changes wrought in the state by the Lincoln legacy amendments.

CHAPTER 7

The Constitution of 1870

Progressive Foundation for a Century

Agitation for changes in the 1848 constitution resumed as soon as the Civil War ended. The inadequacies and defects of that constitution, which had motivated the legislature and voters of the state to call for a convention in 1860, not only had continued but also had become even more serious. The extremely low compensation levels for state officeholders and judges were circumvented by "expense money" for the governor or extra compensation for other officers and judges in payment for trivial services said to have been rendered to the state. Such violations of the letter of the constitution were dangerous precedents that raised concerns of moral laxity. The most serious defect was the increasing proliferation of special-interest laws and private bills, culminating in the Twenty-Sixth General Assembly in 1869 enacting seventeen hundred private laws on almost every conceivable subject, dwarfing the number of public laws passed in the same sessions and stimulating suspicions of bribery and corruption.[1]

Increases in railroad and warehouse rates and corporate combinations in the years of the war and after had precipitated cries for constitutional action, as had movements urging state support for education and other reforms. The restrictions on blacks in the 1848 constitution were glaringly exposed by the military service of blacks during the Civil War and the Civil War amendments to the U.S. Constitution. The war and its aftermath also revealed the sharp differences of

attitudes between the north and south of the state that threatened to split political and civil society and impede public policy making.

Renewed Efforts to Revise the 1848 Constitution

In November 1866 the *Chicago Tribune* staked out a position in favor of "A New
Constitution." The paper asserted, "There is an universal demand by the people
of all parties in the State of Illinois for a thorough revision and amendment to
the Constitution of the State. . . . [T]he inefficiency of our present constitution
is generally admitted." Further,

> {"?}Every department of the Government, Executive, Legislative, and Judi-
> cial, was surrounded by constitutional restrictions which utterly impair their
> efficiency and destroy their usefulness. The result has been that for fifteen
> years there has been a persistent effort to evade the Constitution, and this
> effort has been approved by the people because of the necessity of the case.[2]

Six weeks later, on January 1, 1867, the *Tribune* started the new year with a long
essay pushing for a constitutional convention, concluding, "There is no just or
legal objection to having a Constitutional Convention without delay."[3]

Governor Richard Oglesby took the first step toward the convening of Illinois's
fourth constitutional convention in his message to the legislature on January
7, 1867. After commending the present constitution as containing "many wise
and salutary provisions," he asserted that "what was then prudent, and suitably
adapted to the condition of our people, does not now accord with the requirements of our growth and prosperity."[4]

The governor outlined several defects of the 1848 constitution, including "the
odious discrimination against personal liberty, which ought to be expunged," a
reference to the provisions barring black settlement in Illinois. He asked that the
general assembly call for a referendum at the next general election to hold a constitutional convention. The legislature did just that, adopting a joint resolution
to put to the voters in November 1868 the question of holding a convention.[5]

The call for a convention received immediate and strong newspaper support.
The public displayed scant interest, however. At the general election on November 3, 1868, the proposition was approved by a majority of only 726 votes. The
general assembly in February 1869 enacted legislation calling for the election of

eighty-five delegates at the general election later that year, in November 1869, with the convention to meet in Springfield the next month.[6]

The enabling legislation imposed no condition specifying whether the candidates could run as partisans of a political party. Citizen groups made efforts to avoid partisanship by organizing into a bipartisan "People's Party." Former state supreme court judge J. D. Caton and others called for election without partisan considerations. Fiercely partisan newspapers rejected this conciliatory stance, however, and called for the election of men who would write a Republican or Democratic constitution, the latter to include a specific prohibition on blacks' voting, contrary to the Fifteenth Amendment that the Illinois General Assembly had ratified in March and which was rapidly approaching ratification by the necessary number of states.[7]

The election of delegates on November 2, 1869, resulted in an almost equal number from nominally Republican and Democratic districts. The forty-four delegates elected from Republican districts, however, included the entire nonpartisan People's Party ticket elected in Cook County. This fifteen-person delegation held the balance of power and helped create a tone in which few delegates were inclined to promote political squabbles. Reflecting the sharp divisions in the state following the Civil War and exposing a condition that needed to be recognized by the convention, all except two of the delegates from southern Illinois and the Military Tract in west-central Illinois were Democratic. All but four of the Republican delegates came from northern and east-central counties.[8]

The delegates' occupations reflected two decades of change. Lawyers for the first time were an overwhelming majority. While farmers had outnumbered lawyers in the 1847 convention, in 1869 the fifty-three lawyers outnumbered the fourteen farmers almost 4 to 1. The lawyers as a group were also younger than other occupations; twenty-five of the thirty delegates under age forty were lawyers. The others were merchants, bankers, traders, physicians, and one editor, the redoubtable Joseph Medill of the *Chicago Tribune*.

Prominent historian John Moses in 1892 described the members as "unquestionably the ablest deliberative body that ever convened in the State."[9] Many were men of statewide prominence. The best known was Orville H. Browning of Quincy, former Whig and close friend of Lincoln, appointed Republican U.S. senator by Governor Yates to fill the Douglas vacancy from 1861 to 1863, then secretary of the interior and attorney general under Andrew Johnson until 1866.

By the time of the convention, his strong conservative views and opposition to black suffrage had caused him to reject any party affiliation, although he was elected to the convention as a Democrat. Others of note, in addition to Medill, a Republican Party founder and Chicago delegate, included Reuben Benjamin of Bloomington, an authority on constitutional law who played a leading role in revising the bill of rights and convincing his colleagues to impose restrictions on railroad corporations, and Elliott Anthony, a Chicago lawyer, a member of the 1862 convention who was also active in the 1869 convention proceedings and who later wrote a constitutional history of Illinois.[10]

The Convention Organizes

The convention began on December 13, 1869, in the representatives' chamber of the capitol. The patina of civility and nonpartisanship that overlay the delegates' political animosities was tested immediately in the fight over a temporary president. Republicans from northern Illinois outside Cook County wanted to organize the convention on a partisan basis. They promptly nominated William Cary of Galena. Democrats, who could not dominate a partisan convention on their own, nominated John Dement with the support of Cook County Republicans. Dement, a Democrat, was an "old pioneer" who had held office over the years as sheriff, representative, soldier in the Black Hawk War, state treasurer, receiver of public money in the U.S. Land Office, and delegate to the 1847 and 1862 constitutional conventions; in the latter he had been elected temporary president. A voice vote was taken, but did not settle the matter. Partisans of both declared that their man had been elected. With no one qualified to rule on the matter, Cary and Dement both mounted the rostrum, claimed the chair, and, amid considerable good-natured banter between them and from their backers, for more than an hour each refused to give up the chair and proceeded to rule on motions. Finally, appeals to nonpartisanship won out, and Dement was elected temporary president by a vote of 44 to 32.[11]

A long wrangle over the wording of the oath that the delegates should take consumed three and one-half days of the convention's time. This same question had provoked convention delegates in 1862. Some objected to taking an oath to support the constitution of Illinois, as prescribed by the enabling legislation, when the delegates had been elected to change that constitution. While the issue seemed trivial to many, and it could be argued that the existing constitution itself provided for the process of change, including a new convention, the entire question of the function of a convention was argued at length. In the end, members agreed that not taking the oath would risk public disapproval of the convention's work; thus, those who wished to do so voluntarily would take the oath. Many but not all of the delegates did so.[12]

The maneuvering over organization continued with the election of permanent officers. Democrats joined with the independent group from Cook County to elect as president Charles Hitchcock of Chicago, an attorney who had never held another office of importance. Republicans in opposition supported Joseph Medill for the position but lost by a narrow 45–40 vote. The Cook County independents' plan was to alternate all the officers between the two parties, and the independent/Democrat coalition prevailed, carrying most of the votes by narrow margins.[13]

When the convention undertook substantive work, some articles of the 1848 constitution remained essentially unchanged. These included the preamble, the boundaries article, and, in most respects, the bill of rights. Under Reuben Benjamin's leadership, archaic language was changed and the bill of rights was streamlined, shortened, and clarified in some sections. The prohibition of slavery and involuntary servitude of Section 16 and the disqualification from office, oath, and penalties for persons involved in duels of Sections 25 and 26 of the 1848 bill of rights were dropped.[14]

A substantial part of the convention's work consisted of curing faults of the 1848 constitution, particularly in the articles dealing with the structure and powers of the three branches of government.

Reallocating Government Structures

THE EXECUTIVE

The power of the executive branch was expanded. The governor was to be elected for a four-year term; the restriction against serving consecutive terms was eliminated. The governor's veto power was strengthened: a two-thirds majority of each house of the general assembly was required to override. The governor was given a new power to remove any state official that he could appoint. As before, a lieutenant governor, secretary of state, auditor of public accounts, and state treasurer were to be elected. The office of attorney general and the new office of state superintendent of public instruction also were made elective. All the elective officers except the treasurer and superintendent of public instruction were to stand for election to four-year terms at the same time as the governor. The education superintendent was also to be elected for a four-year term, but at the off-year general election two years after the others. The treasurer was to serve a two-year term, with election at the general election of other officers. Instead of penurious salaries fixed inflexibly, as in 1848, the convention left the question of compensation of public officials to future legislatures.[15]

THE LEGISLATIVE

The legislative article was changed substantially. After extended debate, the convention lowered age requirements for representatives and senators to twenty-one and twenty-five years, respectively; these were the age requirements in the 1818 constitution before being raised to twenty-five and thirty years in the 1847 convention. Citizenship, five years' residence in the state, and two years' residence in the legislative district also were required. The number of members in each house was increased substantially: senators from twenty-five to fifty-one and representatives from eighty-five to 153, with three elected from each senate district. The restriction on salaries and the time limit on the duration of sessions were removed. Although no limit was imposed explicitly on the length of legislative sessions, the practical time limit for a session was June 30 because of the provision that all legislation would take effect on the first day in July after its passage unless two-thirds of both houses specified there was an "emergency" and set a different effective date. Safeguards were also imposed against the hurried passage of bills by the requirement that bills be read on three different days in each house, with no exceptions.[16]

The matter of special legislation and private bills that had become a pernicious legislative practice and a primary motivation for calling a convention was dealt with by sharply curbing the legislature's powers. The new constitution prohibited special laws if a general law could be made applicable. For emphasis, it barred legislation on twenty-three specific subjects that made up most of the private acts enacted by previous legislatures. These included granting divorces, changing names of persons or places, vacating roads, streets, or alleys, regulating county and township affairs, providing for changes of venue in civil or criminal cases, incorporating cities, towns, or villages, regulating the rate of interest on money, remitting fines, penalties, or forfeitures, and many other matters. Of considerable importance, also forbidden was "granting to any corporation, association, or individual any special or exclusive privilege, immunity, or franchise whatever" or releasing or extinguishing, "in whole or in part, the indebtedness, liability, or obligation of any corporation or individual to this State or to any municipal corporation therein." In the way of specific prohibitions, the constitution also forbad lotteries and extending the term of any public officer after his election or appointment.[17]

Treating prohibited subjects in this way was not original with this convention. Nearly all these subjects had been prohibited specifically in the 1851 constitution of Indiana and revised constitutions of Maryland in 1864, Missouri in 1865, and Florida in 1868. The Illinois constitution departed from these, however, when it mandated or specifically suggested the passage of laws on other subjects. In the way of mandates, it provided that "the General Assembly *shall pass* liberal Homestead and Exemption laws" and "*It shall be the duty* of the General Assembly to pass such laws as may be necessary for the safety and protection of miners" (emphasis added). The legislature also was directed to pass laws regulating railroads as public highways and to establish reasonable maximum rates and charges for railroads and warehouses.[18]

Several provisions read as permissions to the legislature to pass laws on specific subjects. For example, Section 30 on connecting private roads and Section 31 concerning drains and ditches, both added to the constitution to overturn the holdings of two supreme court cases in 1866 that the legislature did not have the enumerated powers.[19]

Remembering well the internal-improvements fiascos of 1837, the delegates fixed a debt limitation of not more than 5 percent of the valuation of the state's taxable property and required referendum approval at a general election for total borrowing in excess of $250,000. By 1870 the increasing expense for construction of a new capitol building in Springfield had become a highly controversial matter, also described as a fiasco by some. A limitation of $3.5 million was placed on expenditures for the statehouse, unless additional funds were approved by referendum.[20]

Leading lawyers in the convention opposed adoption of these detailed sections, in particular the mandatory and precatory provisions, arguing that the measures were properly for consideration by the legislature and that incorporation of such matters in a constitution was ill advised. Their inclusion, however, was demanded by those, always present in such a body, who wanted to control the future in accord with their ideas, reinforced by the agricultural community and numerous signed petitions.[21]

THE JUDICIARY

All parts of the state wanted more and better-paid judges. The needs in Chicago, however, had become acute. The city's rapidly growing population had resulted in increased legal business of all types. The civil courts were congested with disputes over land sales, grain elevators, and Board of Trade transactions. The plethora of probate matters that could be taken on by a special court increased their burden. Criminal courts were necessary to handle the increase in robbery, thefts, and murder.[22]

Chicago's requirements for many more courts in comparison to the rest of the state led to a push for a separate, special court system for Cook County. Many downstate members strongly opposed the Cook County provisions. Some did so because of a sincere belief that there should be no constitutional distinctions between localities. Many others greatly resented the claimed need for special treatment for Cook County, resulting in antagonistic and acrimonious debates. John Tincher of Vermilion County (Danville), who spoke frequently and often sarcastically in the convention, used ridicule. Regarding the claimed greater amount of litigation, he said, "Chicago, where they are all commercial gentlemen . . . where they do a commercial business, there must necessarily grow up a great deal of litigation. . . . When they have a trade they begin to study how they can get out of it by having a small lawsuit, and if they can they will go into a lawsuit."[23]

The convention adopted a judicial article that included many more courts, provisions for more local judges and state's attorneys, all to be elected, better pay of judges, and special provisions for Cook County. With little discussion, the convention increased the number of supreme court judges from three to seven, to be elected from seven districts for nine-year terms. Circuit courts were established to have original jurisdiction of cases in law and equity. For the first time, an Illinois constitution provided for appellate courts between the circuit court and supreme court levels. They could be created by the legislature to hear appeals from the lower courts; their judges were to be circuit court judges designated to hear cases in the appellate courts. Each county was also to have a county court with one judge, and probate courts if established by the general assembly. All judges were to be elected by the people for six-year terms, with their compensation established by legislation.[24]

A state's attorney was to be elected in each county to serve a four-year term. Justices of the peace, police constables, and magistrates were to be elected from districts as provided by law.[25]

Cook County was to be one judicial circuit, with five judges at the outset and more as might be provided by law. The Superior Court of Chicago was to continue as the Superior Court of Cook County. The general assembly was authorized to provide for an additional judge of either court for every increase of fifty thousand people over a population of four hundred thousand. All judges were to be elected for six-year terms. This structure, which in effect meant that downstate judges could serve as many as one hundred thousand people, while in Chicago judges would serve fifty thousand or fewer, drew particular fire and antagonism from downstate delegates. Tincher again spoke out: "The people of rural districts are a quiet, honest, and industrious people, and do not require a judge for every forty thousand, as they do in those cities where there are people who propose to live off each other, by just peeling each other every time they pass upon the street."[26]

Despite the opposition's ridicule, it was apparent that Chicago in fact had greater needs for more courts, and the delegates either had to provide them or stand by a principle of equality by establishing more courts for downstate areas, which they made no claim of needing. In the end, the judicial article included the special provisions for Cook County, and the matter was not considered controversial enough to require a separate submission to the voters.[27]

African Americans' Civil Rights

Three substantive matters raised in the convention related specifically to African Americans' rights and treatment. Racial animosity and opposition to black empowerment and social and political equality were strong among many Democratic delegates, particularly from southern Illinois. They fiercely opposed the effects of the Fourteenth and Fifteenth Amendments to the U.S. Constitution. Although the Illinois General Assembly in 1867 and earlier in 1869 had ratified both amendments with overwhelmingly favorable votes, some delegates derided the amendments as intrusion by the federal government and "centralization of power which by force, and physical force alone," imposed on the state.[28]

Two of the three matters, the right to vote and militia segregation and command authority, were debated vehemently and at length. The third, proposing school segregation, was tabled without substantive discussion. Significantly, in the end, the 1870 constitution became Illinois's first to contain no provisions referring to blacks or mulattoes.

School Segregation

James Washburn, Democratic delegate from far south Jackson and Williamson Counties, introduced a resolution on February 16 "that white children should not be permitted to attend the public schools for the colored people of the State, and that colored children should not be permitted to attend the schools for the white people of the State, and that the colored children of the State shall be educated in schools separate from the white children of the state." Moreover, Washburn proposed that no part of "taxes paid by the white people of the State should be appropriated to the education of the colored people of the State" and, vice versa, no taxes paid by colored people should be used for the education of white people.[29]

Speaking in support of this proposal, Washburn referred to "the prospective settlement of the negro suffrage question" (by the Fifteenth Amendment) and warned that "the question of mixed schools has greatly agitated the public mind in some portions of the State, and the question is growing every day more important." Since his propositions were "so plain" and "so manifestly just and equal that they need no argument in support," he urged prompt adoption of his resolutions to settle and quiet "all future agitation of the public mind on this vexed question."[30]

The convention tabled Washburn's resolution the next day by a vote of 42 to 27, with 16 not voting. The convention took no further action relating to school segregation.[31]

The Militia

The military affairs committee report provided the first occasion for the convention to debate consequences of the Fourteenth or Fifteenth Amendments. On January 26 Daniel Cameron, Republican of Cook County, presented the report signed by a six-person majority of the committee. Section 1 stated, "The militia of the State of Illinois shall consist of all able bodied male persons, resident of the

State, between the ages of eighteen and forty-five, except such persons as now are, or hereafter may be, exempted by the laws of the United States, or of this State."[32]

The following day, the committee minority presented its report. Echoing the substance of the 1818 and 1848 constitutions, it provided that the militia would consist of "all the male able bodied persons, (negroes, mulattoes, and Indians excepted)."[33] When the committee of the whole debated the matter later in the month, it became clear that, if necessary, the minority would require militia service only of white males in order to avoid white and colored men serving together or whites serving under the command of colored men.

Speaking for the majority proposal, Chairman Cameron referred to the Fourteenth Amendment, stating it would be unconstitutional, "if military service is considered a privilege," for it to be restricted to whites. If a duty, "there certainly can be no reason that the colored race should be exempted" from it. Cameron also observed that in "the war which has just closed," blacks were enrolled in the militia, drafted, fought, and "some fell in discharge of their duty." He concluded, "a great revolution has taken place since the adoption of our present constitution. . . . [No] distinction should any longer exist in our organic law on the question of race or color."[34]

In response, Democrat William Vandeventer of Pike and Scott Counties offered an amendment to provide, "No colored officer shall ever be assigned to command white militia in this State." It was voted down immediately, 34–24, with 27 not voting. Democrat George Wendling of Shelby County then proposed another amendment to require segregated service: "The legislature shall make provision for the separate organization of negroes and whites." In support, Wendling stated that "a great deal of prejudice was involved" in the words used here, and "we are striking that prejudice . . . as strong a blow by the adoption of this article . . . as we are by removing the word 'white' from any part of the constitution. Adoption of this article," he warned, has "signed and sealed a contract for seventy-five thousand votes against the Constitution." He added, "not one of all that party to which we belong . . . together with a great many of other parties in this State, will ever vote for a constitution that may force the white men of Illinois to stand side by side with negroes in the militia."[35]

Curiously, Cameron attempted to pacify these protesting southerners by referring to Section 2 of the militia article, which states that the militia is to conform to regulations of the U.S. government. He observed that "the laws of Congress provide that colored troops shall be organized separately. The only reason why we did not provide for this in direct language," he explained, "was that we were unwilling to recognize in the Constitution distinctions of race or color, which the higher law of the United States Constitution has now obliterated."[36]

After further debate, which challenged the prediction that ratification votes would be lost "if we do not pander to the popular prejudice on the question of color," members rejected the amendment on a voice vote. The militia article was adopted as offered in the majority report, the membership consisting of "all able bodied male persons," with no exception for negroes, mulattoes, and Indians.[37]

Elections and Suffrage

As had been true in every previous convention, the question of suffrage was a bitterly contested issue. By 1870 women of the state were demanding the right to vote, a large proportion of the population was foreign born, and the Fifteenth Amendment to the U.S. Constitution was about to go into force. Four groups were pressing for their rights to be recognized in the convention: white male citizens, white male noncitizens, women, and blacks.

The controversy was one of the first brought to the floor of the convention. On January 11, 1870, John Dement, chairman of the committee on right of suffrage, presented the majority report, which entitled only white males to vote, defined as "every white male inhabitant who was a voter in this State on the first day of April, A.D. 1848, and every white male citizen of the United States, above the age of twenty-one years, who shall have been a resident of this State one year." The majority report also recommended a separate vote by the people to decide whether the word "white" should be stricken.[38]

Three northern Republicans and Independent Republican Harvey Buxton from the south presented a minority report, which began by stating, "The spirit of the age demands equality in both civil and political rights." They asserted that the people of Illinois called the convention "to remove from their organic law all traces . . . of that ill-founded prejudice which belongs to the past age." Instead of making the choice contrary to the majority by submitting a proposal eliminating the word "white," however, they proposed to "place the matter before the people in a more acceptable light" by leaving the first section of the proposed article blank and letting the voters choose whether to insert the word "white."[39]

A lengthy wrangle followed about when to debate and vote on the issues raised by the reports, with many members urging prompt action despite acknowledging that the Fifteenth Amendment's pending ratification might greatly affect the controversy's resolution. Finally, the convention voted to put the matter over until February.[40]

In February the committee presented a different majority report and two minority reports. Six of the nine committee members signed the new majority report, which extended the vote to "every male citizen" over age twenty-one and also "grandfathered" in all those persons who, although noncitizens, had the right to vote on April 1, 1848. Four of the six, who had signed the earlier minority report and were now part of the majority, submitted a new minority report, asserting that the vote should not be restricted to males, but that the voters should be given the option of extending the franchise to women as well. The other three members of the suffrage committee, all Democrats from far southern counties, offered a second minority report proposing that the word "white" should remain a requirement to vote, as it had been in previous constitutions.[41]

By the time the controversy was brought to the convention floor on April 15, there could no longer be any doubt that the Fifteenth Amendment was the law of the land. Nevertheless, the three-member minority and many other Democrats maintained their position against blacks voting. They condemned the Fifteenth Amendment, criticized its supporters, and sharply discussed the place of the black person in society and government.[42]

The debate began, however, with a vigorous argument over allowing noncitizen foreign-born males to vote. Democrat John Dement led off the first afternoon. He argued at length that allowing noncitizens to vote would give them privileges in directing the government without imposing on them corresponding responsibilities. Referring to the Civil War, Dement asserted that "these foreign-born [voters in Illinois] that had not naturalized under the laws of the country came in when there was a danger of the draft and plead [sic] the protection of their sovereign, their allegiance to whom they had never renounced. While the naturalized citizens and our native citizens were putting down the rebellion, they were basking at home, protected by their allegiance to the sovereign of a foreign government."

He continued, "If we enfranchise them and should be so unfortunate as to engage in another war, it is doubtful whether we could draft these enfranchised foreigners into our ranks to fight for this government that was so kind and liberal to them as to give them the right of suffrage and the right to elect the officers of our government."[43]

Opponents of that assertion met Dement's remarks head on. Democrats had traditionally favored and benefited from immigrant voting, and several took sharp issue with Dement. Democrat James Washburn was first: "I do not think the government proposes to go into war soon, and if it should unfortunately, I apprehend there will be no necessity to draft these foreigners at all; for I apprehend that they will all enlist, go and fight for the country voluntarily, without being drafted, just as they did in the late civil war."[44] Democrat George Wendling followed: "[T]he thousands and tens of thousands of foreigners in this country, who came up from their various vocations, and enlisted in . . . a war for the Constitution and the Union, should plead in louder terms for the enfranchisement of the foreign element, than this evasion of the draft on the part of a few foreigners should speak against it. There were Irishmen, Germans, and foreigners of every clime in the late contest," he continued. "The vast and overwhelming majority, who came forward and so many times, more than counterbalanced those few [evaders]."[45]

Several framed their argument using the Fifteenth Amendment: "I think that motives of right and justice should compel us to give these foreigners the right of suffrage. . . . [There is] no good reason for refusing them this right—the same right that the fifteenth amendment . . . confers upon citizens who are certainly no better qualified to vote than they are."[46] Some who strongly opposed the amendment took a different tack. Democrat Edward Rice stated that he would vote against conforming the state constitution to the Fifteenth Amendment, adding, "I am surprised that any gentleman who has gone so far as to extend suffrage to the colored men, should now be inclined to take a step backward in respect to the people of any nationality that choose to make America their home."[47]

O. H. Wright added, perhaps facetiously, that he also proposed extending the vote to white men from Ireland, France, and Germany. When asked whether he would give the vote to fifty thousand Chinese as well, an issue exposed in earlier reference to California, Wright made clear that he had racial enmities that extended beyond African Americans. "I do not propose to give it to those pigtailed fellows," he said. "I am for a white man's government, claiming to be white myself, straight hair, 'free born, and well recommended'. . . I go for . . . a white man's vote for a white man's government."[48]

After an impassioned statement by Democrat Lewis Ross arguing the fairness of immigrant voting, Republican Joseph Medill jumped into the fray. Decrying the discussion as "of the nature of buncombe and demagoguery," he made the important point that the state constitution had "nothing to do with the right of the colored man to vote. . . . It is not in the power of this convention to take it away from him." He then offered some invective of his own, challenging the motives of those "asking the Convention to bestow the power and privilege of citizenship upon those whose allegiance is due to a foreign power." The attempt to do so, he said "can not be made in good faith, but is offered here with an hostile intent, for the purpose of bringing our work into disrepute and odium, and causing the people to trample it under foot."[49]

Others forcefully decried Medill's language, stressing the sincerity of their belief in the rightness of giving the vote to those who had sought refuge in this country, worked hard to build its railroads and canals, and contributed much to its development. Medill's accusations of bad faith must be considered as well against the facts that the Illinois constitutions of 1818 and 1848 and the failed constitution of 1852 all had allowed alien voting, at least to some extent. Further, in arguing against immigrant voting, Medill and his Republican colleagues were continuing a position that Whigs and Republicans from canal counties and Chicago had been espousing for three decades.

In the end, the convention left the matter essentially where the elections committee had started, giving the vote to citizens and those noncitizens entitled to vote in 1848, but also extending the privilege to those who had "obtained a certificate of naturalization, before any court of record in this State," before January 1, 1870.[50]

Women's suffrage also received serious consideration but consumed much less time. When a motion was made to delete "male" as a voting requirement after the suffrage committee first offered its report on April 15, it was greeted by ridicule and given short shrift. Democrat Robert Hanna moved promptly to substitute the word "female" for "male," saying, "if the females are to vote at all, I want them to do all the voting." That motion failed for lack of a second, but the convention proceeded immediately to approve deletion of the word "male," defeating it decisively, 12 yeas to 48 nays.[51]

The following day, however, the members took a major step forward. Harvey Buxton, an Independent Republican from the south of the state, moved to submit the question of woman suffrage to the voters separately. Republican William Underwood of St. Clair County led the opposition. He contended that "in no state are women more highly favored and protected than in Illinois." However, "it will hardly be questioned," he said, "that men are generally, and always will be, better qualified to judge of the character and qualifications of candidates for office." Further, women's "greatest power is by moral and religious influence to restrain and control men. . . . Their domestic cares and their present field of action is broad enough and large enough to engage their whole time and attention, and we cannot afford to spare them from its sacred and solemn duties" for such a task as voting. Shortly, however, the submission of women's vote as a separate question was approved, 40–21.[52]

In May, the convention members changed their minds, apparently at least in part as a result of antagonizing lectures by suffrage leaders. L. D. Whiting, a supporter of the suffrage cause, argued that delegates' "character for good sense and stability" should lead them to overlook the comments of "the first lady lecturer here this winter" (Mrs. Willard) who "advanced as her theory . . . that men are out of their places in legislative halls and on the judicial bench—that these places should be wholly given to women, and the men go to the fields and workshops." Although he contended slyly that it would give support to her point if one or two lectures should change the delegates' opinions, the convention struck the woman suffrage proposal out of its submission to the voters. The vote was a close 33–28, with 22 abstaining.[53]

Revenue

The revenue article in general reaffirmed the property tax as the most fair and equitable way of supporting government. This tax by valuation was part of each earlier Illinois constitution and constituted the means of raising virtually all state taxes. The two-mill tax for the retirement of canal bonds and the controversial poll tax, both imposed in the 1848 constitution, were removed. The convention greatly increased the list of articles that the legislature could specially tax and placed limits on tax rates for county and other local government purposes.[54]

Although delegates lost considerable time on diversions and paid much attention to backward-looking matters, the convention also gave serious consideration to the state's future needs and drafted important provisions that would have a significant impact.

The Illinois and Michigan Canal

One of the first substantive matters the convention dealt with related to the Illinois and Michigan Canal. In the two decades since its opening in 1848, the canal had proven to be a success, in contrast to the rest of the vast system of internal improvements that had been undertaken in the 1830s. In the context of the bitter sectional differences that existed in the state by the time of the convention, however, that success helped make it the subject of downstate delegates' animosity.

In January both the committee on canals and canal lands and committee on internal improvements proposed that the canal and any addition or extension that might be made to it "should never be sold, leased, or otherwise disposed of" but instead should "remain forever the property of this State and under its management and control." On Thursday, January 27, the proposed article was taken up by the full convention. Debate on the matter extended for more than a week.[55]

Delegates from the south denounced the canal as a sectional enterprise, benefiting only those living in its vicinity. Silas Bryan, of far south Marion County, argued that canal expenditures had been a poor investment and the legislature should not be precluded from leasing or selling the canal if it were advisable to do so. He charged that some were seeking special constitutional protection for the canal because "the gentlemen who live along the line [of the canal] have a multitude of friends to be well paid for the services they render to the State of Illinois, have rendered, and will render in the future . . . and to preserve them, they want to tie up the hands of the Legislature" and did not want "more scrutinizing eyes and a more judicious management."[56] James Allen, from Crawford County, also in the south, argued that state management of state enterprises everywhere had been woefully weak and that it was especially so in Illinois. Other opponents of protecting the canal argued that if the state were to engage in transportation, it should be in railroads, which, they claimed, were far superior to canals.[57]

These points, or variants on them, were made repeatedly. Added to them was other rhetoric that reflected downstate animus to the growing urban giant of the north, a sectional hostility that manifested itself in numerous other issues later in the convention and remains pervasive to present times. Thus, downstate delegates charged that the canal was a "running sore" and that the state would be made the scavenger of Chicago by turning the Chicago River to flow into the canal. They complained of the distribution of school funds, the number of Cook County criminals in the penitentiary, the treatment of downstate visitors by Chicago merchants, and the wealth of Chicagoans generally.[58]

The *Chicago Journal* on February 1 described such remarks as the "shrieks of locality" being voiced unfairly against an enterprise that was "a great national work, which has been committed to the state in trust." Supporters of the provision protecting state ownership of the canal retaliated with sectional disparagements of their own, deriding opponents as complainers who represented counties that paid little or no taxes, that benefited from state largess in supporting local undertakings, or that profited greatly from railroads that had received free public lands or subsidies that bolstered their economies.[59]

Speaking to the merits of the issue, supporters of the canal contended that it was now a profit-making enterprise that benefited the entire state in numerous ways. Elliott Anthony of Chicago led the debate. Citing the huge growth of the state's population, which now numbered close to three million, he argued that a large part of the state's prosperity had occurred because of agricultural and commercial development due to the canal. The canal, he said, was "earning the State of Illinois more than $132,000 per year, over and above expenses." The growth of Chicago and Cook County had bolstered the state treasury. "The State of Illinois has never spent a dollar in Chicago," he said. No "public institution, educational or eleemosynary [had been] planted by the State in her midst." Cook County, he added, "has one eighth of the state's population, but pays one fifth of the taxes."[60]

Anthony, Elijah Haines of Lake County, Joseph Medill, and others observed as well that the canal and Illinois waterway to the Mississippi had become "the great public highway belonging to the people of the State."[61] It not only had amplified prosperity and growth in cities along the waterway but also had benefited farmers and the public because it had held down rates of the railroad monopolies by providing alternative means of shipping their harvests. Far from being sold, they contended that the canal should be enlarged and promoted in order to furnish competition for railroads and their rate schedules.[62]

The debate continued thus for days. Substitutes and amendments were offered and defeated, without altering the state of the matter. Finally, on February 4, Orville Browning offered an entirely new article, which provided simply that the canal could "never be sold or leased until the specific proposition for the sale or lease thereof" should first have been approved by a majority of the state's voters in a referendum held at a general election. The convention adopted his substitution on February 5 and later voted that the provision be submitted separately to the voters for ratification.[63]

Railroad and Warehouse Regulation

In the two decades preceding the convention, railroads had transformed the state. Particularly in the north, they fostered development and population growth through commerce and trade to the east and west. The era of railroads built by private corporations had reached Illinois in 1848. State policy theorists, who pushed for development projects to be entirely within Illinois and not benefit other states and cities, held sway in the legislature for five years. Railroad lines spread quickly across the prairies. By the end of 1855, Illinois had 2,005 miles of track, more than any other western state.[64]

Chicago business leaders did not subscribe to theories that trade should stop at state lines. They promoted their own rail lines into Iowa and Wisconsin and welcomed the arrival of railroads from the East. The east-west axis across the Great Lakes and by the Erie Canal across New York State gave Chicago an economic partner in New York City, which soon outdistanced its rivals of Boston, Philadelphia, and Baltimore in commerce with the West.[65]

Lake Michigan was not only a waterway serving Chicago but a 320-mile-long natural barrier forcing railroads and wagons to go around its southern end. Chicago, with the only good harbor at the tip of the lake, inevitably became the rail center for eastern lines. By 1857 eleven main lines of track radiated westward from the city. Their four thousand miles of direct connections brought to the city immense quantities of farm products and hauled from it merchandise, lumber, and immigrants who built up the city's trade territory in the hinterlands.[66]

After Senator Douglas moved to Chicago in 1847 and invested heavily in strategically located real estate, he revived the projected Illinois Central Railroad north from Cairo. In Washington, Douglas overcame opposition to making federal grants to such a project by providing in his bill for similar land grants to Mississippi and Alabama. A federal grant of more than 2.5 million acres to Illinois in 1850 was transferred to the Illinois Central Railroad Company, which proceeded to build a line from Cairo to East Dubuque at the Mississippi with a "branch" line from the new town of Centralia to Chicago. With extensions to other states from Chicago, building the 705-mile railroad, the world's longest, was described as a bigger public works project than the Erie Canal.[67]

Chicago, which had refused permission for other railroads to enter the city center, did its part by granting to the Illinois Central a three-hundred-foot-wide right-of-way just offshore in Lake Michigan to build a causeway on which to enter the city. Although many considered the structure an eyesore, it created a breakwater protecting the city's shoreline and favoring, particularly, the mansions on the city's south side. Other lines spread across northern Illinois. In 1853 the Rock Island Railway began the first continuous rail service from Chicago to the Mississippi River, 181 miles west. Train service from the East also reached Chicago in 1852. By the late 1850s, Chicago's reputation as the nation's railroad capital was firmly established, with the state-covering Illinois Central as its backbone.[68]

The explosive development of railroads also brought problems. Numerous local governments, captivated by visions of handsome economic returns, competed to attract railroads and other ventures, invested heavily in capital stock, and lent or pledged their credit to such enterprises to lure promoters to their communities. Many of these projects were unsound financially, leaving communities seriously in debt and often on the verge of bankruptcy.[69]

The constitutional convention proposed a simple article intended to prevent such future investments. The provision stated that no local government "shall ever become subscriber to the capital stock of any railroad or private corporation, or make any donation to or loan its credit in aid of, such corporation." Because the subject caused considerable controversy in the convention, it was submitted for a separate ratification vote.[70]

By the time of the 1870 convention, local railroad monopolies caused by single lines or combinations of competitors were imposing excessive or discriminatory rates on farmers. Added to the problem was the ability of warehouses at shipping points to charge exorbitant rates for their services. Grangers and other farm groups beseeched the constitutional convention to take some sort of action.[71]

Early in the convention, the opinion expressed by several delegates, including Robert Hanna of Wayne County and Joseph Medill of Cook, was that more competition was the only remedy. "Build competing lines, hold out liberal inducements for capitalists to come . . . and invest their capital," said Hanna. For his part, Medill pronounced, "[Railroads] must be governed by the same common and general laws, under which we all live." In his modest way, he added, "I am not able, with what investigation I have given this subject for years, and with all the light I have been able to extract from able and astute lawyers, to conceive of any adequate and sufficient means of checking railroad overcharges and rapacity, by statute law of this State."[72]

Despite such opinions, one astute lawyer, Reuben Benjamin of Bloomington, who had reshaped the bill of rights in April, persuaded the convention in May to take a pioneering position by placing railroads under state regulation. On May 3, the committee on railroad corporations presented a report, providing, "It shall be the duty of the General Assembly to pass such laws as will correct abuses and prevent extortion in the rates of freight and passenger tariffs" on state railroads. Benjamin spoke in support, expressing entirely new grounds for legislative action. "Corporations, and especially railroad corporations, have, within the last few years, assumed and exercised powers incompatible with the public welfare," he began. "In theory, railroad corporations are created for the public good. In practice, they become oppressive by being allowed . . . to fix their rates of toll for the transportation of persons and property." They had been given the power to take private property, "even the very homestead," he said, but they remained under the domain of the legislature, which had as much right to regulate rates on railroads as unquestionably it did for bridge, ferry, plank road, and turnpike companies, and numerous other businesses. Taking what was then an advanced stand, he asserted that corporate rights could not be superior to the interests and rights of the public.[73]

Benjamin's arguments swung the views of the convention to the side of regulation. While lawyer members readily accepted his constitutional positions, even the old guard began advancing his arguments. In a complete reversal, Joseph Medill spoke out on the power of the constitution to authorize the legislature to control railroads. His years-long "investigation" and the "light" he had "extracted" from numerous lawyers were forgotten. In a lengthy oration, he extolled the power of the people acting through "this Convention and the State Legislature to assert their sovereignty and supremacy" and set aside any power of the railroads to charge extortionate rates.[74]

In its new mood, the convention promptly passed, by a 35–16 vote, a substitute to the committee proposal, adopting Benjamin's language and declaring that "Railways . . . in this State are hereby declared public highways, and shall be free to all persons for the transportation of person and property thereon, under such regulations as may be prescribed by law." Added to that language by a similar vote was a direction that the legislature shall establish reasonable maximum rates for transportation of persons and property.[75]

As the convention was completing four days of debate on the railroad provisions, on May 6 it added the section on rates originally proposed by the committee. The section confirmed the direction to the legislature to pass laws regulating railroad rates: "The General Assembly shall pass laws to correct abuses and prevent extortion in the rates of freight and passenger tariffs on the different railroads in this State, and to enforce such laws by adequate penalties, to the extent, if necessary for that purpose, of forfeiture of their property and franchises."[76]

During the same days in May as its action on railroads, the convention also took a pioneering stand by imposing regulation on warehouses. Declaring as "public warehouses . . . all elevators and storehouses where grain or other property is stored for a compensation," the article comprised seven sections establishing in some detail requirements for weights and charges, recordkeeping, reporting, weighing and measuring, issuing receipts, and safe delivery. The article also directed the general assembly to pass laws to prevent issuance of "false and fraudulent" documentation and to provide for inspection "for the protection of producers, shippers, and receivers of grain and produce."[77]

The 1870 convention's action in placing railroads and warehouses under state regulation was a pioneering position that had important consequences for the nation as well as for Illinois. Regulation of railroads was one of the principal objectives of the Granger movement of the 1860s and 1870s. The mandate to the legislature to pass laws regulating rates for passenger and freight traffic was heeded in 1871, when the general assembly established a railroad and warehouse commission to regulate and fix maximum rates. The Illinois precedent was widely followed, and was upheld by the supreme court in 1871. In a landmark ruling, the court affirmed that the state indeed had the power to regulate businesses affected with the public interest.[78]

The Illinois Central Railroad

Earlier in the week, on May 2, the convention had taken up the question of the financial relationship between the Illinois Central Railroad and the state. In 1851, in return for the donation of public lands, the Illinois Central charter had provided for it to pay a total of at least 7 percent of its gross revenues to the state, to be applied to the payment of state debt. In return, it was to be exempted from all other taxes. Counties along the railroad's lines were agitating to have the legislature provide them with some of those receipts, arguing that they were suffering because the railroad was protected from local taxes.[79]

Support was widespread for a constitutional provision to prevent the legislature from succumbing to local pressures to relieve the railroad from its obligation. The debate was heated, with delegates from across the state scathingly denouncing the minority, principally representatives of the "suffering" railroad counties. "Those counties got what they had bargained for," proponents said. Moreover, they argued, those counties "have all its advantages." "Why, gentlemen, the Illinois Central railroad has made you rich," said James Allen of Crawford County. "It has poured into the laps of those counties millions of wealth. It has built up large towns and cities all along its line, while the other sixty odd counties have not had one dollar's benefit from it, except as they have derived it from the taxes paid into the State treasury."[80]

In the end, the convention voted to lock in the 7 percent payment of the railroad charter by a constitutional provision that none of the railroad's obligations to pay into the state treasury "shall ever be released, suspended, modified, altered, remitted, or in any manner be diminished or impaired by legislation or other authority." The provision was adopted by a vote of 33 to 18, with a stipulation that the section would be submitted separately to the voters.[81]

Public Education

No one in the convention objected to including as a separate article a provision on public-school education. The first section of the article, as proposed by the education committee and ultimately adopted by the full convention, instructed the general assembly to "provide a thorough and efficient system of free schools, whereby all children of this State may receive a good common school education."[82]

A proposed amendment to strike out all the words after "schools" and substitute for "children" the words "for all persons in the state" was much debated. Deleting the word "children," it was argued, would open the state to potentially great expense to educate adults. The argument was made generally about a man or woman "who has reached his or her majority," but also specifically about the great number of blacks who had immigrated to the southern parts of the state—persons whom delegate James Washburn referred to several times as "fifteenth amendments." Proponents of the change met the argument squarely, asserting that educating adults was a good thing for the state. A second objection was made to the term "common schools." In brief argument on that point, supporters of retaining the term contended that it indicated that special and "collegiate" educations were not to be supported by taxation.[83]

The proposed deletion of "children" from Section 1 was rejected on a voice vote. The section ultimately was included in the constitution as proposed by the committee.[84]

Section 2, concerning the handling of school property and funds, and Section 3, drawing a sharp line against use of public funds in aid of church or sectarian schools, were adopted promptly without debate. Controversy and extensive debate arose, however, over proposed Section 4, which provided that no teacher or school officer "shall ever be interested in the sale, proceeds, or profits of any book, apparatus or furniture, used or to be used, in any school in this State." Delegate Jesse Fox of Schuyler County argued that the section "was a very obnoxious principle . . . legislating against a class. Teachers," he said, "are a class, a profession." Elliott Anthony of Chicago echoed Fox: teachers, he said, "may be a humble class, but a very worthy one." Experienced educators, he argued, should not be barred in the constitution from writing out their views learned from experience or be deprived of their vocation by becoming authors. If there was a problem, they argued, it should be dealt with by legislation. The motion to exclude the section failed, and it eventually was adopted in the constitution.[85]

A torrent of impassioned debate was unleashed by the proposal of delegate James G. Bayne of Woodford County to permit Bible reading in the public schools. The argument continued for most of Saturday, May 7. On Monday the matter was sent back to the committee, and in the end the proposal never was reported out. The education article was finished with no reference to Bible reading.[86]

Minority Representation in the General Assembly

The convention created a distinctive and progressive means for electing members of the house of representatives by a process of cumulative voting, or minority representation. The procedure, unique among states at the time, was intended to help solve the persistent problems created by the sharp geographical division between northern and southern parts of the state. In the previous half-century, sentiment on the slavery issue and treatment of blacks had become increasingly different between north and south as the population grew proportionally much greater in the north. With the advent of the Republican Party and the hostilities of the Civil War, by 1870 almost every legislative district in southern and western Illinois was Democratic, while Republicans dominated the eastern and northern sections of the state. Thus, of the eighty-five members of the 1869 house of representatives, only eight of the sixty Republicans were from south of Springfield and only five of the twenty-five Democrats represented districts north of Springfield. This geographical division not only left unrepresented the views of great numbers of minority voters in large areas of the state, it also made politics in the state more divisive and hostile between regions.[87]

Within days of the convention's start, Robert Hanna of Wayne County recommended a plan to give minority voters in each district a way to choose a representative, proposing a method of allocating votes in representative districts, "to the end that minorities might be represented in the Legislature of the State in proportion to their numbers."[88] Joseph Medill, chairman of the committee on electoral and representative reform, refined and proposed the plan to the convention in February. In his thoughtful paper, "Theory of Representative Government," he observed that in winner-take-all elections, only the victor's supporters are represented. Voters supporting losing candidates were unrepresented, which, he stated, was contrary to principles of representative government as manifested in a traditional town meeting, where losing factions can be heard.[89]

The committee's solution was to have three-member districts, with each voter having three votes that could be marked all for one candidate, split equally between two, or given one to each of three candidates. In districts where the minority comprised at least one-third of the voters, they were assured of electing one of three representatives by cumulating their votes for one person. "The perfect rule of the majority is thus preserved and unimpaired, while the minorities, who are now entirely excluded, will secure a sufficient portion of representation to enable them to be heard on all questions," Medill wrote.[90]

For reasons that do not appear in the debates, the plan was not brought to a vote in February but was presented to the convention on May 6 instead. Medill spoke in support, observing that John Stuart Mill was advocating such a system in England, and that others in Europe were considering it. Illinois would be the first to adopt it in the United States. Its effect, Medill asserted, would be to "secure representation for our long enduring republican friends in Egypt, and give the swallowed-up and buried under democrats of northern Illinois a chance."[91]

It will, he said, "secure to both parties representation from all parts of the state." Other convention members were not so enthusiastic, but they did agree, 46–17, to put the provision on the ballot for a separate ratification vote.[92]

Wilbur F. Storey, whose Democratic *Chicago Times* for a decade had stridently criticized Lincoln, Republicans, and Medill, and the Republican *Tribune* lavishly praised the provision, urging a favorable ratification vote:

> In Chicago and elsewhere in the state most journals have declared in favor of the proposed constitutional provision for proportional representation in the general assembly.... The more carefully and critically it is examined the more converts it makes. There has never been advanced [a measure] which so speedily commended itself to the approval of thoughtful men or which so promptly found advocacy in all the leading organs of public sentiment.[93]

Voters approved the plan, but by the narrowest favorable margin of all the matters put before them. In practice, it did result in election of a minority party representative in virtually all districts in the state, thus providing cross-representation spanning the geographical north/south party divide as intended. The effect of the system, however, was virtually to eliminate competition between candidates of different parties. The majority party often nominated only two candidates and the minority party one, leaving general election voters no choice but to ratify the parties' nominations. On occasions when the minority party nominated two candidates, the choice between them was left to an intraparty fight in the general election. Experience also showed that in districts with a very dominant majority party, the minority representative often owed his seat to the good graces of the majority party voters and political machines, resulting in "me too" representatives whose political existence depended on cooperation with the majority party.

Submission to the Voters

On May 13, 1870, the convention completed its work with the adoption of a schedule for submission of the constitution to the voters at a special referendum on Saturday, July 2. In addition to the basic document, eight separate propositions were offered for approval or rejection. The strategy was to minimize the chance that the whole constitution might be defeated by opposition to controversial subjects, such as the provision that the Illinois and Michigan Canal could never be leased or sold, or provisions for railroad and warehouse regulation or minority voting.[94]

Seventy-nine members signed the new constitution the same day. The convention then adjourned, five months after it first met.[95]

The day the convention adjourned, the *Chicago Tribune* gave the constitution effusive praise as a nonpartisan document and urged its ratification:

> There is not a single section or paragraph in the whole document of a partisan nature. There is no reason why a Republican would be more in favor of it than a Democrat, or a Democrat than a Republican. In this respect, the new constitution appeals to each man as a citizen and a taxpayer—as a member of a commonwealth that will live long after existing political parties are forgotten. We can see no reason, therefore, why it should not be cordially supported by men of all shades of political and religious belief.[96]

The next day the *Chicago Times* in its turn lauded the new constitution:

> Considered as a whole, the new constitution is not only a vast improvement upon the existing one, but it is the best one that has ever been framed in Illinois.... The people of this state might go further and fare a great deal worse than they will in ratifying this instrument, in all its parts and provisions.[97]

The *Illinois State Journal* weighed in with more measured language:

> No one, we are sure, can fail to observe how much better adapted to the present wants and necessities of the State the new Constitution is than the old. That such will be the judgment of the people upon the comparison, we most heartily trust and hope.[98]

During the seven-week period before the special election, almost all influential government figures and much of the press urged approval of the proposed constitution. A week before the ratification vote, the *Tribune* claimed, "nearly the whole press of the State and the leading men of both parties, have pronounced in favor of the new constitution." The only opposition, it said, came from a few Democratic newspapers that were firmly opposed to black civil rights and from "professional bummers, lobbyists, and barnacles who oppose reform." One of the papers singled out by the *Tribune* was the *Quincy Herald*, which lamented that the new constitution did not require separate schools for blacks and whites.[99]

The morning of the ratification referendum on July 2, the *Chicago Times* stressed the importance of voters going to the polls: "Indeed the people in no portion of the state have so direct a personal interest in the ratification of the new constitution as in Cook County. The *Times* ardently hopes that everyone will feel that it is his personal duty to vote today, even if you never propose to vote again."[100]

Illinois voters on July 2 ratified the constitution and the eight separate submissions without difficulty. The basic constitution was approved by a large majority, 134,277 to 35,443. The closest vote on the separate articles was for the provision establishing minority representation in the legislature, which was favored 99,022 to 70,080. Cook County, in particular, and other northern counties gave it strong enough support to gain approval despite the fact that the section was opposed by a majority of voters in forty counties.[101]

Celebrating the ratification on July 7, the *Chicago Times* singled out several provisions for praise, including the prohibition on special legislation. The publisher then concluded grandly, "In the science of government, Illinois, at one great forward stride, has taken the lead of all American states, and . . . stands head and shoulders above all the rest."[102]

The new constitution went into effect on August 8, 1870. It remained the state's fundamental law, with amendments, for just over one hundred years, until the constitution drafted by the Sixth Illinois Constitutional Convention in 1970 became effective on July 1, 1971.

Epilogue

The 1870 constitution was Illinois's third in fifty-two years. It remained in effect for one hundred and one years, and even then the voters ratifying the proposed 1970 constitution refused to change four key provisions of the 1870 constitution.

State constitutions reflect the states of their time. The first constitution in 1818 reflected a state in which the white settlement occupied a small portion in the south of the state's entire territory. The populace was much concerned with the ownership and control of slaves and servants held in bondage, and with the structures and powers of the branches of government after years of authoritarian territorial administration. Apart from dealing with occasional Indian troubles, they had little involvement with or interest in the state's northern half. The area in the north added by the boundary amendment in the 1818 enabling act for the first constitution was basically irrelevant.

By 1848 the constitution reflected a more modern society occupying, even if sparsely, the state's entire land area. Black bondage was expiring and would be gone legally within a decade. The immigration and presence of free blacks had become a concern. The development of commerce, agriculture, and river, canal, and overland transportation, along with the immigration of easterners and foreigners, especially in the north, and the rapid growth of Chicago and Cook

County were changing the character of the state. The boundary extension area was the base on which the substantial part of these changes were occurring.

Twenty-one years later, by the time of the 1869 constitutional convention, continued rapid population increases, the economic growth of the Civil War years, increasing industrial growth in the 1860s, the expansion of railroads, with the beginning of rail commerce to the West Coast and rail and water commerce to the ocean in the East, made Illinois a leading state. The ongoing influx of immigrant populations, the growth of the Republican Party, Lincoln's election, the effects of the war victory, and changes wrought to the society by the Lincoln legacy amendments to the U.S. Constitution made a state very different from that of 1848.

These changes largely were grounded on the land area added by the 1818 boundary extension. Except for that land area and the foundation it created for the state of 1870, Illinois would have been a much smaller and less significant part of the Union.

Despite the Chicago Fire of 1871, which devastated large portions of the city a year after the new constitution, Chicago's geographical advantages remained, and its expansion and that of the north continued. Chicago's population nearly doubled in the 1870s. By 1880 it had become the nation's fourth-largest city. Ten years later, in 1890, it was second in size only to New York. The state, too, was growing rapidly, moving from fifth-largest in the nation in 1870 to second in population two decades later. Again, the much greater part of the growth was in the north boundary extension area.[1]

The essential qualities of the 1870 constitution contributed to its durability. The matter of treatment of blacks, the subject of detailed provisions in the earlier constitutions, was gone. Several measures hailed as forward looking at convention's conclusion proved to be so. Among them were the provisions for minority representation in the legislature, the structure and jurisdiction of the courts, with the election of judges and a different organization of the courts in Cook County, the regulation of railroads and warehouses, and the purchase and lease of the Illinois and Michigan Canal.[2]

Notably, the provisions of the constitution authorizing regulation of railroads were challenged promptly in the courts. After the legislature's first attempt in 1870 to pass such regulations was invalidated, the general assembly in 1873 passed a new law empowering a commission to regulate rates. The U.S. Supreme Court upheld the law in 1877 in the landmark case of *Munn v. Illinois*. Soon, other states followed Illinois's lead, passing similar laws.[3]

Other factors explain the durability of the 1870 constitution. Constitutional revision is challenging to accomplish because of difficulty marshaling the requisite numbers of votes to approve amendment proposals. This begins in the general assembly, where under the 1870 constitution a two-thirds vote of all the members of both houses was required, something that is difficult to obtain, especially with the minority representation system governing the election of representatives. Further, the obstacle often has been apathy and failure on the part of the electorate to vote on proposed revisions. Partisan fights and bitter animosities among Chicago, suburban Cook County, other "collar" counties around Chicago, and "Downstate" also have hampered efforts to achieve change.[4]

In the first twenty years to 1890, five proposed amendments to the 1870 constitution were adopted without difficulty. In that period, political parties printed ballots that were cast at elections by their supporters. Parties printed on the ballots their position "for" or "against" constitutional amendments.[5]

After an official ballot law was passed in 1891, government printed ballots and voters were required to fill out their choices at the polling place. Over the next seventy-eight years, until November 1968, numerous failures and a few successes marked efforts at constitutional revision in Illinois. Part of that record of failure was a constitutional convention that lasted two years and nine months during 1920–1922. Partisanship, absenteeism, interruptions, and recesses caused such dissatisfaction on the part of the electorate that the proposed constitution, when finally submitted to the voters, was emphatically rejected 5:1 statewide and 20:1 in Cook County.[6]

Another factor in the inability to muster support for constitutional changes is that measures pushed by advocates as necessary to resolve deficiencies of the 1870 document did not create sufficient interest and force for change among the public. Although proponents of change increasingly derided the 1870 constitution as a "straitjacket on progress," three significant amendments passed in a thirteen-year period with broad support: in 1950 a so-called Gateway Amendment easing the revision process gained voter approval; a reapportionment amendment was approved in 1954; and a judicial reorganization amendment ratified in 1962.[7]

Practical revision is achieved also when the state courts change their interpretation of its constitution. That occurred in Illinois in 1969. The accepted doctrine that an income tax was not permitted under the 1870 constitution changed when the Illinois Supreme Court approved as constitutional an income tax law passed by the general assembly earlier in 1969. Notably, the supreme court's action came after the public in 1968 had overwhelmingly approved a call for the state to hold its sixth constitutional convention in 1970 and as the election process for delegates to the 1970 convention was underway. The convention in turn included an income tax as part of a comprehensive revenue article.[8]

The Sixth Illinois Constitutional Convention worked for nine months, from December 1969 until early September 1970. It produced a draft constitution that voters ratified in December 1970. The convention submitted four issues for separate considerations. On all four, the electorate by large majorities opted to keep in force the provisions of the 1870 constitution. Three-member house of representative districts with cumulative voting was approved over single-member districts. The election of judges was retained instead of adopting an appointment system. The voting age was kept at twenty-one instead of lowering to eighteen, and the proposal to abolish the death penalty was defeated.[9]

Within a decade, two of those ratification results had been reversed. In a period of just four months from March to June 1971, before the Illinois constitution went into effect on July 1, the Congress proposed and the required thirty-eight states ratified the Twenty-Sixth Amendment to the U.S. Constitution lowering the voting age for federal office to eighteen, also effective on July 1. Illinois was the thirty-sixth state to ratify by general assembly vote on June 29, 1971. The 1970 Illinois constitution was not amended to lower the age to eighteen for state and local elections until seventeen years later, in 1988.[10]

In 1980 the initiative provision of the 1970 constitution, which allowed amendments to the legislative article to be proposed by citizen petition for voter ratification, was used successfully to achieve the first amendment to the 1970 constitution. The so-called Cutback Amendment eliminated three-member house districts with cumulative voting after 110 years and provided for two single-member house districts in each senate district.

The initiative provision was vigorously debated in the 1970 convention. Proponents contended that it was a means to achieve constitutional reforms that self-interested legislators would never propose. Opponents argued that it would open the way, as in other states, to detailed legislative-type proposals by special interests to freeze into the constitution their pet issues. Both views have proved to be true.

Proponents of the initiative were proved correct with the ratification of the Cutback Amendment in 1980. Opponents' fears were justified with the ratification in November 2016 of the so-called Safe Roads Lockbox Amendment. In the latter case, a lengthy and detailed provision was adopted that requires the use of funds derived from gasoline taxes and other sources to be used only for roads, bridges, and other infrastructure. Conceived and put forth by road builders, contractors, unions, and other special interests, and promoted by a multimillion-dollar media campaign, the amendment was ratified by a 3,796,654 to 1,014,46 vote.[11]

The 1970 constitution also mandates that the question of calling a constitutional convention be proposed to the voters every twenty years unless the general assembly calls for one in the interim. The proposal at the 1988 general election for a convention was defeated 3–1. The call proposal was rejected again in 2008, 2–1. The Illinois experience is not unique. Fourteen states have provisions for periodic convention calls to be presented to the voters. Eight such referendums were held from 2000 through 2008. All were defeated.[12]

The passage of almost 150 years, including the constitutional revisions in that time, did not change the basic character of the state of Illinois from that of 1870. At this writing, approaching the bicentennial of Illinois statehood, it can fairly be said that the Abraham Lincoln we venerate and the Land of Lincoln we celebrate were created by events of the fifty-three years spanning the Congress's enabling act of 1818 and the three nineteenth-century constitutions of 1818, 1848, and 1870.

Of paramount importance, the land area added to the state by the amendment to the constitution enabling act that Nathaniel Pope achieved in the Congress in April 1818 provided the base for Illinois to become one of the most populous and economically strong states in the nation by 1870. As Illinois was populated in large part by immigrants from eastern states and from abroad who provided the economic power, the state's political character was changed by the antislavery attitudes of these newcomers. The added land area furnished the voting base for Republican Party victories statewide in 1856, 1858, and 1860, and for Lincoln's winning of the state's electoral votes in 1860.

The Lincoln presidency, his assassination, and the outcome of the Civil War changed the state in the 1860s—as they did the nation. In a first significant step in 1862, the Illinois electorate rejected the last overt advocacy of oppression of blacks—the subject that long had preoccupied public discourse in Illinois—when it refused to ratify the new constitution proposed by the partisan 1862 wartime convention.

By the time of the 1869 constitutional convention, the Illinois legislature had ratified promptly the Thirteenth, Fourteenth, and Fifteenth Amendments to the U.S. Constitution and, in 1865, repealed the black anti-immigration law of 1853 and all other black laws. The 1869 convention delegates rebuffed attempts to enforce segregation in schools or the militia and to deny blacks the right to vote or hold office. Instead, the 1870 constitution was the first in Illinois to make no reference to African Americans.

The 1870 constitution included other provisions to bridge post–Civil War animosities and look to the future, including the provision for three-member districts and minority representation in the House of Representatives. It remained in effect for a century and reflected the state's history to 1870 that enabled Illinois to become known as the Land of Lincoln.[13]

ACKNOWLEDGMENTS

The seed that germinated into this book first was planted by my friend Russell Lewis, executive vice president and chief historian of the Chicago History Museum. As I was pondering book ideas, following publication of my previous book, Russell suggested I consider something concerning Chicago or Illinois history. My own tentative thoughts to write about the 1970 constitutional convention, combined with my strongly held belief that state constitutions in large part reflect the state history that precedes them, matured quickly to the conclusion that I should do both; thus this book about Illinois's four eighteenth-century constitutional conventions and the history that preceded them.

The enthusiastic response by David Spadafora, president of the Newberry Library, William Furry of the Illinois State Historical Society, and others to the concept of a history comprising these elements motivated me to push ahead. I owe thanks to David and to other friends who read drafts of the manuscript, made valuable suggestions, and warmly encouraged me to complete this work. First among them are my former law colleague, and later judge, John Ferren, himself a distinguished biographer; my former law partner, and later president of Knox College, Roger Taylor; and Wayne Whalen, whom I first met in December 1969, when we both were young Chicago lawyers and delegates-elect to the 1970 constitutional convention. Other old friends and helpful critics who read and commented on drafts in process included Judge Ruben Castillo, Frank Babb, Doug and Norma Madsen, Roberta Rubin, Robert and Lynn Rubright, Mary Sasse, and Stuart Struever.

I am grateful for the comments, thoughtful criticism, suggestions, and encouragement of scholars I came to know as this work progressed, including Daniel Greene, Bradford Hunt, Ann Durkin Keating, Robert Morrissey, Junius Rodriguez, and Susan Sleeper-Smith. They contributed much to the contents and organization of the book.

From my law firm, I received immense help from my longtime secretary and assistant Laura Czukla, who can do most anything, and from research specialist Mary Beth Kamraczewski, who can find most anything. I thank them, and also Michael Hensler, Amy Montero, and David Sokol, for their contributions to the finished work.

Over several years, I was assisted in the search for historical materials by the excellent staff of the Abraham Lincoln Presidential Library and Museum. Lincoln Collection Curator James Cornelius, Gwenith Podeschi, Jane Ehrenhart, Jennifer Ericson, Roberta Fairburn, Debbie Hamm, Kathryn Harris, and Ian Hunt all gave me their assistance on numerous occasions, and I thank them all.

In addition to Russell Lewis, staff of the Chicago History Museum were ready with help when called upon, in particular those who staffed the research desk and the image and rights facilitators.

Many people at the Newberry Library, in addition to David Spadafora and Bradford Hunt, willingly gave me their time and suggestions, even on creative questions of mine that proved not to have answers. I thank in particular James Akerman, Martha Briggs, Diane Dillon, and Matthew Rutherford.

I thank research assistants Lori Mattten and Eric Barrone for their labors in the early stages of this project, and give special thanks to Shannon Pennefeather Gardner, whose editing work and suggestions over the years contributed great value to the final product.

I am indebted to Laurie Matheson, director of the University of Illinois Press, for taking on my project, and give special thanks to Daniel Nasset, senior acquisitions editor, for his editing, advice, and encouragement. I am grateful to them and to Jennifer Comeau, Dustin Hubbart, and others on the staff of the press who made it possible for this book to appear in time for Illinois's bicentennial.

This book would not have been what it is and never would have been finished and worthy of publication without the unfaltering support of my wife, Jan Cicero, to whom the book is dedicated. From discussion of my earliest ideas through the reading of every sentence of every draft, her comments, suggestions, criticism, encouragement, and advice have shaped the final product and maintained my enthusiasm through the process.

This work is also written for our daughters, Erica Cicero and Caroline Cicero, their husbands, Edward Chrapla and Craig Detweiler, and, especially, our grandchildren, Zoe Grace Detweiler, Theo Cicero Detweiler, and Leo Cicero Chrapla, who were born and live thousands of miles from the Land of Lincoln. It may help them, like other readers, understand the state in which three generations of their grandparents lived and the struggles and fortuities from which President Abraham Lincoln emerged.

NOTES

Preface

1. Putnam, *Illinois and Michigan Canal*, 10.

Introduction

1. Herndon, *Herndon's Lincoln*, 1:79.

2. Cronon, *Nature's Metropolis*, 54.

3. Basler et al., *Collected Works* [hereafter, *CW*], 4:67, written by Lincoln in summer 1860 in his presidential campaign biography.

4. Moses, *Illinois*, 2:1198. Similarly, from the time party identifications became recorded for congressional races, Democrats held all three Illinois house seats from 1835 to 1839; 2:1 Whig from 1839 to 1843; and 6:1 Whig in the five terms from 1843 to 1853. Party success changed from 1853 to 1855, with four Whigs and five Democrats, and from 1855 to 1863 with four Republicans and five Democrats. Moses, *Illinois*, 2:1199–1200.

5. Allen and Lacey, *Illinois Elections*, 137–39.

6. Ibid., 141–43; Moses, *Illinois*, 2:621.

7. Allen and Lacey, *Illinois Elections*, 144–45.

8. Moses, *Illinois*, 2:638.

Chapter 1. Illinois before Statehood:
Slave Country of the Northwest Territory

1. Davis, *Frontier Illinois*, 64–75. Clark was born in Albemarle County, Virginia, on November 19, 1752. His youngest brother, William Clark, would lead the Lewis and Clark expedition.

2. Alvord, *Illinois Country*, 323–24.

3. The "American Bottom" is the nickname that evolved to describe the fertile flood plain in far southwestern Illinois, along the east bank of the Mississippi River, which had been occupied for more than six decades, from 1699 until 1763, by settlements that were colonies of France. With the exception of Green Bay, Wisconsin, first established as a mission in 1634, these former French colonies remain today as the oldest settlements in the Northwest Territory. For a discussion of the French explorations in the seventeenth and early eighteenth centuries in Illinois, see Alvord, *Illinois Country*; Parkman, *LaSalle*.

4. Ekberg, *French Roots*, 34–35. The first Fort de Chartres was built in 1720 on the east bank of the Mississippi River. Floods destroyed it and a successor. A handsome limestone replacement was erected in the 1750s farther from the river. Abandoned after the end of French rule, a substantial part of the structures and walls, which enclosed a four-acre site, still stands. The structures in their pastoral setting are now a registered historic landmark managed by the Illinois Historic Preservation Agency.

5. Alvord, *Illinois Country*, 322–27; Moses, *Illinois*, 2:146–47.

6. Cahan, *Court That Shaped America*, 4.

7. Alvord, *Illinois Country*, 320–32; Cayton, *Frontier Indiana*, 70–73; Howard, *Illinois*, 53–54. American settlers complained that Hamilton encouraged Indian raids and incited barbarous behavior by paying bounties for scalps and for captives at the same rate.

8. Alvord, *Illinois Country*, 327–35; Howard, *Illinois*, 53–54.

9. Alvord, *Illinois Country*, 335–47; Moses, *Illinois*, 1:158–61.

10. Howard, *Illinois*, 54.

11. Alvord, *Illinois Country*, 339–40.

12. Ibid., 348–78.

13. Ibid., 356.

14. Ibid., 354–57.

15. Ibid., 357, 357n47. One of the causes of the war was that the British did not withdraw from all the Great Lakes forts as required by the Treaty of Paris.

16. Ibid., 339–59; Howard, *Illinois*, 54–60, 58n7.

17. Alvord, *Illinois Country*, 358, 372–78.

18. Ibid., 380; Moses, *Illinois*, 1:174.

19. Howard, *Illinois*, 62; Moses, *Illinois*, 1:174.

20. Alvord, *Illinois Country*, 383; Moses, *Illinois*, 1:176–80; Howard, *Illinois*, 62.

21. Buck, *Illinois in 1818*, 181; Howard, *Illinois*, 62; Moses, *Illinois*, 1:176–81.

22. Ekberg, *French Roots*, 35–128; Ekberg, *Stealing Indian Women*, 32, 41. Under Jesuit tutelage, many couples, slave pairs and mixed, sanctified their relationship with the sacrament of marriage and had their children baptized. By the 1720s three villages of Illinois Indians were close to the French settlements. The village of the Kaskaskia Indians was close to Kaskaskia; a village of the Michigamea and Kaskaskia was near Chartres; the village of the Tamaroa and Cahokia was just outside Cahokia. Alvord, *Illinois Country*, 222; Morrissey, *Empire by Collaboration*, 128; Tanner, *Atlas*, 58–59, 63, 93–94.

23. Alvord, *Illinois Country*, 154, 190–209; Ekberg, *French Roots*, 33–34,147.

24. Ekberg, *Colonial Ste. Genevieve*, 11–43; Ekberg, *French Roots*; Ekberg, *Stealing Indian Women*, 51. Creole or French-Creole were descendants born in Louisiana territory of unions between French and Indian or, occasionally, black slaves. See, for example, Ekberg, *Stealing Indian Women*, 2, 5, 63–64, 71.

Ste. Genevieve, Missouri, exists to this day and retains structures and features of French colonial life from the eighteenth century, including vertical log houses, square residential lots, a common, and other topographical features.

25. Ekberg, *French Roots*, 150–52, table 1; Ekberg, *Stealing Indian Women*, 41; Morrissey, "Empires, Identities, and Communities," 231. There is a slight discrepancy between the census numbers in the references cited by these two authors. There were one hundred troops at Fort de Chartres in 1722, a considerable presence in the population. The garrison was reduced to forty-one men by 1732. Morrissey, "Empires, Identities, and Communities," 231.

26. Ekberg, *French Roots*, 157; Huston, *Calculating the Value*, 26–29; Levine, *House of Dixie*, 3.

27. Alvord, *Illinois Country*, 386–87; Howard, *Illinois*, 62, 62n11. The names invented by Jefferson were Assenisipi, Chersonesus, Metropotamia, Michigania, Polisipia, Polypotamia, and Sylvania.

28. Cayton, *Frontier Republic*, 8–14.

29. Middleton, *Black Laws*, 9–10, 10n11.

30. Cayton, *Frontier Republic*, 22–25.; Middleton, *Black Laws*, 9. Southern votes may have been motivated by anticompetitive considerations. The Virginia delegate explained his vote by saying that the antislavery clause would prevent the raising of tobacco, cotton, and indigo north of the Ohio River. Moses, *Illinois*, 1:187.

31. Ordinance of July 13, 1787, Sections 3–6.

32. Ibid., Section 7.

33. Ibid., Section 9.

34. Middleton, *Black Laws*, 23, 23n21. The 1800 federal census recorded only 337 blacks in the Ohio area of the Northwest Territory—none of whom were slaves—out of a population

of more than forty-five thousand. Although Republicans in Ohio pushing for statehood sought the black vote, the small number of blacks was no threat to the predominately white population.

35. Ordinance of July 13, 1787, Section 13, Article V.

36. Ibid., Article VI.

37. Finkelman, "Evading the Ordinance," 24–25; Harris, *History of Negro Servitude*, 6, 6n3; Middleton, *Black Laws*, 12–13, 13n29. Harris cites the St. Clair letter to President Washington communicating his interpretation.

38. Alvord, *Illinois Country*, 403; Moses, *Illinois*, 1:196–98.

39. Alvord, *Illinois Country*, 404. A portion of the original area of St. Clair County still exists as a county with the same name. It is one of Illinois's largest counties, across the Mississippi River from St. Louis. Many other Illinois counties were later formed out of the original county.

40. Moses, *Illinois*, 1:196.

41. Ibid., 1:198.

42. 1818 Constitution, Schedule, Section 14.

43. Cayton, *Frontier Republic*, 38–39.

44. Alvord, *Illinois Country*, 407.

45. Recent research suggests that the venerable narrative that Harrison died because he caught pneumonia from talking too long in the rain is not entirely accurate. More likely, Harrison died from septic shock caused by one of two strains of enteric fever. The source of the infection was contamination of the White House water supply from a nearby waste depository in the city, which had no sewer system. Two other presidents, James K. Polk and Zachary Taylor, also developed severe gastroenteritis while living in the White House. Jane McHugh and Philip A. Mackowiak, "What Really Killed the President," *New York Times*, April 1, 2014.

46. Alvord, *Illinois Country*, 419; Howard, *Illinois*, 69; Moses, *Illinois*, 1:213.

47. Alvord, *Illinois Country*, 407; Howard, *Illinois*, 69–70.

48. Alvord, *Illinois Country*, 407–8; Howard, *Illinois*, 70–72.

49. Alvord, *Illinois Country*, 422–29; Finkelman, "Evading the Ordinance," 25–34, 30n25; Moses, *Illinois*, 1:184–85, 185n.

50. Ohio Constitution of 1802, Article 7, Section 2. Indentured servitude had long been common in the American colonies and, later, the states. Hundreds of thousands of immigrants, for example, made their voyages across the Atlantic under indenture contracts, legally enforceable in the courts, that paid for their passage and obligated them to terms of service in the new country. Indentures of blacks became widespread in the American colonies founded on the legal fiction that the contracts were voluntary and for specified periods, therefore were not slavery or involuntary servitude.

51. Alvord, *Illinois Country*, 423.

52. Ibid., 423–24.

53. Philbrick, *Laws of Indiana Territory*, 136–39.

54. Ibid., 203–4. The law, passed December 3, 1806, went into effect on January 1, 1807, and is generally referred to as the 1807 law. Finkelman, "Evading the Ordinance," 35, 35nn.

55. Smith, "Salines of Southern Illinois," 246.

56. Dexter, *Bondage in Egypt*, 165; Howard, *Illinois*, 132; Smith, "Salines of Southern Illinois," 246–47.

57. Slave numbers upward of one thousand seem high and are not substantiated by census records. Censuses, however, which record only 168 slaves in Illinois Territory, do not include the number of leased slaves required for the scale of operations in the salines. Dexter, *Bondage in Egypt*, 165–68; Howard, *Illinois*, 132–33; Smith, "Salines of Southern Illinois," 246–52.

58. The law also said that leasing must end in the saline on January 1, 1826. However, indentured servitude continued beyond that time. Dexter, *Bondage in Egypt*, 165–68; Howard, *Illinois*, 132–33; Moses, *Illinois*, 1:265–66.

59. Buck, *Illinois in 1818*, 189–92.

60. Alvord, *Illinois Country*, 425; Buck, *Illinois in 1818*, 192; Philbrick, *Laws of Indiana Territory*, 139, 204.

61. Kenney and Hartley, *Heroic and Notorious*, 4–8; Moses, *Illinois*, 1:242, 264.

62. Moses, *Illinois*, 1:226, 244.

63. Angle, "Nathaniel Pope," 151, 179–81.

64. Ibid., 113–14.

65. Ibid., 115–17.

66. Ibid., 117–20.

67. Ibid., 120.

68. Ibid., 121–23.

69. All officers of the Illinois Territory and their terms of service are set forth at Moses, *Illinois*, 1:264n*.

70. Alvord, *Illinois Country*, 429; Edwards, *History of Illinois*, 22.

71. Howard, *Illinois*, 76–77; Howard, *Mostly Good Men*, 20–21.

72. Howard, *Illinois*, 139–40; Howard, *Mostly Good Men*, 33; Kenney and Hartley, *Heroic and Notorious*, 121–13. While Edwards was territorial governor, Edwards County was created and named after him in 1814, as was the city of Edwardsville, which was built by his business enterprises, in 1815. Moses, *Illinois*, 1:272.

Edwards was often a benefactor to needy friends and neighbors. Having had some medical training, in 1833 he remained in residence in Belleville when a cholera epidemic struck; he refused to flee and instead gave aid and comfort to other residents until the illness ended his life on July 20, 1833.

73. Moses, *Illinois*, 1:244.

74. Angle, "Nathaniel Pope," 124–27; Moses, *Illinois*, 1:244–45; Simeone, *Democracy and Slavery*, 21.

75. Howard, *Illinois*, 70.

76. Moses, *Illinois*, 1:245–46.

77. Ferguson, *Illinois in the War of 1812*, ch. 5; Keating, *Rising Up from Indian Country*, 136–47, 136n1; Quaife, *Chicago and the Old Northwest*, 127–261. In recent years, the description of the two-centuries-old event, long remembered as the Fort Dearborn Massacre and celebrated as a potent image of Chicago's past, has been challenged. Growing controversy over calling the events of August 15, 1812, a massacre led to the removal from public view in 1998 of a notable monument with the same title that had occupied the entry lobby of the Chicago Historical Society for more than fifty years. Historians and others have argued that the attack was a battle on a far western outpost in Indian country, and that it should be described as a battle. See Keating, *Rising Up from Indian Country*, 136–50, and, especially, the epilogue, "Why It Was Not a Massacre," 235–48. Keating argues that even the killing of young children and women traveling in rear wagons was justified in battle because they might "travel back to their villages and potentially serve some useful purpose."

But see also Ferguson, *Illinois in the War of 1812*, published the same year as Keating, *Rising Up from Indian Country*. Unabashedly calling the event a massacre, Ferguson describes in detail the characteristic Indian manner of carrying out the attack on the soldiers, the women, and the children, and the subsequent ordeals of those carried away as prisoners. The Indians' conduct, which would be characterized as savagery by whites, undoubtedly stimulated the description as a massacre.

78. Howard, *Illinois*, 90–91; Moses, *Illinois*, 1:252–54.

79. Alvord, *Illinois Country*, 446; Angle, "Nathaniel Pope," 132–33.

80. Philbrick, *Laws of Illinois Territory*, 177–78.

81. Angle, "Nathaniel Pope," 136.

82. Ibid., 139–41.

83. Buck, *Illinois in 1818*, 207.

84. Ibid., 209.

85. Ibid.; Burns and McLean, "Daniel P. Cook," 427; Ford, *History of Illinois*, 73. Cook married Edwards's eldest daughter, Julia, in 1821.

86. Alvord, *Illinois Country*, 458; Buck, *Illinois in 1818*, 209.

87. Angle, "Nathaniel Pope," 145; Buck, *Illinois in 1818*, 209.

88. Buck, *Illinois in 1818*, 209; Edstrom, "With . . . Candour and Good Faith," 242, 242n8.

89. Buck, *Illinois in 1818*, 220.

90. Ibid., 210–11.

91. *Western Intelligencer*, November 20, 1817, p. 3, col. 2.

92. *Western Intelligencer*, November 27, 1817, p. 3, cols. 2–4.

93. Alvord, *Illinois Country*, 459; Buck, *Illinois in 1818*, 212.

94. *Intelligencer*, December 11, 1817, qtd. in Buck, *Illinois in 1818*, 213.

95. Buck, *Illinois in 1818*, 213.

96. Ibid., 213.

97. Letter to Rufus King, April 10, 1818, qtd. in Edstrom, "With . . . Candour and Good Faith," 244, 244n15.

98. *Annals of Congress*, 15th Cong., 1st Sess., p. 782; Angle, "Nathaniel Pope," 144; Buck, *Illinois in 1818*, 221.

99. Alvord, *Illinois Country*, 459; Buck, *Illinois in 1818*, 21–24.

100. Buck, *Illinois in 1818*, 222. The select committee in the House decided to interpret the Northwest Ordinance specification that any two future northern states in the territory should be "*In* that part of said territory which lies north of an east and west line drawn through the southerly bend or extreme of Lake Michigan" (emphasis added) as meaning that such states should be *within* the area north of that line, not necessarily *at* the line.

101. *Annals of Congress*, 15th Cong., 1st Sess., p. 814; Buck, *Illinois in 1818*, 224.

102. *Western Intelligencer*, March 4, 1818; Buck, *Illinois in 1818*, 221.

103. *Western Intelligencer*, March 11, 1818, p. 2, col. 4; Angle, "Nathaniel Pope," 145.

104. Putnam, *Illinois and Michigan Canal*, 1–6.

105. Grover, "Indian Treaties," 385–89.

106. *Niles' Weekly Register*, August 6, 1814, 394; Putnam, *Illinois and Michigan Canal*, 4, 4nn1–2, 5. Putnam adds, "The fact that boats of light burden frequently passed from the Chicago river to the Des Plaines during periods of high water was well known."

107. Edwards, *History of Illinois*, 172. Chouteau, a businessman and second-generation French settler in the American Bottom, was a founder of St. Louis and businessman there as well.

In the 1820s, Illinois and Missouri were allied in Congress in seeking financial support for the canal project. Governor Edwards, in a letter to Henry Clay in 1825, noted, "A favorable object, and indeed a political hobby, that supercedes [*sic*] all others, in this State and Missouri, is a canal to connect Lake Michigan and the Illinois River." Edwards, *History of Illinois*, 173.

108. Alvord, *Illinois Country*, 449–50; Howard, *Illinois*, 196.

109. "Canal to Connect the Illinois River with Lake Michigan," *American State Papers: Miscellaneous*, 2:555–57, https://memory.loc.gov/ammem/amlaw/lwsplink.html, accessed January 4, 2017.

110. Angle, "Nathaniel Pope," 145; *Western Intelligencer*, April 22, 1818, p. 2, col. 2.

111. Angle, "Nathaniel Pope," 146; Buck, *Illinois in 1818*, 224–26.

112. Richard Mentor Johnson of Kentucky, a member of the House subcommittee, exploited such patronage opportunities promptly. From 1819 or 1820 until 1825, Johnson and his brother, Colonel James Johnson, also of Kentucky, owned a concession to mine lead at Galena. They used a workforce of black slaves. Howard, *Illinois*, 167; Murphy, *Gathering of Rivers*; Thwaites, "Notes on Early Lead Mining."

113. *Annals of Congress*, 15th Cong., 1st Sess., p. 1677; Alvord, *Illinois Country*, 460; Buck, *Illinois in 1818*, 225–26.

114. Ford, *History of Illinois*, 23.

115. Ibid., 23; Buck, *Illinois in 1818*, 25–26.

116. Ford, *History of Illinois*, 23.

117. Moses, *Illinois*, 1:278.

118. *Annals of Congress*, 15th Cong., 1st Sess., p. 1677.

119. Angle, "Nathaniel Pope," 146–47; Enabling Act, Buck, *Illinois in 1818*, 226.

120. *Annals of Congress*, 15th Cong., 1st Sess., p. 1678; Edstrom, "With . . . Candour and Good Faith," 255, 258, 261; Meese, "Nathaniel Pope," 17–19.

121. Angle, "Nathaniel Pope," 146–47; *Annals of Congress*, 15th Cong., 1st Sess., p. 1678; Buck, *Illinois in 1818*, 226.

122. Angle, "Nathaniel Pope," 147; *Annals of Congress*, 15th Cong., 1st Sess., p. 1678; Buck, *Illinois in 1818*, 227–29.

123. *Western Intelligencer*, May 6, 1818, p. 3, col. 3 (emphasis added).

124. Buck, *Illinois in 1818*, 229–30.

125. Moses, *Illinois*, 1:281–82.

Chapter 2. The Constitution of 1818:
Slavery, a Bogus Census, Feeble Executive Power

1. Barnhart, "Southern Influence," 373. Barnhart notes that at least two-thirds of the delegates were of southern origin, and the number of slaves owned by delegates was greater than the number of delegates.

There is doubt about the site of the convention. While there is a certain romance to the thought of delegates crowding into Bennett's tavern, reported as the site by some historians (see, for example, Buck, *Illinois in 1818*, 262), others maintain that a more likely site was the building that had been the French commandant's house, which had served as the territorial legislative hall. The only substantial two-story building in town, it was owned by Dr. George Fisher at the time and was rented to the First General Assembly after Illinois became a state.

Kaskaskia, founded on a low-lying peninsula between the Mississippi and Kaskaskia Rivers, experienced a flood in 1844 that caused substantial damage to the town and forced removal of the seat of Randolph County to nearby Chester, located on the bluff above. The next big flood in 1881 destroyed the town and cut a new channel that left Kaskaskia

Island, a part of Illinois, on the Missouri side of the river. Whatever evidence might have existed of the structures of 1818 was submerged under the river.

2. Buck, *Illinois in 1818*, 259–60.

3. Ibid., 212.

4. Alvord, *Illinois Country*, 461–62.

5. Ibid., 462.

6. Ibid., 461.

7. Buck, *Illinois in 1818*, 215–17.

8. Ibid., 218.

9. Howard, *Illinois*, 131.

10. Buck, *Illinois in 1818*, 218.

11. Ibid., 218.

12. Ibid., 243 (emphasis in original).

13. Cornelius, *Constitution Making*, 6–9.

14. The *Journal of the Illinois Constitutional Convention of 1818* was published verbatim in the *Journal of the Illinois State Historical Society* 6 (October 1913): 355–424. It is a brief document that summarizes the actions, textual revisions, and numerical votes at the convention but not verbatim remarks or the names of delegates voting yea and nay. It will be referred to here as *1818 Journal* and cited by page numbers from the historical society publication and, in parentheses, to the original journal as well. Carpenter and Kitchell, "Illinois Constitutional Convention," 327–424.

15. Buck, *Illinois in 1818*, 232. The same issue carried the announcement that Daniel Pope Cook, the same age as Kane, was a candidate to represent the new state in the House of Representatives.

16. *1818 Journal*, 357 (5).

17. Ibid., 359 (7).

18. Ibid., 360 (8), 368–86 (16–34).

19. 1818 Constitution, Article II, Sections 5, 31.

20. *1818 Journal*, 373 (21); Buck, *Illinois in 1818*, 270–71.

21. *1818 Journal*, 405 (53).

22. Ibid., 373 (21); *Intelligencer*, October 14, November 11, 1818.

23. Cayton, *Frontier Republic*, 76–80; Middleton, *Black Laws*, 31–37.

24. *1818 Journal*, 374–75, 389, 397.

25. Ibid., 413, 415.

26. 1818 Constitution, Article III, Section 19.

27. Schedule, Section 10; *1818 Journal*, 415 (63).

28. Schedule, Section 14; Ekberg, *French Roots*, 109, 227, 271. Menard's elegant home, now a state historic site, still stands on its beautiful wooded site partway up the bluff above old Kaskaskia. An imposing statue of Menard stands prominently on the sweeping front

lawn of the State House in Springfield, the capitol building of Illinois. It is a remarkable tribute to one whose highest office was lieutenant governor.

29. 1818 Constitution, Article III, Sections 2–5.

30. 1816 Indiana Constitution, Article V, Section 7.

31. Buck, *Illinois in 1818*, 282; Harris, *History of Negro Servitude*, 18.

32. Opinion on including the slavery prohibition was sharply divided in the Ohio constitutional convention. The provision to prohibit slavery was ultimately approved by one vote, a weak endorsement of Article VI. Middleton, *Black Laws*, 37.

33. Indiana Constitution, 1816, Article XI, Section 7.

34. *1818 Journal*, 401, 411 (49, 59); 1818 Constitution, Article VI.

35. Middleton, *Black Laws*, 30.

36. *1818 Journal*, 400 (48); 1818 Constitution, Article VI.

37. See, for example, Dexter, *Bondage in Egypt*, 72–73.

38. Compare indentures, originals in the Abraham Lincoln Presidential Library and Museum, Springfield [hereafter, ALPLM], manuscript collection, folio SC 1320, with those in folio 3090. See also Dexter, *Bondage in Egypt*, 72–73.

39. *1818 Journal*, 401 (49).

40. Ibid., 411 (59).

41. Ibid., 406–7 (54–55), 411–12 (59–60).

42. 1818 Constitution, Articles V, VII.

43. Ibid., Article VIII; *1818 Journal*, 412 (60); Buck, *Illinois in 1818*, 283–84.

44. 1818 Constitution, Article VIII; *1818 Journal.* 413 (61).

45. 1818 Constitution, Article VIII, Section 8.

46. *1818 Journal*, 407 (55), 409 (57), 416 (64), 423 (71); Buck, *Illinois in 1818*, 286–92.

47. *Intelligencer*, September 2, 1818.

48. Buck, *Illinois in 1818*, 299.

49. Ibid., 297–99.

50. Ibid., 300–302.

51. For biographical information of the first state officers, see Moses, *Illinois*, 1:287–99. Elias Kent Kane served as secretary of state until 1824. That year he was elected U.S. senator. He served in that office from March 1825 until his death in Washington at age forty-one on December 12, 1835. On January 16, 1836, the Illinois legislature formed Kane County, named in his honor.

52. Buck, *Illinois in 1818*, 303–5.

53. Ibid., 311–12.

54. Ibid., 312–13.

55. Ibid., 311–13; Moses, *Illinois*, 1:283–84.

56. Buck, *Illinois in 1818*, 313–14; Moses, *Illinois*, 1:283–84.

57. Buck, *Illinois in 1818*, 315; Moses, *Illinois*, 1:284.

58. *Annals of Congress*, 2nd sess., p. 23, 26, 31–32, 38, 342.

59. Moses, *Illinois*, 1:295. Missouri petitioned the U. S. House of Representatives for admission on March 18, 1818. In February 1819 the House went into a Committee of the Whole to discuss the question. Harris, *History of Negro Servitude*, 27n1.

60. Moses, *Illinois*, 1:314.

61. Ibid., 1:323.

62. Ibid., 1:307.

63. Guasco, *Confronting Slavery*, 71, 78–83, 182–84; Howard, *Illinois*, 183–87; Moses, *Illinois*, 1:307–8.

64. Moses, *Illinois*, 1:309–10.

65. Ibid., 1:315.

66. Ibid., 1:317.

67. Ibid., 1:318.

68. Ibid., 1:319.

69. Ibid., 1:320–21.

70. Ibid., 1:320.

71. Ibid., 1:322.

72. Ibid., 1:321–22.

73. Ibid., 1:323–24.

74. Ibid., 1:332–33.

75. Spencer, "Edward Coles," 153, 153n13.

76. Moses, *Illinois*, 1:326, 342.

77. Ibid., 1:342.

78. Guasco, *Confronting Slavery*, 155–237; Moses, *Illinois*, 1:332–33.

Chapter 3. Black Codes and Bondage, Settling the North, Legislative Follies

1. Davis, *Frontier Illinois*, 20. The state's first capital was a stucco-and-brick house in Kaskaskia, rented from Dr. George Fisher for four dollars a day. The low-ceilinged rooms in which the members conducted their business were also used by Daniel Pope Cook as his law office. Howard, *Illinois*, 117.

2. Stroble, *Okaw's Western Bank*, 11–12.

3. Ibid., 12–13.

4. Ibid., 14–18.

5. Ibid., 78–83, 123–32.

6. Enabling Act of 1818, Section 6.

7. Pease, *Frontier State*, 44–46. The Seventh General Assembly in 1831 amended the criminal code, substituting imprisonment in the penitentiary for whipping and imprisonment in the pillory. Moses, *Illinois*, 1:356–57.

8. "An Act Respecting Free Negroes, Mulattoes, Servants and Slaves," March 1819.

9. Act approved, February 1827; *Illinois Revised Statutes*, 1833, p. 496.

10. *Revised Laws of Illinois*, 6 G. A. (1828–29), 109.

11. Illinois State Archives, online Service and Emancipation Records, accessed August 22, 2012.

12. Dexter, *Bondage in Egypt*, 76–77; Illinois State Archives, online Service and Emancipation Records, accessed August 22, 2012; Norton, *Illinois Census Returns, 1820*, 237.

13. Dexter, *Bondage in Egypt*, 537–52; Harris, *History of Negro Servitude*, 14–15.

14. Davis, *Frontier Illinois*, 166; Danzer, *Illinois*, 79.

15. Simon, *Lincoln's Preparation*, 121–22, citing Ethan A. Snively, "Slavery in Illinois," 55.

16. St. Clair County Will Records and St. Clair County Probate Case files for Ninian Edwards, Office of the Secretary of State, Illinois Regional Archives Depository, Special Collections, Morris Library-1632, Southern Illinois University, Carbondale, reference no. 2837, accessed March 2013.

17. Dexter, *Bondage in Egypt*, 497; Simon, *Lincoln's Preparation*, 28, 122, 122n3.

18. Harris, *History of Negro Servitude*, 121, 121n2.

19. Blackwell, *Decisions*, 1:50.

20. Dexter, *Bondage in Egypt*, 125, 125n467.

21. Ibid., 125, 125n468.

22. Blackwell, *Decisions*, 1:50–52.

23. Ibid., 1:336.

24. Ibid., 1:129.

25. Ibid., 1:131.

26. *Nance v. Howard*, Blackwell, *Decisions*, 1:112.

27. Even the poorest slave owner knew the economic value of owning a "breeder" female slave who, forced to mate with a male slave, produced slave children that were an addition to the owner's wealth. See, for example, Douglass, *Narrative*, 94.

28. Wiencek, *Master*, 30. Ironically, George Washington, who received Jefferson's calculation, later freed his slaves because slavery had made human beings into money, like "Cattle in the market."

29. Ibid., 31.

30. Ibid., 31.

31. Blackwell, *Decisions*, 1:50.

32. Harris, *History of Negro Servitude*, 14.

33. 1818 Constitution, Article VI, Section 1.

34. Enacted in December 1826, the act went into force on July 1, 1827.

35. 1833 Revised Laws, 68–73.

36. 1833 Revised Laws, Section 4.

37. 1833 Revised Laws.

38. Dexter, *Bondage in Egypt*, 130–31.

39. Ibid., 529–32.

40. Thomas Schwartz, "The Lincoln 'Apprentice': Part 1," from Out of the Top Hat: A blog from the ALPLM, entry posted March 21, 2011, http://www.alplm.org/blog/tag/ninian-edwards/, accessed January 24, 2013.

41. Hart, *Lincoln's Springfield*, 56, 212; Schwartz, "The Lincoln 'Apprentice.'"

42. Hart, "Springfield's African Americans"; Schwartz, "The Lincoln 'Apprentice.'" {Add Frederick Douglass citation]

43. Hart, "Springfield's African Americans"; manuscript files, ALPLM, folio SC 1327–5. The manuscript files contain about the same number of apprenticeship indentures of white children as blacks.

Other leading citizens of Springfield who signed children to apprenticeship indentures in the 1840s that bound them to long years of service included James F. Owings, clerk of Nathaniel Pope's U.S. district court at Springfield, William Hickman, a justice of the peace, and Robert Irwin, Abraham Lincoln's banker. As late as 1849, Mary Ferguson indentured eight-year-old Elizabeth West to serve until February 1859, when she would reach age eighteen. Hart, "Springfield's African Americans"; manuscript files, ALPLM, folio SC 1327–5.

44. Manuscript files, ALPLM, N. W. Edwards collection; Hostick collection.

45. Edwards, *Papers*, 243n*.

46. Session Laws, 1826, Act on Apprentices, Sections 9–12.

47. House Journal, 1836–37, 241–44; Simon, *Lincoln's Preparation*, 132–33.

48. House Journal, 1836–37, 241–44; Simon, *Lincoln's Preparation*, 130–33.

49. House Journal, 1835–36, 236; Simon, *Lincoln's Preparation*, 130.

50. Simon, *Lincoln's Preparation*, 127, 127n20.

51. The Black Hawk War was unnecessary, avoidable, expensive, and overrated. It lasted fifteen weeks. Only seventy settlers and soldiers died, a small toll as wars go. Two U.S. presidents, Zachary Taylor and Abraham Lincoln (the latter elected captain by the small militia of New Salem); Jefferson Davis, president of the Southern Confederacy; General Winfield Scott, presidential candidate and the most notable soldier of his generation; and senators, governors, and generals in profusion maintained the war's status in Illinois legend. Hauberg, "Black Hawk War," 91–134; Howard, *Illinois*, 147–52; Pease, *Frontier State*, 154–71; Quaife, *Chicago and the Old Northwest*, 323–39.

52. Gerwing, "Chicago Indian Treaty," 118–42.

53. Quaife, *Chicago and the Old Northwest*, 357.

54. Ordinance of 1787, Section 14, Article III.

55. Conzen and Carr, *Illinois and Michigan Canal*, 65–70; Moses, *Illinois*, 1:385–87, appendix 1.

56. Secretary of State, *Origin and Evolution of Illinois Counties*, March 2010, 37 (Exs. 7–1), 51 (Ex. 7–2), 59 (Exs. 7–4, 7–5, 7–6), maps of population density 1820, 1830, 1840; Pease, *Frontier State*, 4, 174, 384; Moses, *Illinois*, 1:385.

57. Cronon, *Nature's Metropolis*, 29; Davis, *Frontier Illinois*, 209–10.

58. Angle, "Nathaniel Pope," 153; Cahan, *Court That Shaped America*, 9–10; Howard, *Illinois*, 85; Pease, *Frontier State*, 173–76; Pooley, "Settlement of Illinois," 397–419.

59. Pooley, "Settlement of Illinois," 397.

60. Cahan, *Court That Shaped America*, 9–10; Pooley, "Settlement of Illinois," 397.

61. Howard, *Illinois*, 154–56; Young, *Chicago Transit*, 6, 12.

62. Davis, *Frontier Illinois*, 220–21; Howard, *Illinois*, 147, 157, 157n13, 222; Young, *Chicago Transit*, 8–9.

63. Conzen and Carr, *Illinois and Michigan Canal*, 6–22; Putnam, *Illinois and Michigan Canal*, 8–18. The single most authoritative publication on the canal is Putnam's detailed and comprehensive work, published by the Chicago Historical Society at the centennial of statehood in 1918. Conzen and Carr's reference book includes superb introductory essays and a 250-page guide to sources. See also Lamb, *Corridor in Time*.

64. Howard, *Illinois*, 194–96; Lamb, *Corridor in Time*, 15; Putnam, *Illinois and Michigan Canal*, 35–37.

65. Davis, *Frontier Illinois*, 226–29. Howard, *Illinois*, 195–96; Putnam, *Illinois and Michigan Canal*, 36–37, 42–44.

66. Conzen and Carr, *Illinois and Michigan Canal*, 63–64; Putnam, *Illinois and Michigan Canal*, 62.

67. For firsthand descriptions of travel along the canal, see J. H. Buckingham, "Chicago to Springfield and Towns along the Way," and Arthur Cunynghame, "Travel on the Illinois and Michigan Canal," in Angle, *Prairie State*, 237–53, 254–59; Howard, *Illinois*, 240.

68. Putnam, *Illinois and Michigan Canal*, 96–97, 106–7, 154–58.

69. Conzen and Carr, *Illinois and Michigan Canal*, 65–67; Howard, *Illinois*, 242–48.

70. Conzen and Carr, *Illinois and Michigan Canal*, 67–68; Davis, *Frontier Illinois*, 232–37; Howard, *Illinois*, 237–49.

71. Conzen and Carr, *Illinois and Michigan Canal*, 64; Davis, *Frontier Illinois*, 232; Howard, *Illinois*, 123–25.

72. Moses, *Illinois*, 1:292–94.

73. Simon, *Lincoln's Preparation*, 49–50.

74. Qtd. in Simon, *Lincoln's Preparation*, 51.

75. Johannsen, *Stephen A. Douglas*, 3–22.

76. Ibid., 38–42; Simon, *Lincoln's Preparation*, 34–35.

77. Johannsen, *Stephen A. Douglas*, 30–72; Simon, *Lincoln's Preparation*, 116.

78. Johannsen, *Stephen A. Douglas*, 92–96; Simon, *Lincoln's Preparation*, 116–17.

79. Howard, *Illinois*, 295: Johannsen, *Stephen A. Douglas*, 117–23, 186–87.

80. Davis, *Frontier Illinois*, 230–32.

81. *CW*, 1:5–9.

82. Donald, *Lincoln*, 46, 53.

83. Ibid., 60–61; Simon, *Lincoln's Preparation*, 147–48; Edwards's wife, Elizabeth Todd Edwards, was Mary Todd Lincoln's older sister.

84. Burlingame, *Abraham Lincoln*, 1:112–20; Simon, *Lincoln's Preparation*, 45–52, 76–90.

85. Moses, Illinois, 410; Pease, *Frontier State*, 214.

86. Pease, *Frontier State*, 214.

87. Moses, *Illinois*, <vol.?>:412; Pease, *Frontier State*, 215.

88. *Sangamo Journal*, March 4, 1837, qtd. in Simon, *Lincoln's Preparation*, 31.

89. Moses, *Illinois*, 412.

90. Burlingame, *Abraham Lincoln*, 1:118; Donald, *Lincoln*, 64; Moses, *Illinois*, 1:411–13; Simon, *Lincoln's Preparation*, 58–60.

91. Howard, *Illinois*, 193–207, 227–31; Moses, *Illinois*, 1:413–16; Pease, *Frontier State*, chs. 11, 16, 17; Simon, *Lincoln's Preparation*, 173–78, 184–90.

92. Howard, *Illinois*, 200.

93. Ibid., 202–6; Davis, *Frontier Illinois*, 232–34.

94. Howard, *Illinois*, 200–202.

95. *Choisser v. Hargrave*, Breese (Hamilton edition), 1:336; *Boon v. Juliet*, Breese (Hamilton edition), 1:311.

96. Dexter, *Bondage in Egypt*, 129–31; Harris, *History of Negro Servitude*, 104–5, 105n1; Howard, *Illinois*, 189–90.

97. *Kinney v. Cook*, Scammon 3:231 (December Term 1840); *Bailey v. Cromwell*, Scammon 3:70, 71 (July Term 1841); Dexter, *Bondage in Egypt*, 262–63, 274; Finkelman, "More Perfect Union," 266; Harris, *History of Negro Servitude*, 105.

98. *Kinney v. Cook*, 233.

99. Bailey v. Cromwell, Scammon 3:70–72 (July Term 1841). Abraham Lincoln was one of the most ambitious and active lawyers in Illinois. He and his partner, William Herndon, took on whatever clients came their way. Between 1838 and 1847, when he left for Washington to serve his one term in Congress, by one count he was said to have been in at least seventeen cases involving slavery issues. He represented whites in most cases, including slave owners and opponents of slavery. He represented some free blacks. In some cases for whites he raised antislavery arguments, as in the Bailey case. In others, as for slave owner Robert Matson, he tried, unsuccessfully, to recover runaway slaves. Finkelman, "Abraham Lincoln," 134; Donald, *Lincoln*, 103. "Lincoln [was not] squeamish about the social implications of the cases that he argued. . . . His business was law, not morality." Donald, *Lincoln*, 103–4.

100. Harris, *History of Negro Servitude*, 109.

101. Ibid., 109, 109n2, 110.

102. Finkelman, "More Perfect Union," 263–64; Harris, *History of Negro Servitude*, 110–13; Howard, *Illinois*, 189; *Richard Eels v. The People*, Scammon 4.

103. Finkelman, "More Perfect Union," 254–55; Harris, *History of Negro Servitude*, 114.

104. Harris, *History of Negro Servitude*, 106.

105. Dexter, *Bondage in Egypt*, 132–33.

106. Ibid., 133; Harris, *History of Negro Servitude*, 106–9, 122–23; Fuhrig, "Lincoln and Koerner," 119; Howard, *Illinois*, 190–91.

107. *Jarrot v. Jarrot*, Gilman 2:1–25 (December Term 1845).

108. Finkelman, "Abraham Lincoln," 134; Harris, *History of Negro Servitude*, 118–19, 179.

Chapter 4. The Constitution of 1848:
Reconstructing Government, Balancing Powers, Oppressing Free Blacks

1. Cornelius, *Constitution Making*, 25–28; Howard, *Illinois*, 232; Moses, *Illinois*, 2:553.

2. Cornelius, *Constitution Making*, 28.

3. Ibid., 29; *Journal*, Illinois House of Representatives, Fifteenth General Assembly, Session 1, February 17, 1847, 422, 426 [hereafter, *1847 Journal*]; *Laws of Illinois*, 1847, 33.

4. Donald, *Lincoln*, 11–14; Howard, *Illinois*, 136–37.

5. Eisenhower, *So Far from God*, 183; Greenberg, *Wicked War*, 113–18, 135–40; Moses, *Illinois*, 1:490–96. Illinois treated returning volunteers as heroes, with special honors for those who were wounded in action. Baker, Bissell, Shields, and numerous others all later held high public office. Pease, *Frontier State*, 406; Kenney and Hartley, *Heroic and Notorious*, 37–41, 63–71.

6. Burlingame, *Abraham Lincoln*, 194–98, 218–24, 231–41, 248; Donald, *Lincoln*, 114–15; Greenberg, *Wicked War*, 135–36; Moses, *Illinois*, 1:509–10; Howard, *Illinois*, 241; Temple, *Lincoln's Connections*, 27.

7. Moses, *Illinois*, 1:496; Pease, *Frontier State*, 405–6.

8. *1847 Journal*, 148–49; Cole, *Constitutional Debates of 1847*, 345–50.

9. Cornelius, *Constitution Making*, 30.

10. Ibid., 30. The 162 total number of delegates was the largest to attend any of the state's six constitutional conventions. The 1818 constitution set the total, specifying that the number of delegates was to equal the number of members of the general assembly. 1818 Constitution, Article VII.

11. Cornelius, *Constitution Making*, 30, 30n15, 31.

12. Fraker, *Lincoln's Ladder*, 36–149. Davis was a prolific letter writer. During the 1848 convention he and his wife exchanged letters three times a week. In letters to her and to others, Davis revealed many of his thoughts about the convention. On June 19, at the end

of the convention's second week, he wrote, "The convention is composed of a better body of men than I have seen in the state," in contrast to the legislature as "full of drunkards." Letter, June 19, 1848, Davis Family Papers, ALPLM, box 7, folder B-2.

13. In an act of parsimony that was cured only seventy-two years later by private initiatives, the convention voted not to provide funds to print its debates. In 1919 a valuable reconstruction of the proceedings was drawn from accounts during the convention published in the *Illinois State Register* and its partisan rival, the *Sangamo Journal*. The *Constitutional Debates of 1847* was edited by Arthur Charles Cole of the University of Illinois and published by the Illinois State Historical Library.

14. Ford, *History of Illinois*, 27; Angle, "Review," 99–104. David Davis voiced the unhappiness of many, especially Whig delegates, concerning the legislature. On June 25, he wrote, "Reforms were greatly needed, many salutary ones have been already agreed on. The legislature has been the Great Source of Evil in the state. If there had been none in session for 10 yrs. Illinois would have been a very prosperous State." Letter, June 25, 1848, Davis Family Papers, ALPLM, box 2, folder A-7.

15. 1848 Constitution, Article III, Sections 3, 4; Cole, *Constitutional Debates of 1847*, 292.

16. 1848 Constitution, Article III, Section 6; Cole, *Constitutional Debates of 1847*, 293–303.

17. 1848 Constitution, Article III, Section 24; Cornelius, *Constitution Making*, 34.

18. 1848 Constitution, Article III, Section 7.

19. Cornelius, *Constitution Making*, 35.

20. 1848 Constitution, Article IV, Sections 1, 2, 14, 22.

21. *1847 Journal*, 61–63.

22. Cole, *Constitutional Debates of 1847*, 361–90.

23. 1848 Constitution, Article IV, Sections 5, 23, 24, Article V, Section 10; *1847 Journal*, 157–58, 165, 171, 319; Cole, *Constitutional Debates of 1847*, 376–82, 392–95, 736. In contrast, the Northwest Ordinance set the salary for territorial governors at $2,000, plus a thousand-acre land grant.

24. *1847 Journal*, 176–77; Cole, *Constitutional Debates of 1847*, 404–5, 442.

25. *1847 Journal*, 317–19, 322–23.

26. Moses, *Illinois*, 2:553, 556–57. Indiana Constitution of 1816, Article V, Section 7. Virginia in 1864 and Mississippi in 1868 returned to the method of legislatures selecting judges.

27. Moses, *Illinois*, 2:1146.

28. Ibid., 1:443–44. Lockwood, a prominent Whig, was elected to and served in the constitutional convention in 1847 while remaining on the court.

29. 1818 Constitution, Article II, Section 27.

30. Moses, *Illinois*, 1:444.

31. Ibid., 1:444–45.

32. Ibid., 1:445.

33. 1848 Constitution, Article V, Sections 2–6.

34. Ibid., Article V, Section 3; Cole, *Constitutional Debates of 1847*, xxvi, 450–514, 742–86.

35. 1848 Constitution, Article V, Sections 7, 15, 16, 19; Cole, *Constitutional Debates of 1847*, 760–800.

36. 1848 Constitution, Article V, Section 10; Cole, *Constitutional Debates of 1847*, 775–87.

37. 1848 Constitution, Article III, Sections 32, 33, 35, 36, 37.

38. Ibid., Article X, Section 1; Cornelius, *Constitution Making*, 38–39.

39. One observer, former Democratic governor Thomas Ford, calculated that more than nine thousand of about ten thousand foreign votes in Illinois went to the Democrats, more than enough to be decisive in close elections. Ford, *History of Illinois*, 214–15.

Shortly after the 1840 elections, David Davis, writing to a relative, expressed a charge that has been a consistent refrain to the present day by "downstaters" about alleged vote fraud in the north, particularly by Democrats in Cook County. Davis wrote, "We think that if the *Irish* did not vote more than *3 times* we could carry the State. . . . The Irish vote along the line of the [Illinois and Michigan] Canal increased most wonderfully, and in nearly every other county of the State, the Whig vote has enlarged greatly." Letter to father-in-law, November 16, 1840, Davis Family Papers, ALPLM, box 2.

40. Cole, *Constitutional Debates of 1847*, xxiv–xxv.

41. Ibid. 527.

42. Ibid., 525, 528–29.

43. Ibid., 552–54, 578–80; Moses, *Illinois*, 2:556.

44. 1848 Constitution, Article VI, Sec 1.

45. *1847 Journal*, 76; Cornelius, *Constitution Making*, 37.

46. 1848 Constitution, Article VI, Section 2.

47. Ibid., Article VI, Section 9.

48. Cornelius, *Constitution Making*, 39.

49. Cole, *Constitutional Debates of 1847*, xxii–xxiv, 68–70.

50. Ibid., 101–4; Cornelius, *Constitution Making*, 39; *1847 Journal*, 53–53.

51. 1848 Constitution, Article X, Sections 3–5; Cole, *Constitutional Debates of 1847*, 312–14, 690–99, 707–19.

52. *1847 Journal*, 50; Cole, *Constitutional Debates of 1847*, 90–99.

53. 1848 Constitution, Article IX, Section 1; Cole, *Constitutional Debates of 1847*, 100; *1847 Journal*, 52. The final constitution included the substance of this resolution, but with the amount of the tax to be "not less than fifty cents nor more than one dollar each." 1848 Constitution, Article IX, Section 1.

54. 1848 Constitution, Article XIII, Section 16; *1847 Journal*, 463; Cole, *Constitutional Debates of 1847*, 868.

55. *1847 Journal*, 92; Cole, *Constitutional Debates of 1847*, 201–2; Fishback, "Illinois Legislation on Slavery," 427.

56. Cole, *Constitutional Debates of 1847*, 204, 206, 210.

57. Ibid., 212, 216, 218, 221. Residents of the state's southern counties, particularly those across the Ohio River from Kentucky or the Mississippi River from Missouri, complained that slave owners from slave states dumped aged or infirm slaves in Illinois. They also asserted that the much greater numbers of free blacks were visible and a public nuisance, while slaves were controlled and confined to their masters' premises. Whatever the cause, the data show that free blacks in Illinois's thirty-four southernmost counties greatly outnumbered slaves. The 1845 state census, completed just before the 1847 convention, recorded 142 "slaves/servants" in the thirty-four southernmost counties and 3,190 "free blacks." Dexter, *Bondage in Egypt*, 470.

58. Cole, *Constitutional Debates of 1847*, 228.

59. *1847 Journal*, 94–95, Cole, *Constitutional Debates of 1847*, 219, 228.

60. 1848 Constitution, Article XIV; *1847 Journal*, 453; Fishback, "Illinois Legislation on Slavery," 427.

61. Cole, *Constitutional Debates of 1847*, 855–58.

62. Ibid., 860–61.

63. *1847 Journal*, 455–56; Cole, *Constitutional Debates of 1847*, 863.

64. 1848 Constitution, Article XIII, Sections 15, 16; Cole, *Constitutional Debates of 1847*, 869–72; *1847 Journal*, 465–66, 472–73.

65. Howard, *Mostly Good Men*, 87–91; Moses, *Illinois*, 2:603–6.

66. Moses, *Illinois*, 2:994.

67. Howard, *Illinois*, 275; Moses, *Illinois*, 2:995–96.

68. Cole, *Constitutional Debates of 1847*, 65–74, 953.

69. Enabling Act of 1818, Section 6; Moses, *Illinois*, 2:989–92.

70. *1847 Journal*, 78–79; Cole, *Constitutional Debates of 1847*, 172–86.

71. *1847 Journal*, 496; Cole, *Constitutional Debates of 1847*, 898–99.

72. *1847 Journal*, 496; Cole, *Constitutional Debates of 1847*, 898–99.

73. *1847 Journal*, 496–97; Cole, *Constitutional Debates of 1847*, 900–921.

74. Cole, *Constitutional Debates of 1847*, 552–54.

75. *1847 Journal*, 496–506; Cole, *Constitutional Debates of 1847*, 921–26. Education advocates' effort to achieve passage of a state law continued. Well-attended conventions, one in 1852 and two in 1853, one of them organized by teachers' associations, campaigned for school betterment. Laws were enacted. The first, in 1851, allowed townships to levy property taxes for educational purposes. In 1854 the general assembly created the office of state superintendent of public instruction. Governor Joel Matteson appointed Ninian W. Edwards to the position. Edwards's consultations and surveys of the state resulted in

an 1855 law establishing the principle that the state should use its taxing power to support schools. By 1860 the superintendent's report showed that four out of five persons of school age were enrolled in almost nine thousand districts that maintained public schools. Education was raised to constitutional importance with the inclusion of an article on education in the proposed 1862 constitution. Howard, *Illinois*, 273–75; Moses, *Illinois*, 2:995–1002.

76. Hall, Hyman, and Sigal, *Constitutional Convention*, vi–vii, 9–11.

77. 1848 Constitution, Article X.

78. *1847 Journal*, 488; Cole, *Constitutional Debates of 1847*, 885–87; Moses, *Illinois*, 2:559.

79. 1848 Constitution, Article XV; *1847 Journal*, 513, 535; Cole, *Constitutional Debates of 1847*, 929–39.

80. *1847 Journal*, 515, 569–70.

81. Ibid., 570–73; Cole, *Constitutional Debates of 1847*, 944–45.

82. Letter, August 29, 1847, Davis Family Papers, ALPLM, box 7.

83. Cole, *Constitutional Debates of 1847*, xxix–xx; Cornelius, *Constitution Making*, 43; Koerner, *Memoirs*, 523–24; Moses, *Illinois*, 2:559–60; Pease, *Frontier State*, 407–8.

84. 1848 Constitution, Schedule, Section 13; *1847 Journal*, 570; Cornelius, *Constitution Making*, 44; Moses, *Illinois*, 2:559; Pease, *Frontier State*, 409.

85. Wisconsin Historical Society, "Turning Points," http//www.wisconsinhistory.org/turning points/search.asp?id=1627, accessed February 26, 2014; Moses, *Illinois*, 2:553.

86. Howard, *Illinois*, 234–35.

87. Wisconsin Constitution of 1848, Article II, Section 1; Howard, *Illinois*, 234–35; Moses, *Illinois*, 1:278–80; Strong, *History*, 312–14.

Chapter 5. Two Transformative Decades: 1848–1868

1. Angle, "Nathaniel Pope," 176.

2. Ibid., 156–67; Cahan, *Court That Shaped America*, 8–9.

3. Angle, "Nathaniel Pope," 178–79.

4. Ibid., 178–79.

5. Ibid., 179–80.

6. Fifteen more counties were added from 1841 to 1859, bringing the number to the final total of 102. Secretary of State, *Origin and Evolution of Illinois Counties*, March 2010, 58; Bogart and Thompson, *Industrial State*, 1; Cahan, *Court That Shaped America*, 9–10; Hirsh, "Economic Geography," 254–60.

7. Young, *Chicago Transit*, 27–29.

8. Johannsen, *Stephen A. Douglas*, 304, 395, 435.

9. 1848 Constitution, Art XIII, Section 16; Article XIV.

10. Dexter, *Bondage in Egypt*, appendix A.

11. 1848 Constitution, Article XIV.

12. Fishback, "Illinois Legislation on Slavery," 427–28.

13. Harris, *History of Negro Servitude*, 119.

14. *Hone v. Ammons*, 14 Illinois Reports, 31.

15. "An Act to Prevent the Immigration of Free Negroes," February 5, 1853, *Laws of Illinois, 1853*, 57.

16. *Rodney*, 19 Illinois 42 (1857).

17. Howard, *Illinois*, 286, 294.

18. Burlingame, *Abraham Lincoln*, 1:368–70.

19. Donald, *Lincoln*, 140–41.

20. Davis and Wilson, *Lincoln-Douglas Debates*, xii–xiii.

21. Ibid., xii–xv.

22. *CW*, 4:67.

23. Roske, *His Own Counsel*, 22–23. Trumbull's career in many ways closely resembled that of Stephen Douglas. Born in Connecticut in 1813, he attended a private academy and taught school in the state until 1833. At age twenty he moved to Georgia to head another academy, after which he studied law, was admitted to the bar, and practiced in Georgia until 1837, when he moved to Alton, Illinois. He soon became a well-known lawyer. Between 1839 and 1848, he argued eighty-seven cases before the Illinois Supreme Court. He was not reluctant to represent black people in court. He represented the free slaves who were the prevailing parties in *Kinney v. Cook* in 1841 and *Jarrot v. Jarrot* in 1845. Trumbull was elected as a Democrat to the Illinois House of Representatives in 1840, and the next year to the office of secretary of state, where he served until 1843. Elected to the new supreme court in 1848, he resigned that position in 1854 to campaign against the Kansas-Nebraska Act. He was elected to Congress that year and elevated to the Senate in 1855. Trumbull was a distinguished senator from 1855 until 1873, the first Illinois senator to serve three terms. Over the course of his political career he was a Democrat, then a Republican, a Liberal Republican, and again a Democrat. *Biographical Directory of the United States Congress*; Simon, *Lincoln's Preparation*, 312–13; Kenney, *Heroic and Notorious*, 42–50; Finkelman, "More Perfect Union," 266.

24. Roske, *His Own Counsel*, 20–23.

25. Burlingame., *Abraham Lincoln*, 1:375–76.

26. Donald, *Lincoln*, 178–79; Roske, *His Own Counsel*, 22–23.

27. Burlingame, *Abraham Lincoln*, 1:392.

28. Ibid., 1:401–2; Roske, *His Own Counsel*, 24–25.

29. Burlingame, *Abraham Lincoln*, 1:402–3; Roske, *His Own Counsel*, 24–25.

30. *CW*, 2:382–83 (emphasis in original).

31. Moses, *Illinois*, 2:596–97.

32. Howard, *Illinois*, 289–90; Moses, *Illinois*, 2:598–99.

33. Howard, *Illinois*, 290–91; Howard, *Mostly Good Men*, 89–90; Moses, *Illinois*, 2:599–601.

34. Howard, *Mostly Good Men*, 87–91; Moses, *Illinois*. 2:603–6.

35. 1848 Illinois Constitution, Article VI, Sections 25, 26; Howard, *Mostly Good Men*, 90.

36. Howard, *Illinois*, 291; Moses, *Illinois*, 2:602–8.

37. Howard, *Mostly Good Men*, 90–91; Moses, *Illinois*, 2:606, 626.

38. Allen and Lacey, *Illinois Elections*, 137–39.

39. Howard, *Illinois*, 293.

40. Guelzo, "Houses Divided," 398; Moses, *Illinois*, 2:609–10.

41. *CW*, 2:461–69; Finkelman, "More Perfect Union," 248–49.

42. *CW*, 2:461–69; Finkelman, "More Perfect Union," 248–49.

43. Finkelman, "Dred Scott," 24–25; Finkelman, "More Perfect Union."

44. Burlingame, *Abraham Lincoln*, 1:472; Howard, *Illinois*, 292.

45. Burlingame, *Abraham Lincoln*, 1:467–69; Howard, *Illinois*, 292.

46. Davis and Wilson, *Lincoln-Douglas Debates*, xx–xxiv; Howard, *Illinois*, 292–94; Johannsen, *Stephen A. Douglas*, 662–63. Douglas's beautiful and regal second wife, Adele Cutts, generally accompanied him throughout the campaign. Douglas, who wished to appear a commanding figure, traveled in a flag-bedecked special train, fitted out for comfort and campaigning, to which was attached a flatcar carrying a brass cannon labeled "Popular Sovereignty." The cannon loudly announced the approach of the Douglas entourage at every speaking location. Douglas himself spoke in a handsome blue suit with silver buttons and "immaculate linen," cutting the figure of a great U.S. senator appearing before his constituents. Johannsen, *Stephen A. Douglas*, 655–56.

Lincoln deliberately cultivated a different image. He traveled in the regular passenger cars on trains, mingling with the people. During the debates he wore his regular clothes, described as "a rusty black frock-coat with sleeves that should have been longer" and black trousers that "permitted a very full view of his large feet."

Mary Lincoln, elegantly dressed, with her aristocratic bearing, accompanied Lincoln only to the final debate in Alton. Davis and Wilson, *Lincoln-Douglas Debates*, xx–xxiv; Donald, *Lincoln*, 215, quoting Carl Schurz, the German American leader; Guelzo, "Houses Divided," 405–10; Johannsen, *Stephen A. Douglas*, 662–63.

47. Davis and Wilson, *Lincoln-Douglas Debates*, 43–44.

48. Donald, *Lincoln*, 211.

49. Ibid., 215–18.

50. Guelzo, "Houses Divided," 412.

51. Ibid., 412–13.

52. Davis and Wilson, *Lincoln-Douglas Debates*, 45, 62.

53. *CW*, 2:266; Davis and Wilson, *Lincoln-Douglas Debates*, 127, 131; Donald, *Lincoln*, 215–21; Howard, *Illinois*, 292–94. The importance of the Declaration of Independence in Lincoln's political philosophy is indicated by the fact that, five years later in the Gettysburg Address, Lincoln would return to it rather than to the U.S. Constitution to make his points.

54. Donald, *Lincoln*, 221–23; Howard, *Illinois*, 294–95. In the 1840s, Lincoln had expressed interest in colonization plans, such as those of the American Colonization Society. The option of colonization was also an issue he discussed in internal councils of his administration in 1862. Burlingame, *Abraham Lincoln*, 2:383–90.

55. Davis and Wilson, *Lincoln-Douglas Debates*, 266 (Douglas at the Alton debate), 96 (Jonesboro), 184 (Charleston); Johannsen, *Stephen A. Douglas*, 570–71, 725.

56. Allen and Lacey, *Illinois Elections*, 11; Donald, *Lincoln*, 227–29; Guelzo, "Houses Divided," 415. Douglas carried some of the legislative districts by very narrow margins: 75 votes in one, 90 and 150 votes in two others. A different result in those districts alone would have changed the legislative vote in Lincoln's favor. Guelzo, "Houses Divided," 415.

57. Allen and Lacey, *Illinois Elections*, 141–43; Guelzo, "Houses Divided," 417.

58. Burlingame, *Abraham Lincoln*, 1:550; Donald, *Illinois*, 228.

59. Baringer, "Campaign Techniques in Illinois," 207–9.

60. Ambrose, *Nothing Like It*, 23–26, 270–71; Miers, *Lincoln Day by Day*, 2:258.

61. Donald, *Lincoln*, 236.

62. *CW*, 3:523–50.

63. Ibid., 3:550.

64. Finkelman, "Dred Scott," 24–25; Finkelman, "More Perfect Union," 77.

65. Johannsen, *Stephen A. Douglas*, 749–59.

66. Ibid., 767–73.

67. Baringer, "Campaign Techniques in Illinois," 223–27.

68. Ibid., 222.

69. Ibid., 226–41.

70. Wood was elected lieutenant governor in 1856. In March 1860 he became governor for the unexpired term when William Bissell died. He served in that position until January 14, 1861, when Republican Richard Yates, who had been elected governor in 1860, took office.

71. Donald, *Lincoln*, 255–56.

72. John Wooley and Gerhard Peters, "The American Presidency Project," www.presidency.ucsb.edu/showelection.php?year=1864#, accessed September 27, 2013.

73. Allen and Lacey, *Illinois Elections*, 144–45.

74. Moses, *Illinois*, 2:635, 638. The vote for Trumbull over Samuel Marshall was 54 to 36, the exact reversal of Douglas's election over Lincoln two years earlier.

75. Karamanski, *Rally 'Round the Flag*, 51–59.

76. Burlingame, *Abraham Lincoln*, 1:685–702; Donald, *Illinois*, 258–59.

77. Donald, *Illinois*, 260.

78. Burlingame, *Abraham Lincoln*, 1:757; Donald, *Illinois*, 271–72.

79. *CW*, 4:190–91.

Chapter 6. Civil War, a Partisan Convention, the Decisive Later 1860s

1. Moses, *Illinois*, 2:638.

2. Howard, *Mostly Good Men*, 101–7; Moses, *Illinois*, 2:638.

3. Donald, *Lincoln*, 277–79.

4. Johannsen, *Stephen A. Douglas*, 805–7.

5. Ibid., 820–34.

6. Ibid., 809–26.

7. Ibid., 838–39.

8. Ibid., 840–42.

9. Ibid., 862.

10. Howard, *Illinois*, 297–98; Johannsen, *Stephen A. Douglas*, 868.

11. Johannsen, *Stephen A. Douglas*, 867–69, 868n33; Simon, *Lincoln's Preparation*, 118–19.

12. Howard, *Illinois*, 298; Johannsen, *Stephen A. Douglas*, 870–74; Simon, *Lincoln's Preparation*, 120–21.

13. Regiments ostensibly comprised eight hundred men, but they often had as many as several hundred less.

14. Moses, *Illinois*, 2:643.

15. Ibid., 2:645.

16. Biles, *Illinois*, 107–8; Howard, *Illinois*, 300–301.

17. Moses, *Illinois*, 2:649–51.

18. 1848 Constitution, Article VIII; Proposed 1862 Constitution, Article V.

19. Another 2,154 died from "other," unspecified causes. Howard, *Illinois*, 318.

20. Cornelius, *Constitution Making*, 46n2.ß

21. Ibid., 45.

22. Ibid., 45.

23. Verlie, *Illinois Constitutions*, xxvi.

24. Cornelius, *Constitution Making*, 47; Moses, *Illinois*, 2:655.

25. Proposed 1862 Constitution, Article V, Section 1, Articles XIX, XX; *Journal of the Constitutional Convention of the State of Illinois*, Convened at Springfield, January 7, 1862 [hereafter, *1862 Journal*], 58–60, 114, 1082, 1098, 1099; Cornelius, *Constitution Making*, 48–49.

26. *1862 Journal*, 58–60, 114; *Chicago Tribune*, January 22, 1862; *New York Times*, January 24, 1862; Moses, *Illinois*, 2:656–57; Verlie, *Illinois Constitutions*, xxvii.

27. *1862 Journal*, 236.

28. *1862 Journal*, 421.

29. Letter from Governor Yates to Senator Lyman Trumbull, February 14, 1862, Trumbull Papers, Illinois Historical Survey, qtd. in Cole, *Era of the Civil War*, 267. Yates believed the situation so serious as to require a regiment of well-armed soldiers to be stationed at Springfield. Cole, *Era of the Civil War*, 267n36.

30. *1862 Journal*, 216–17.

31. Cornelius, *Constitution Making*, 49.

32. Proposed 1862 Constitution, Article XVIII; *1862 Journal*, 653, 691–93, 1098.

33. *1862 Journal*, 691–93.

34. Cornelius, *Constitution Making*, 53n24.

35. *1862 Journal*, 1076.

36. Proposed 1862 Constitution, Article VIII, Section 1; *1862 Journal*, 725, 794–95, 1091.

37. Proposed 1862 Constitution, Article V, Section 17, Article VI, Section 4, Article IV, Section 23.

38. Ibid., Article V, Section 14

39. Proposed 1862 Constitution, Article IV; *1862 Journal*, 1095.

40. Proposed 1862 Constitution, Article IV, Section 35; *1862 Journal*, 1081.

41. Proposed 1862 Constitution, Article IV, Sections 22, 30; Verlie, *Illinois Constitutions*, xxvi.

42. Cornelius, *Constitution Making*, 51–52.

43. Proposed 1862 Constitution, Article XVII; *1862 Journal*, 936–38, 1097–98.

44. Proposed 1862 Constitution, Article IV, Section 38; *1862 Journal*, 148, 838, 1082.

45. Howard, *Illinois*, 274–76.

46. *1862 Journal*, 766–878.

47. *1862 Journal*, 923–24; Dickerson, "Constitutional Convention of 1862," 399 (15). The ordinance went into effect, the election on the proposal was held in April, and the vote carried in favor of Chicago electing its own officers. When the constitution was defeated, however, the city government continued to exist as before.

48. *1862 Journal*, 835.

49. Ibid., 1114.

50. Cornelius, *Constitution Making*, 53–55; Howard, *Illinois*, 306.

51. Cornelius, *Constitution Making*, 54, 54n28, 55n29.

52. Ibid., 53–54.

53. *Nelson*, 33 Illinois, 390–98 (1864). The court also ruled that the provisions of Section 8 of the law that required a claiming owner to pay part or all of any fine was a violation of the federal Fugitive Slave Act of 1850, but he could be required to pay court costs. That narrow ruling, it held, did not render other parts of the act unconstitutional.

54. Cremin, *Grant Park*, 17–19. The term "wigwam" was commonly used in this period to refer to a political meeting place. The 1860 Illinois Republican party convention in Decatur met in a Wigwam, as did the famous 1860 Republican national convention in Chicago that nominated Abraham Lincoln for the presidency.

55. Karamanski, *Rally 'Round the Flag*, 199–203.

56. Ibid., 203–6; Moses, *Illinois*, 2:707–8.

57. Moses, *Illinois*, 2:707–8.

58. Ibid., II:704.

59. Donald, *Lincoln*, 503–8.

60. Wooley and Peters, "American Presidency Project," www.presidency.ucsb.edu/showelection.php?year=1864#, accessed June 13, 2014; Moses, *Illinois*, 2:709.

61. Moses, *Illinois*, 2:710.

62. Biles, *Illinois*, 128; Howard, *Illinois*, 304–5, 575; Karamanski, *Rally 'Round the Flag*, 165–67, 173–75.

63. Cole, *Era of the Civil War*, 362; Karamanski, *Rally 'Round the Flag*, 165, 172–73.

64. Karamanski, *Rally 'Round the Flag*, 168–70.

65. Biles, *Illinois*, 128; Karamanski, *Rally 'Round the Flag*, 168–70.

66. Karamanski, *Rally 'Round the Flag*, 162–63.

67. Cole, *Era of the Civil War*, 362–63; Cronon, *Nature's Metropolis*, 301–8; Howard, *Illinois*, 304; Karamanski, *Rally 'Round the Flag*, 160–61, 173–74.

68. Karamanski, *Rally 'Round the Flag*, 94–132; Moses, *Illinois*, 2:755–60.

69. Biles, *Illinois*, 139; Cole, *Era of the Civil War*, 357–59; Moses, *Illinois*, 2:778–79.

70. Cole, *Era of the Civil War*, 368–72.

71. Illinois Public Laws, Twenty-Fourth General Assembly, Joint Resolution, February 1, 1865, 135; Richard J. Oglesby to Abraham Lincoln, telegram, February 1, 1865, Abraham Lincoln Papers, Library of Congress; Rick Beard, "The Birth of the 13th Amendment," http://opinionator.blogs.nytimes.com/2014/04/08/the-birth-of-the-13th-amendment/, accessed April 11, 2014; Burlingame, *Abraham Lincoln*, 2:751; Donald, *Lincoln*, 563; Howard, *Illinois*, 324. The amendment introduced the word "slavery" into the constitution for the first time. Amendments to the U.S. Constitution do not require concurrence by the president.

72. Moses, *Illinois*, 2:722.

73. Burlingame, *Abraham Lincoln*, 2:825; Cremin, *Grant Park*, 20–21; Karamanski, *Rally 'Round the Flag*, 245–49.

74. Howard, *Illinois*, 323.

75. Moses, *Illinois*, 2:768, 784–85. Both amendments were ratified by straight party votes; the Fourteenth Amendment by a 17 to 8 vote in the senate and a 60 to 25 vote in the house, and the Fifteenth Amendment by an 18 to 7 vote in the senate and a 58 to 27 vote in the house.

76. Harris, *History of Negro Servitude*, 240–42.

Chapter 7. The Constitution of 1870: Progressive Foundation for a Century

1. Bogart and Thompson, *Industrial State*, 1–2; Moses, *Illinois*, 2:784–85. The Twenty-Fifth General Assembly in its 1867 session passed 1,071 private and only 202 public laws. The twenty-sixth in 1869 passed 1,188 private and 385 public laws. In 1869, private bills granted charters to sixty-seven banks, fourteen loan and trust companies, and thirty-six insurance companies, none of which were placed under the jurisdiction or supervision of the state. They incorporated private manufacturing companies, hotels, banks, land companies, and dozens of other types of enterprises, all intended to create profitable monopolies. Howard, *Illinois*, 333.

2. "A New Constitution," *Chicago Tribune*, November 16, 1866.

3. "A Constitutional Convention," *Chicago Tribune*, January 1, 1867.

4. "Governor Oglesby's Biennial Message," *Chicago Tribune*, January 8, 1867.

5. Cornelius, *Constitution Making*, 44.

6. Enabling act to provide for calling a convention, February 25, 1869, *Debates and Proceedings of the Constitutional Convention Convened at the City of Springfield, Illinois, Tuesday, December 3, 1869* [hereafter referred to as *Debates, 1869 Constitutional Convention*], 2:1893.

7. Cornelius, *Constitution Making*, 45.

8. Ibid., 45, 45n11, 12.

9. Moses, *Illinois*, 2:788.

10. Cornelius, *Constitution Making*, 60–61; Moses, *Illinois*, 2:788.

11. *Debates, 1869 Constitutional Convention*, 1:1–6; *Journal of the Constitutional Convention of the State of Illinois*, Convened at Springfield, December 13, 1869 [hereafter, *1869 Journal*], 6.

12. *Debates, 1869 Constitutional Convention*, 1:7–49.

13. Ibid., 1:50–53.

14. 1870 Constitution, Article II; *Debates, 1869 Constitutional Convention*, 2:1258–91.

15. 1870 Constitution, Article V.

16. Ibid., Article IV, Sections 3, 6, 7, 8, 13.

17. Ibid., Article IV, Sections 22, 23, 27, 28.

18. Ibid., Article IV, Sections 29, 32 (emphasis added); Moses, *Illinois*, I2:709.

19. 1870 Constitution, Article IV, Sections, 30, 31 (emphasis added).

20. Ibid., Article IV, Sections 18, 33; Cornelius, *Constitution Making*, 51.

21. Moses, *Illinois*, 2:790.

22. Bogart and Thompson, *Industrial State*, 22; Cornelius, *Constitution Making*, 53.

23. *Debates, 1869 Constitutional Convention*, 2:1117.

24. 1870 Constitution, Article VI.

25. Ibid., Article VI, Sections 22, 23.

26. *Debates, 1869 Constitutional Convention*, 2:1117.

27. 1870 Constitution, Article VI, Sections 6, 13, 18, 20, 23–28; *Debates, 1869 Constitutional Convention*, 2:1105–29; Bogart and Mathews, *Modern Commonwealth*, 320–29.

28. Delegate O. H. Wright, representing Menard and Mason Counties, referring specifically to the Fifteenth Amendment during argument on the right of suffrage on April 15, 1870. *Debates, 1869 Constitutional Convention*, 2:1291.

29. Ibid., 1:679.

30. Ibid.

31. Ibid., 1:703.

32. Ibid., 1:293.

33. Ibid., 1:307.

34. Ibid., 1:860.

35. Ibid., 1:865–66.

36. Ibid., 1:865.

37. 1870 Constitution, Article XII, Section 1; *Debates, 1869 Constitutional Convention*, 1:866. No reference was made to Indians during the debates on the militia article, or with respect to any other substantive matter at any other time in the convention. The discussions about race were framed in terms of "whites," on the one hand, or "negroes" and its synonym, "colored," on the other.

38. *Debates, 1869 Constitutional Convention*, 1:157.

39. Ibid., 1:157.

40. On January 11, 1870, amid a debate in which southerners attacked the speed with which Illinois had become the third state to ratify the Fifteenth Amendment in 1869, the convention by a straight party vote adopted a resolution commending the Illinois legislature's ratification of the amendment. The vote was 38 Republicans for and 36 Democrats against. *1869 Journal*, 110–11; *Debates, 1869 Constitutional Convention*, 1:165–66.

41. *Debates, 1869 Constitutional Convention*, 1:858.

42. *1869 Journal*, 603; *Debates, 1869 Constitutional Convention*, 2:1280.

43. *Debates, 1869 Constitutional Convention*, 2:1285.

44. Ibid., 2:1285.

45. Ibid.

46. Ibid.

47. Ibid., 2:1286–87.

48. Ibid., 2:1291.

49. Ibid., 2:1290.

50. 1870 Constitution, Article VII, Section 1.

51. *1869 Journal*, 604; *Debates, 1869 Constitutional Convention*, 2:1291.

52. *Debates, 1869 Constitutional Convention*, 2:1308–9.

53. *1869 Journal*, 853–54; *Debates, 1869 Constitutional Convention*, 2:1725–26. In April and May, during the closing weeks of the convention, almost all votes on important substantive matters were decided with as many as a third of the delegates not voting.

54. 1870 Constitution, Article IX.

55. *1869 Journal*, 209, 228.

56. *Debates, 1869 Constitutional Convention*, 1:311.

57. Ibid., 1:311–15.

58. Ibid., 1:320–97.

59. Ibid., 1:397, qtd. by Elijah Haines of Lake County.

60. Ibid., 1:412, 413, 414.

61. Ibid., 1:414.

62. Ibid., 1:414–10

63. *1869 Journal*, 379, 966.

64. Howard, *Illinois*, 237–47.

65. Ibid., 238.

66. Cronon, *Nature's Metropolis*, 9.

67. Howard, *Illinois*, 244–45.

68. Cronon, *Nature's Metropolis*, 63–70; Mayer and Wade, *Chicago*, 38; Young, *Chicago Transit*, 32–33.

69. Howard, *Illinois*, 246–48.

70. 1870 Constitution, "Sections Separately Submitted"; Braden and Cohn, *Illinois Constitution*, 576; Cornelius, *Constitution Making*, 60.

71. Cornelius, *Constitution Making*, 59; Howard, *Illinois*, 334.

72. *Debates, 1869 Constitutional Convention*, 1:325.

73. Ibid., 2:1641–43.

74. Ibid., 2:1644–46.

75. *1869 Journal*, 815; *Debates, 1869 Constitutional Convention*, 2:1646.

76. *1869 Journal*, 847–48; *Debates, 1869 Constitutional Convention*, 2:1669–70.

77. 1870 Constitution, Article XIII; *1869 Journal*, 811; *Debates, 1869 Constitutional Convention*, 2:1622–25, 1697–1701.

78. *Munn v. Illinois*, 94 U.S. 113 (1876); Cronon, *Nature's Metropolis*, 132–45.

79. Cornelius, *Constitution Making*, 60.

80. *Debates, 1869 Constitutional Convention*, 2:1615.

81. *1869 Journal*, 793–94; *Debates, 1869 Constitutional Convention*, 2:1615–17, 1878.

82. 1870 Constitution, Article VIII, Section 1.

83. *Debates, 1869 Constitutional Convention*, 2:1732–35.

84. 1870 Constitution, Article VIII, Section 1.

85. 1870 Constitution, Article VIII, Section 4; *Debates, 1869 Constitutional Convention*, 2:1734.

86. 1870 Constitution, Article VIII; *Debates, 1869 Constitutional Convention*, 2:1759–61.

87. Bogart and Thompson, *Industrial State*, 17; Cornelius, *Constitution Making*, 50, 50n32.

88. *Debates, 1869 Constitutional Convention*, 1:72.

89. Ibid., 1:560–64.

90. Ibid., 1:561.

91. "Egypt" is a term applied regionally to the southernmost counties of Illinois; more specifically to the southern thirty-four counties. Its precise origin is unclear. Dexter attributes it to "the winter of deep snow in 1830 and 1831" killing the corn crop in northern Illinois and causing farmers to travel to the south to purchase seed corn, thus an analogy to the Israelites going into Egypt in times of drought. Earlier origins are also alleged. Cairo, the southernmost town of Illinois at the juncture of the Ohio and Mississippi Rivers, is the nominal "capital" of the region. Dexter, *Bondage in Egypt*, 41, 41n3–5.

92. *Debates, 1869 Constitutional Convention*, 2:1727.

93. *Chicago Times*, July 1, 1870. Regarding Storey, see L. E. Ellis, "*Chicago Times*," 135–84; Karamanski, *Rally 'Round the Flag*, 177–78, 188–97.

94. *1869 Journal*, 1016.

95. Ibid., 1019–22.

96. *Chicago Tribune*, May 13, 1870, qtd. in Cornelius, *Constitution Making*, 64.

97. *Chicago Times*, May 14, 1970.

98. *Illinois State Journal*, May 14, 1870, qtd. in Cornelius, *Constitution Making*, 64.

99. *Chicago Tribune*, June 23, 1870.

100. *Chicago Times*, July 2, 1870.

101. *Debates, 1869 Constitutional Convention*, 2:1894–95. The eight separately submitted propositions, and the vote approving each one, were: the railroad regulation sections of the article on corporations (144,750–28,525); the article on formation of counties (136,815–31,644); the article on supervision and inspection of warehouses (143,533–29,702); the question of requiring a three-fifths vote to remove a county seat (127,077–41,417); the section relating to the Illinois Central Railroad (147,082–21,310); the section providing for minority representation in the house of representatives (99,022–70,080); the section restricting municipal subscriptions to railroads or private corporations (134,112–34,061); and the section on the Illinois and Michigan Canal (142,540–27,017). *Debates, 1869 Constitutional Convention*, 2:1896.

102. *Chicago Times*, July 7, 1870.

Epilogue

1. Biles, *Illinois*, 124–30.

2. Bogart and Thompson, *Industrial State*, 10.

3. *Munn v. Illinois*, 94 U.S. 113 (1877).

4. Cornelius, *Constitution Making*, xiv, 68–69.

5. Ibid., 67, 67n1. The amendments dealt with drainage ditches, county sheriffs and treasurers succeeding themselves, granting the governor a line-item veto in appropriation bills, the hiring of convict labor, and bond financing of the World's Columbian Exposition of 1893.

6. Howard, *Illinois*, 473. In that period, nine amendments were ratified and eighteen failed to receive enough favorable votes.

7. Cornelius, *Constitution Making*, 95–104; Howard, *Illinois*, 333.

8. Cornelius, *Constitution Making*, 159; Howard, *Illinois*, 562.

9. Illinois Secretary State, election returns, December 15, 1870.

10. Fifth Amendment to the 1970 Illinois Constitution.

11. Illinois State Board of Elections, www.elections.il.gov/Downloads/ElectionInformation VoteTotals/2016, accessed November 16, 2016. The report states that the amendment's promoters spent almost $4 million in support of the proposals against little by opponents. See also *Chicago Sun-Times*, November 6, 2016.

12. Dinan, "Political Dynamics of Mandatory . . . Referendums." 418.

13. The slogan "Land of Lincoln" had come into general use. It was added to Illinois's license plates in 1954; the general assembly adopted it in 1955 as an official slogan of the state, for which the State of Illinois has a copyright for its exclusive use. 2012 14 *Illinois Blue Book*, 421

BIBLIOGRAPHY

Allen, Howard W., and Vincent A. Lacey, eds. *Illinois Elections, 1818–1990: Candidates and County Returns for President, Governor, Senate, and House of Representatives.* Carbondale: Southern Illinois University Press, 1992.

Alvord, Clarence W. *The Illinois Country, 1673–1818.* The Centennial History of Illinois. Chicago: McClurg, 1922.

Ambrose, Stephen E. *Nothing Like It in the World: The Men Who Built the Transcontinental Railroad, 1863–69.* New York: Simon and Schuster, 2000.

Angle, Paul M. "Nathaniel Pope, 1784–1850: A Memoir." *Transactions of the Illinois State Historical Society* (1936): 111–81.

———, ed. *Prairie State: Impressions of Illinois, 1673–1967, by Travelers and Other Observers.* Chicago: University of Chicago Press, 1968.

———. "Review of *A History of Illinois from its Commencement as a State in 1818 to 1847* by Thomas Ford 1854." *Journal of the Illinois State Historical Society* 38, no. 1 (March 1945): 99–104.

Baringer, Wm. E. "Campaign Techniques in Illinois: 1860." *Transactions, Ill. State Historical Society* (1932): 203–81.

Barker, Lucius J., and Twiley W. Barker. *Constitutional Conventions in Illinois.* Springfield, Ill.: Schnepp and Barnes, 1919. Available at http://www.idaillinois.org/cdm/ref/collection/isl2/id/153.

Barnhart, John D. "The Southern Influence in the Formation of Illinois." *Journal of the Illinois State Historical Society* 38, no. 1 (September 1939): 358–78.

Basler, Roy P., et al., eds. *The Collected Works of Abraham Lincoln.* New Brunswick, N.J.: Rutgers University Press, 1953.

Biles, Roger. *Illinois: A History of the Land and Its People.* DeKalb: Northern Illinois University Press, 2005.

Blackwell, Robert S., ed. *Reports of Decisions of the Supreme Court of the State of Illinois; From the December Term, 1819, to the February Term, 1841, Inclusive, Which Were Embraced in Breese, and Volumes One and Two Scammon's Reports.* Chicago: Myers, 1862.

Bogart, Ernest Ludlow, and John Mabry Mathews. *The Modern Commonwealth, 1893–1918.* The Centennial History of Illinois 5. Chicago: McClurg, 1922.

Bogart, Ernest Ludlow, and Charles Manfred Thompson. *The Industrial State, 1870–1893.* The Centennial History of Illinois 4. Chicago: McClurg, 1922.

Braden, George D., and Rubin G. Cohn. *The Illinois Constitution: An Annotated and Comparative Analysis.* Urbana: Institute of Government and Public Affairs, University of Illinois, 1969.

Buck, Solon Justus. *Illinois in 1818.* The Centennial History of Illinois, Intro. vol. Chicago: McClurg, 1918.

Burlingame, Michael. *Abraham Lincoln: A Life.* Vols. 1 and 2. Baltimore, Md.: Johns Hopkins University Press, 2008.

Burns, Josephine E., and John McLean. "Daniel P. Cook." *Journal of the Illinois State Historical Society* 6, no. 3 (October 1913): 425–44.

Cahan, Richard. *A Court That Shaped America: Chicago's Federal District Court from Abe Lincoln to Abbie Hoffman.* Evanston, Ill.: Northwestern University Press, 2002.

Carpenter, Richard V., and J. W. Kitchell. "The Illinois Constitutional Convention of 1818." *Journal of the Illinois State Historical Society* 6, no. 3 (October 1913): 327–424.

Cayton, Andrew R. L. *Frontier Indiana,* Bloomington: Indiana University Press, 1996.

———. *The Frontier Republic: Ideology and Politics in the Ohio Country, 1780–1825.* Kent, Ohio: Kent State University Press, 1986.

Cole, Arthur Charles. *The Era of the Civil War, 1848–1870.* The Centennial History of Illinois 3. Springfield: Illinois Centennial Commission, 1919.

———, ed. *The Constitutional Debates of 1847.* Springfield: Illinois State Historical Library, 1919. *Collections of the Illinois State Historical Library* 14, Constitutional Series 2.

Conzen, Michael P., and Kay J. Carr, eds. *The Illinois and Michigan Canal National Heritage Corridor: A Guide to Its History and Sources.* DeKalb: Northern Illinois University Press, 1988.

Cornelius, James M. "John Hart Crenshaw and Hickory Hill." Final Report for the Historic Sites Division, Illinois Historic Preservation Agency, 2002.

Cornelius, Janet. *Constitution Making in Illinois.* Urbana: Published for the Institute of Government and Public Affairs by the University of Illinois Press, 1972.

Cremin, Dennis H. *Grant Park: The Evolution of Chicago's Front Yard*. Carbondale: Southern Illinois University Press, 2014.

Cronon, William. *Nature's Metropolis: Chicago and the Great West*. New York: Norton, 1991.

Danzer, Gerald A. *Illinois: A History in Pictures*. Urbana: University of Illinois Press, 2011.

Davis, James E. *Frontier Illinois*. Bloomington: Indiana University Press, 1998.

Davis, Rodney O., and Douglas L. Wilson, eds. *The Lincoln-Douglas Debates*. The Lincoln Studies Center Edition. Urbana: Knox College Lincoln Studies Center and University of Illinois Press, 2008.

Debates and Proceedings of the Constitutional Convention of the State of Illinois, Convened at the City of Springfield, Tuesday, December 13, 1869. 2 vols. Springfield, Ill.: Merritt, 1870.

Dexter, Darrel. *Bondage in Egypt: Slavery in Southern Illinois*. Cape Girardeau: Center for Regional History, Southeast Missouri State University, 2011.

Dickerson, P. M. "The Illinois Constitutional Convention of 1862." *University of Illinois: The University Studies* 1, no. 9 (March 15, 1905): 385–442.

Dinan, John. "The Political Dynamics of Mandatory State Constitutional Convention Referendums: Lessons from the 2000s Regarding Obstacles and Pathways to Their Passage." *Montana Law Review* 71 (2010): 395–432.

Donald, David Herbert. *Lincoln*. New York: Simon and Schuster, 1995.

Douglass, Frederick. *Narrative of the Life of Frederick Douglass, an American Slave*. Edited by Benjamin Quarles. Cambridge, Mass.: Belknap Press of Harvard University Press, 1960.

Edstrom, James A. "'With . . . Candour and Good Faith': Nathaniel Pope and the Admission Enabling Act of 1818." *Illinois Historical Journal* 88, no. 4 (Winter 1995): 241–62.

Ellis, Mrs. L. E. "The *Chicago Times* during the Civil War." *Transactions, Ill. State Historical Society* (1932): 135–84.

Edwards, Ninian W., ed. *The Edwards Papers: Being a Portion of the Collection of the Letters, Papers, and Manuscripts of Ninian Edwards; Chief Justice of the Court of Appeals of Kentucky, First and Only Governor of Illinois Territory, One of the First Two United States Senators from the State of Illinois, Third Governor of the State of Illinois*. Vol. 3. Chicago: Chicago Historical Society Collection, 1884.

———. *History of Illinois from 1778 to 1833; and Life and Times of Ninian Edwards*. Springfield: Illinois State Journal Co., 1870.

Eisenhower, John S. D. *So Far from God: The U.S. War with Mexico, 1846–1848*. Norman: University of Oklahoma Press, 2000.

Ekberg, Carl J. *Colonial Ste. Genevieve: An Adventure on the Mississippi Frontier*. Tucson, Ariz.: Patrice, 1996.

———. *French Roots in the Illinois Country: The Mississippi Frontier in Colonial Times*. Urbana: University of Illinois Press, 1998.

———. *Stealing Indian Women: Native Slavery in the Illinois Country*. Urbana: University of Illinois Press, 2010.

Ferguson, Gillum. *Illinois in the War of 1812*. Urbana: University of Illinois Press, 2012.

Finkelman, Paul. "Abraham Lincoln: Prairie Lawyer." In *America's Lawyer Presidents: From Law Office to the Oval Office*, edited by Norman Gross, 128–37. Evanston, Ill.: Northwestern University Press, 2004.

———. "*Dred Scott v. Sandford*." In *The Public Debate over Controversial Supreme Court Decisions*, edited by Melvin I. Urofsky, 24–33. Washington, D.C.: CQ, 2004.

———. "Evading the Ordinance: The Persistence of Bondage in Indiana and Illinois." *Journal of the Early Republic* 9 (Spring 1989): 21–51.

———. "Slavery, the 'More Perfect Union,' and the Prairie State." *Illinois Historical Journal* 80, no. 4 (Winter 1987): 248–69.

Fishback, Mason M. "Illinois Legislation on Slavery and Free Negroes, 1818–1865." *Transactions of the Illinois State Historical Society* (1904): 414.

Ford, Thomas. *A History of Illinois from Its Commencement as a State in 1818 to 1847*. Chicago: Griggs, 1854.

Fraker, Guy C. *Lincoln's Ladder to the Presidency: The Eighth Judicial Circuit*. Carbondale: Southern Illinois University Press, 2012.

Fuhrig, Wolf. "Lincoln and Koerner: Ethnic Germans and the Presidential Election of 1860." *Illinois Heritage* 16, no. 2 (January–February 2013).

Gallay, Alan. *The Indian Slave Trade: The Rise of the English Empire in the American South*. New Haven, Conn.: Yale University Press, 2002.

Gerwing, Anselm J. "The Chicago Indian Treaty of 1833." *Journal of the Illinois State Historical Society* 57 (Summer 1964): 117–42.

Greenberg, Amy S. *A Wicked War: Polk, Clay, Lincoln, and the 1846 U.S. Invasion of Mexico*. New York: Knopf, 2012.

Grover, Frank R. "Indian Treaties Affecting Lands in Illinois." *Journal of the Illinois State Historical Society* 8 (October 1915): 379–419.

Guasco, Suzanne Cooper. *Confronting Slavery: Edward Coles and the Rise of Anti-Slavery Politics in Nineteenth-Century America*. DeKalb: Northern Illinois University Press, 2013.

Guelzo, Allen C. "Houses Divided: Lincoln, Douglas, and the Political Landscape of 1858." *Journal of American History* (September 2007): 391–417.

Haeger, John D. "The American Fur Company and the Chicago of 1812–1835." *Journal of the Illinois State Historical Society* 61 (Summer 1968): 117–39.

Hall, Kermit L., Harold M. Hyman, and Leon V. Sigal. *The Constitutional Convention as an Amending Device*. Washington, D.C.: American Historical Association and the American Political Science Association, 1981.

Harris, N. Dwight. *The History of Negro Servitude in Illinois, and of the Slavery Agitation in That State, 1719–1864*. Chicago: McClurg, 1904.

Hart, Richard E. *Lincoln's Springfield: The Early African American Population of Springfield, Illinois (1818–1861)*. Springfield: The author, 2008.

———. "Springfield's African Americans as a Part of the Lincoln Community." *Journal of the Abraham Lincoln Association* 20, no. 1 (Winter 1999).

Hauberg, John H. "The Black Hawk War, 1831–32." *Transactions, Ill. State Historical Society* (1932): 91–134.

Haydon, J. R. "John Kinzie's Place in History." *Transactions, Ill. State Historical Society* (1932): 183–200.

Herndon, William H. *Herndon's Lincoln: The True Story of a Great Life*. Vol. 1. Springfield: Herndon's Lincoln Publishing, 1921.

Hirsch, Susan. "Economic Geography." In *Encyclopedia of Chicago*. Edited by Janice L. Reiff, Ann Durkin Keating, and James R. Grossman. Chicago: Chicago History Museum, the Newberry Library, and Northwestern University, 2004. Available at http://www.encyclopedia.chicagohistory.org.

Howard, Robert P. *Illinois: A History of the Prairie State*. Grand Rapids, Mich.: Eerdmans, 1972.

———. *Mostly Good and Competent Men: Illinois Governors, 1818–1988*. 2nd ed. Springfield: Illinois State Historical Society, 1988.

Howe, Walter A. *Documentary History of the Illinois and Michigan Canal*. Springfield: State of Illinois Department of Public Works and Buildings, Division of Waterways, 1956.

Huston, James L. *Calculating the Value of the Union: Slavery, Property Rights, and the Economic Origins of the Civil War*. Chapel Hill: University of North Carolina Press, 2003.

Illinois Secretary of State. *Counties of Illinois: Their Origin and Evolution with Twenty-Three Maps Showing the Original and Present Boundary Lines of Each County of the State*. Springfield: Illinois State Journal Co., State Printers, 1919.

"James Thompson's Plat of Chicago: A 150-Year Perspective." *Chicago History* 9, no. 2 (Summer 1980): 66.

Johannsen, Robert W. *Stephen A. Douglas*. New York: Oxford University Press, 1973.

Journal of the Convention, Assembled at Springfield, June 7, 1847, for the purpose of Altering, Amending, or Revising the Constitution of the State of Illinois. Springfield, Ill.: Lanphier and Walker, 1847.

Journal of the Constitutional Convention of the State of Illinois, Convened at Springfield, December 13, 1869. Springfield, Ill.: State Journal Printing Office, 1870.

Journal of the Constitutional Convention of the State of Illinois, Convened at Springfield, January 7, 1862. Springfield, Ill.: C. H. Lanphier, 1862.

Karamanski, Theodore J. *Rally 'Round the Flag: Chicago and the Civil War*. London: Rowman and Littlefield, 2006.

Keating, Ann Durkin. *Rising Up from Indian Country: The Battle of Fort Dearborn and the Birth of Chicago*. Chicago: University of Chicago Press, 2012.

Kenney, David, and Robert E. Hartley. *The Heroic and the Notorious: U.S. Senators from Illinois.* 2003. Carbondale: Southern Illinois University Press, 2012.

Klebaner, Benjamin Joseph. "American Manumission Laws and the Responsibility for Supporting Slaves." *Virginia Magazine of History and Biography* 63, no. 4 (October 1955): 443–53.

Koerner, Gustave. *Memoirs of Gustave Koerner, 1809–1896.* Cedar Rapids: Privately printed, 1909.

Kogan, Vladimir. "The Irony of Comprehensive State Constitutional Reform. *Rutgers Law Journal* 41 (2009–2010): 881–905.

Lamb, John. *A Corridor in Time: 1836–1986, I & M Canal.* Romeoville, Ill.: Lewis University and Illinois Department of Commerce and Community Affairs, Office of Tourism, 1987.

Levine, Bruce. *The Fall of the House of Dixie: The Civil War and the Social Revolution that Transformed the South.* New York: Random House, 2013.

Long, John H., ed. *Illinois: Atlas of Historical County Boundaries.* Compiled by Gordon DenBoer. New York: Scribner's, 1997.

Magnaghi, Russell M. "Red Slavery in the Great Lakes Country during the French and British Regimes." *Old Northwest* 12 (Summer 1996): 201–17.

Margry, M. Pierre. *Mémoires et Documents Pour Servir a l'Histoire des Françaises des Pays d'Outre Mer: Découvertes et Établissements des Français dans l'Ouest et dans le Sud de l'Amérique Septentrionale (1614–1754).* Vols. 1, 2, and 3. Paris: Maisonneuve et Cie, Libraires-Editeurs, 1876–1888.

Mayer, Harold M., and Richard C. Wade. *Chicago: Growth of a Metropolis.* Chicago: University of Chicago Press, 1969.

Meese, William A. "Nathaniel Pope." *Journal of the Illinois State Historical Society* 3, no. 4 (January 1911): 7–21.

Middleton, Stephen. *The Black Laws: Race and the Legal Process in Early Ohio.* Athens: Ohio University Press, 2005.

Miers, Earl Schenk, ed. *Lincoln Day by Day: A Chronology, 1809–1865.* 3 vols. Washington: Lincoln Sesquicentennial Commission, 1960.

Morrissey, Robert Michael. *Empire by Collaboration: Indians, Colonists, and Governments in Colonial Illinois Country.* Philadelphia: University of Pennsylvania Press, 2015.

———. "Empires, Identities, and Communities in Illinois Country, 1673–1772," PhD diss., University of Illinois, 2014.

Moses, John. *Illinois, Historical and Statistical.* Vols. 1 and 2. Chicago: Fergus, 1889, 1892.

Murphy, Lucy Eldersveld. *A Gathering of Rivers: Indians, Métis, and Mining in the Western Great Lakes, 1737–1832.* Lincoln: University of Nebraska Press, 2000.

Norton, Margaret Cross, ed. *Illinois Census Returns, 1810, 1811.* Collections of the Illinois State Historical Library 26, Statistical Series 2. Springfield: Illinois State Historical Library, 1935.

———. *Illinois Census Returns, 1820*. Collections of the Illinois State Historical Library 26, Statistical Series 3. Springfield: Illinois State Historical Library, 1934.

Parkman, Francis. *The Discovery of the Great West: LaSalle*. Edited by William R. Taylor. New York: Rinehart, 1956.

———. *LaSalle and the Discovery of the Great West: France and England in North America*. 11th ed. Boston: Little, Brown, 1902.

Pease, Theodore C. *The Frontier State, 1818–1848*. The Centennial History of Illinois 2. Springfield: Illinois Centennial Commission, 1918.

Philbrick, Francis S., ed. *The Laws of the Illinois Territory, 1809–1818*. Springfield: Illinois State Historical Library, 1950.

———. *The Laws of the Indiana Territory, 1801–1809*. Springfield: Illinois State Historical Library, 1930.

Pooley, William Vipond. "The Settlement of Illinois from 1830 to 1850." *Bulletin of the University of Wisconsin History Series* 1 (1905): 287–595.

Putnam, James William. *The Illinois and Michigan Canal: A Study in Economic History*. Chicago: Chicago Historical Society, 1918.

Quaife, Milo Milton. *Chicago and the Old Northwest, 1673–1835: A Study of the Evolution of the Northwestern Frontier, Together with a History of Fort Dearborn*. Chicago: University of Chicago Press, 1913.

Quitt, Martin H. *Stephen A. Douglas and Antebellum Democracy*. Cambridge: Cambridge University Press, 2012.

Roske, Ralph J. *His Own Counsel: The Life and Times of Lyman Trumbull*. Reno: University of Nevada Press, 1979.

Simeone, James. *Democracy and Slavery in Frontier Illinois: The Bottomland Republic*. DeKalb: Northern Illinois University Press, 2000.

Simon, Paul A. *Lincoln's Preparation for Greatness: The Illinois Legislative Years*. Urbana: University of Illinois Press, 1971.

Sixth Illinois Constitutional Convention. *Record of Proceedings: Verbatim Transcripts, 1969–1970*. Springfield, Ill.: Office of the Secretary of State, 1972.

Sleeper-Smith, Susan. *Indian Women and French Men: Rethinking Cultural Encounter in the Western Great Lakes*. Amherst: University of Massachusetts Press, 2002.

Smith, George W. "The Salines of Southern Ilinois." *Transactions of the Illinois State Historical Society* (1904): 245–58.

Snively, Ethan A. "Slavery in Illinois." *Transactions of the Illinois State Historical Society* (1901): 52–59.

Spencer, Donald S. "Edward Coles, Virginia Gentleman in Frontier Politics." *Journal of the Illinois State Historical Society* 61, no. 2 (Summer 1968): 150–63.

Stroble, Paul E., Jr. *High on the Okaw's Western Bank: Vandalia, Illinois 1819–39*. Urbana: University of Illinois Press, 1992.

Strong, Moses McCure. *History of the Territory of Wisconsin, from 1836 to 1848*. Madison, Wis.: Democrat Printing, 1885.

Tanner, Helen Hornbeck, ed. *Atlas of Great Lakes Indian History*. Norman: University of Oklahoma Press (for the Newberry Library), 1987.

Temple, Wayne C. *Lincoln's Connections with the Illinois and Michigan Canal, His Return from Congress in '48, and His Invention*. Springfield: Illinois Bell, 1986.

Thwaites, Rueben G. *Father Marquette*. New York: Appleton, 1902.

———. *The Jesuit Relations and Allied Documents*. Vol. 59. Cleveland: Burroughs, 1899.

———, ed. "Notes on Early Lead Mining in the Fever (or Galena) River Region." *Collections of the State Historical Society of Wisconsin* 13 (1895): 271–91.

Verlie, Emil J. *Illinois Constitutions*. Springfield: Illinois State Historical Library, 1919.

Wiencek, Henry. *Master of the Mountain: Thomas Jefferson and His Slaves*. New York: Macmillan, 2012.

Young, David M. *Chicago Transit: An Illustrated History*. DeKalb: Northern Illinois University Press, 1998.

INDEX

Frank Cicero Jr. is a senior partner at Kirkland and Ellis LLP and served as a delegate for Illinois's Sixth Constitutional Convention. He is the author of *Relative Strangers: Italian Protestants in the Catholic World.*

The University of Illinois Press
is a founding member of the
Association of American University Presses.

Composed in 10.5/14 Arno Pro
with Trade Gothic LT Std display
by Lisa Connery
at the University of Illinois Press
Cover designed by Dustin J. Hubbart
Cover illustrations: Dome of Illinois State Capitol
Building (Henryk Sadura / Shutterstock.com);
Abraham Lincoln's stovepipe hat (Abraham Lincoln
Presidential Library and Museum).
Manufactured by Sheridan Books, Inc.

University of Illinois Press
1325 South Oak Street
Champaign, IL 61820-6903
www.press.uillinois.edu